WOMEN AND PROPERTY
IN THE EIGHTEENTH-CENTURY
ENGLISH NOVEL

This book investigates the critical importance of women to the eighteenth-century debate on property as conducted in the fiction of the period. April London argues that contemporary novels advanced several, often conflicting, interpretations of the relation of women to property, ranging from straightforward assertions of equivalence between women and things to subtle explorations of the self-possession open to those denied a full civic identity. Two contemporary models for the defining of selfhood through reference to property structure the book, one historical (classical republicanism and bourgeois individualism), and the other literary (pastoral and georgic). These paradigms offer a cultural context for the analysis of both canonical and less well-known writers, from Samuel Richardson and Henry Mackenzie to Clara Reeve and Jane West. While this study focuses on fiction from 1740 to 1800, it also draws on the historiography, literary criticism, and philosophy of the period, and on recent feminist and cultural studies.

APRIL LONDON is Associate Professor of English at the University of Ottawa. She has written widely on eighteenth-century fiction in journals and in essay collections. This is her first full-length book.

WOMEN AND PROPERTY
IN THE
EIGHTEENTH-CENTURY
ENGLISH NOVEL

APRIL LONDON

CAMBRIDGE
UNIVERSITY PRESS

PUBLISHED BY THE PRESS SYNDICATE OF THE UNIVERSITY OF CAMBRIDGE
The Pitt Building, Trumpington Street, Cambridge, CB2 1RP, United Kingdom

CAMBRIDGE UNIVERSITY PRESS
The Edinburgh Building, Cambridge, CB2 2RU, UK   http://www.cup.cam.ac.uk
40 West 20th Street, New York, NY 10011–4211, USA   http://www.cup.org
10 Stamford Road, Oakleigh, Melbourne 3166, Australia

First published 1999

Typeset in Baskerville 11/12.5pt [VN]

A catalogue record for this book is available from the British Library

Library of Congress Cataloging in Publication data
London, April.
Women and property in the eighteenth-century English novel / April
London.
p.   cm.
Includes bibliographical references and index.
ISBN 0 521 65013 5 (hardback)
1. English fiction – 18th century – History and criticism.   2. Women
and literature – Great Britain – 18th century.   3. Property
in literature.   I. Title.
PR858.W6L66   1999
823'.809355 – dc21   98–11651
CIP
ISBN 0 521 650135 hardback

Transferred to digital printing 2004

To my parents

Contents

Acknowledgements

I have been fortunate in the friends and colleagues who have helped me with this book. I would like to thank Linda Merians, Susan Hitch, and David Shore for their scholarly advice, Nicholas von Maltzahn for incisive criticism of the early chapters, Ina Ferris both for her patient and generous reading at a critical point in the book's evolution and for the friendship that has made academic writing a social pleasure, and Annabel and Lee Patterson for engaging and stimulating conversations over many years. Annabel Patterson's astute commentary on the book in its final stages is especially appreciated. Mark Phillips has been throughout the best of critics and I am grateful for the exacting and intelligent commentary he has offered. My most profound debt is to Keith Wilson. From him and our children, Neil and Jamie, has come all that makes life a joy.

I would like to thank the editor of *Eighteenth-Century Fiction* for permission to reprint parts of "Historiography, Pastoral, Novel: Genre in *The Man of Feeling*" and the editor of *Genre* for permission to reprint part of "Novel and Natural History: Edward Bancroft in Guiana." Chapter 12 is reproduced with permission of Oxford University Press from *Tradition in Transition: Women Writers, Marginal Texts, and the Eighteenth-Century Canon* ed. Alvaro Ribeiro and James G. Basker (Clarendon Press, 1996), 56–74.

Introduction

What's *Property*? dear Swift! you see it alter
From you to me, from me to Peter Walter,
Or, in a mortgage, prove a Lawyer's share,
Or, in a jointure, vanish from the Heir,
Or in pure Equity (the Case not clear)
The Chanc'ry takes your rents for twenty year:
At best, it falls to some ungracious Son
Who cries, my father's damn'd, and all's my own.
Shades, that to Bacon could retreat afford,
Become the portion of a booby Lord;
And Hemsley once proud Buckingham's delight,
Slides to a Scriv'ner or a City Knight,
Let Lands and Houses have what Lords they will,
Let Us be fix'd, and our own Masters still.
(Pope, *Imitations of Horace*: Sat.II.ii.167–80)[1]

Pope's enlargement on the terms of his key question – "what's *Property*? dear Swift!" – enlists the discourse of humanism in order to argue for the kinds of virtue possible in a corruptible world. A key part of his strategy in defining virtue involves distinguishing the multiple meanings attaching to property. Considered in its public role as the means by which material value passes from one generation to the next, property "alter[s]" in a process whose degeneration follows a line from father to "ungracious Son," the "booby Lord" who betrays his father's delight. But Pope's lines also distinguish the mobility of real property from a capacity for self-possession that is both "fix'd" and sustained by the companionship of the like-minded. This is not the self-possession of the bourgeois subject – "Scriv'ner" or "City Knight" – with his characteristic acquisitiveness and malleable personality. It is instead a form of identity that reasserts the standard of behavior implicit in the political paradigm of classical republicanism, now threatened in these "*South-sea*

I

days" (line 133). In the complex metalepsis of the final line, Swift and Pope will be "Lords" over the only unsullied variant of "Lands and Houses" that remains to such virtuous individuals: they will be "Masters" of a self that has assumed the "fix'd" characteristics of real property. In short, Pope's reanimation of the Horatian ideal envisions the "middle state" (line 61) as the exclusive preserve of an exemplary masculine virtue that flourishes in the "blessings Temperance can bring" (line 66).

In this brief excerpt, we see eighteenth-century understandings of property played out in a number of different registers: identity, virtue, economics, and the real property of "Lands and Houses." As a figure signifying these complex terms and interactions, property has been interrogated by political theorists, historians of ideas, literary critics, and economists.[2] What is missing from many of these narratives – as it is (at least explicitly) from Pope's – is the presence of women. This book is about the ways in which the signal importance of property to the eighteenth century is both affirmed and complicated when women are included in the account.[3] My particular interest is the form that contemporaries most often saw as feminocentric, the novel. Representations of women in fiction provided a vehicle for the debate concerning the relationship of property (the ownership of things) to propriety (the possession of one's own person). That debate as conducted within the novel had significant implications for the disciplinary terms of such discourses as philosophical history, aesthetics, and political theory.

In developing this claim, I draw on a vocabulary of literary and political tropes that the eighteenth century itself inherited and then adapted. The intersecting languages of genre – pastoral and georgic – and of political theory – civic humanism and bourgeois individualism – are key to the emergent form of the novel. They provided structures for confronting and containing change and for exploring and delimiting the possibilities of self-making. And in their confirmation of the profound connectedness and mutually informing influence of contemporary discourses, these tropes also attest to the appeal of more inclusive interpretative frameworks for literary criticism.

Representations of women in the eighteenth century are central to the ways in which the culture mediated conflicting interpretations of how identity is made, expressed, refined, and also, when necessary, repressed. The pivotal role they play in the novel follows from the fact that women have existence in fiction both as particularized characters and as points of reference for a range of concerns attaching to the relation of identity to property. Such alignments of women and property in part reflect contemporary legal definitions which virtually equate the two and so establish women's susceptibility to male definition. But they also, and more intricately, speak to the ways in which eighteenth-century novels textualize male anxiety about social and economic change. In examining these altered relations of property to person as they are formally rendered in fiction through the intersections of gender, genre, and political paradigm, I consider a range of texts, some canonic, others less familiar. In an effort to suggest, as nearly as possible, the widening scope of contemporary understandings of property as these are realized in novel settings, I include in Parts II and III colonial narratives, utopian fictions, and depictions of imagined communities. And in order to test the argument that representations of women are indeed central to the period's conceptualizing of property, regardless of authorial gender, I discuss both male- and female-authored fiction. Before offering a more detailed account of the book, however, I want to consider briefly the ways in which the paradigms of political philosophy and of genre to which I referred earlier inform my reading of eighteenth-century fiction.

POLITICAL PHILOSOPHY AND ITS ANALOGIES

Contemporary anxieties about change, identity, and social role were often expressed in terms that conflated gender and property. The oppositions that emerged from this unease can be summarized by turning again to Pope's *Imitations of Horace*. The constancy of the self-possession which will allow Pope and Swift to be their "own Masters still," the passage suggests, was once preserved by an elite order (unquestionably masculine) whose authority derived from the inheritance of real property. The bourgeois subject – "Scriv'ner" or "City Knight" – is, conversely, depicted through reference to qualities that align him with women and the marketplace: he profits from the conversion of real to imagined property that can be made through the chicanery of lawyers to "vanish from the Heir"; he is interested, speculative, unfixed.

Historians have developed the complex of notions to which Pope and his contemporaries refer by privileging one or the other of two contrastive structures: classical republicanism and Lockean liberalism. Joyce Appleby and Isaac Kramnick are among those who, in arguing the primacy of the latter position, assert that the bourgeois individualism of the eighteenth-century middle class is rooted in a seventeenth-century political discourse centered on private rights and competition.⁴ Opposition to this model comes primarily from J. G. A. Pocock. He maintains that antipathy to the commercial, oligarchic, and imperial administration that emerged after 1688 revived a civic humanist discourse in which virtue appears the prerogative of a landed class whose disinterestedness is secured by their possession of property.⁵ In literary studies, most notably in the work of John Barrell, these terms have contributed significantly to our understanding of early Augustan modes.⁶ But in relation to eighteenth-century novels, which worry relentlessly about the mobility of both persons and property, the explanatory force of civic humanism is somewhat diminished. Extrapolating from Appleby or Kramnick a model that posited an invariable progressivism would be no less partial: contemporary fiction after all observes with discomfort and not equanimity the loss of the familiar. But however limited republican and liberal models appear in isolation, if we do not insist on seeing them as singular and exclusive, they have much to tell us about the characteristic concerns of eighteenth-century fiction. For, in fact, novelistic representations of property are mutually, if unequally, informed by the paradigms of both bourgeois individualism and civic humanism. Together with the generic structures of pastoral and georgic, they afford contexts for fiction's rendering of identity: Lockean liberalism for the charting of the processes of self-making which stand at the center of many novelistic plots, civic humanism for the resolution or displacement of disruptiveness through the novel's closing emphasis on the value of real property.

GENRE: PASTORAL, GEORGIC, NOVEL

Large numbers of eighteenth-century novels shape their plots in accordance with the generic assumptions provided by two classical antecedents, pastoral and georgic, that again define selfhood in relation to property. The currency pastoral and georgic retain in eighteenth-century literature has much to do with the work that genre itself does in providing a matrix for problem-solving, a way of rendering intelligibility through characteristic and historically specific structures.⁷ The novelists' incorporation of georgic and pastoral conventions within their fictions attests to their desire to participate in the continuity of a classical tradition whose subject was the individual's relation to leisure and labor. But for those engaged in the writing of novels, intelligibility also demanded that existing discursive practices should be attentive to the unprecedented, the range of experiences believed to have been formerly unrepresented.

Classical literature served these two intersecting needs, providing models (as the long history of their adjustment to particular cultural contexts affirms) that were both powerful and flexible. In the seventeenth century, georgic and pastoral had both undergone significant transformations of meaning, transformations that would further their ideological usefulness as points of reference within the novel. The preference for georgic over pastoral that is so marked a feature of Augustan poetry (one that effectively reversed the relative status of each in the previous century) depended on economic and political affiliations that came to define the opposition between the two modes.[8] James Thomson's 1748 *Castle of Indolence* emblematizes the distinction in its contrast of "that soul-enfeebling wizard, Indolence" and the "Knight of Arts and Industry" whose vigor resists his antagonist's "luxury" and "torpid sluggishness" in order to bring to "new-created men" the joys of labor.[9] Pastoral sloth is here defeated by georgic industriousness in ways that confirm the adaptability of the Virgilian original to the problems associated with the new economic order. Georgic enables a purposive construction of the uncertainties inherent in a world increasingly imagined in transactional terms. As John Chalker writes, "[o]n the one hand [georgic] promotes awareness of the instability of civilized values, and on the other the ethic of work, and of the need to build patiently by mastering the fundamental resources of life."[10]

For those who wished to affirm the values to which georgic gave expression – the civilizing capacity of labor, the vindication of empire, an ideal of progress – the mode continued to provide an admirable vehicle. But those same qualities appeared to many as ciphers of degeneration, as a leveling of necessary distinction, a dangerous engagement with colonial otherness, a wilful abandonment of the civic humanist ideal of disinterestedness. Hence georgic and pastoral are transformed in the eighteenth-century novel from contrastive modes to combative ones that are both mutually informing and antagonistic. This shift signals not only the loss of their straightforward denotative function as the first two terms in the Virgilian triad (pastoral, georgic, and epic), but also the destabilizing of the distinct scope of their representational spheres (respectively leisure, work, and martial heroism). Because their meanings emerge from such defined positional contexts, pastoral and georgic in contemporary novels always implicitly invoke the competing mode. For those writing within the georgic mode, pastoral thus comes to stand for an effeminate, pleasure-seeking aristocracy; conversely, for those who align themselves with pastoral, georgic signals the undifferentiated embrace of change and male acquisitiveness, qualities associated with a new middling class.

GENRE, GENDER, AND THE NOVEL

When eighteenth-century novelists draw on the conventions of pastoral and georgic, their appropriations of poetic genres are informed by correlative assumptions about social identity. Central to these conjectures are questions of gender. Within mid-century culture, as numbers of critics have detailed from a wide range of perspectives, the place of women was highly contested.[11] Among the most persuasive of the accounts of the critical role played by gender in discourse formation is that of Nancy Armstrong.[12] Her argument about the novel's encoding of social processes accepts as fundamental the gendering of subjectivity as female. Reading back from the paradigms of nineteenth-century fiction (ones that she accepts as normative), she focuses on Samuel Richardson and on conduct literature to detail the origins of the "domestic woman." But the representations of women's dual relations to property that underpin much eighteenth-century fiction complicate this teleology. Women's embodiment of customary and more modern understandings of property derives from two sources: on the one hand, the extrinsic signification women carry in their legal status as the property of father and husband and, on the other, the intrinsic meaning they potentially exercise as possessors of their own persons. Through its plots and generic adaptations, the novel negotiates these conflicting perspectives in ways that ultimately pertain to both genders. Representations of women and property enable exploration, in other words, of the grounds of both male and female subjectivity and its realization in social practices. Lacking the programmatic impulses of the political treatise (or its domestic equivalent, the conduct book), the novel allows for the suspension of argumentative rigor in favor of a flexibility that proved immensely attractive to growing numbers of readers.[13] Its hero is consequently not the classically modeled humanist of Pope's poem, but the emergent liberal male subject whose historical development from Lockean paradigms has been charted by Joyce Appleby.[14] In the novel's construction and critique of this hero – often by way of feminocentric plots – a revelation of female difference is also made possible.

Modern criticism perceives the "hero" of eighteenth-century fiction through the double lens of the residual and emergent cultures and sees that over the course of the period identity was increasingly imagined as self-generated, rather than hierarchically determined. But contemporaries made no such discrete differentiation, nor did they, in the main, respond with equanimity or disinterest to the changes they witnessed. One gauge of such complexities can be found in the novel's uneasy attempt to assimilate the impulse toward "horizontal" solidarity or definition by class to the customary "vertical" hierarchies. In a recent attempt to historicize patriarchy, Michael McKeon argues that its modern incarnation depends on the contemporaneous emergence of the "language and assumptions of 'class'" with a system of gender difference.[15] The defeat of earlier forms of patriarchalism that this entailed had consequences to which the culture responded with varying degrees of intensity and acceptance, variations that followed closely the ways in which the new liberal subject of Appleby and Kramnick's model was constituted. The definition of that subject, enabled by the "revolutionary and antihierarchical principle of equality in difference" (315) and by the "structural separation of the genders" (300) was never intended, McKeon emphasizes, to extend either to women or to unpropertied men. Nevertheless, I will argue, the critical role played by women in eighteenth-century fiction depends on their witnessing to the processes of "horizontal solidarity" that enabled differentiation of class and gender and that contributed to the consolidation of a specifically modern patriarchy.

Plot is crucial to this process. Its characteristic structures suggest how women at once represent the possibilities of self-making through horizontal affiliations and are denied the rewards of coherent selfhood. Eighteenth-century novels consistently locate female characters within plots that allow them to exercise reformative agency (both individual and social) by drawing on their properties of industriousness and by realizing selfhood through active relationship with the things of this world. That agency is then relocated within male characters by way of endings that assert the primacy of real property and hence women's subordination to the men who control it. This double structure (sustained through a distinction of self-possession from actual property) by which change is both enabled and contained engages the political and the poetic ways of constructing identity that I have already outlined. On the one hand, novels employ a Lockean understanding of selfhood as a process of active making, a process most often generically expressed in the terms provided by georgic. On the other, they deflect the dangerous potential of this self-making by focusing at the novel's end on a civic humanist reading of real property as the guarantor and inescapable condition of selfhood. Novels that resist mutability tend, conversely, to exchange georgic for pastoral conventions, adapted to episodic plots that favor regression over advance. But whether georgic or pastoral is chosen as the appropriate mode for expressing the achievement or loss of identity, at novel's end land ownership appears the correlative of virtue. Since the characteristic fates of eighteenth-century heroines – marriage or death – render them women without property, they are finally made subject to the terms of a discourse that returns the exclusive authority to confer meaning to male characters.

In the properties ascribed to women and in the plots that enact these for the reader, eighteenth-century audiences saw the possibilities of self-making realized in ways that significantly amended customary notions of the individual subject. But the novelty of the amendments was tempered by the associations carried by the key terms invoked: the refiguring of community, the civilizing capacity of labor, the engagement of individuals within a new economic order, the articulation (and domestication) of an imperial mode. Virgilian georgic, in short, enabled the novel's assimilation of historically specific problems to an existing framework sympathetic to change but anchored in precedent. And pastoral in turn allowed for the expression of a powerful counterposition antipathetic to change and to the characteristic features of possessive individualism.

The range of responses to the question that georgic posed to the eighteenth century – "And various Arts in order did succeed / (What cannot endless Labour urg'd by need?)" – shapes the inquiry I pursue in the following chapters.[16] The terms of labor, need and invention invoked in Dryden's translation are diversely textualized through the novel's representations of woman as property and as a figure for property relations. The reference to "various Arts," however, underscores the need to consider the novel within the larger context of two further questions: how do reading and writing – the work that is done in the making of meaning – relate to the Lockean claim to possession that comes when one "mixes one's labour" with the things of this world? And how does the use of pastoral and georgic work to inscribe (or resist) progress within a continuous literary tradition?

In taking up these questions, I organize my inquiry on grounds that are both contrastive and roughly chronological: the paradigms of georgic and pastoral are first established through analysis of two mid-century exemplars, Richardson and Mackenzie respectively, then extended through explorations of the Virgilian imperial theme (both domestic and foreign), and finally tested in the conflict between radical and conservative writing in the crucial decade of the 1790s. The value of such inclusive structures consists in their capacity to register continuities (and disruptions) in the depiction of women's relation to property across the period; the potential danger of schematization will, I hope, be offset by attention to particular texts and close readings. Part I considers Samuel Richardson's investigations of identity through the experiences of a female protagonist, a model that will be elaborated and extended (or resisted and delimited) in many later eighteenth-century novels. The conclusions to his novels involve a double displacement of female energy that also becomes paradigmatic for later fiction. These displacements begin with the shift of attention from the heroine to the altered representations of property that accompany the hero's moral reformation and are completed by the real reader's compact with those characters within the novel who adhere to hierarchical forms of male definition. In the concluding sections of Richardson's novels, the communities of readers regulated by male figures are directed toward documentary evidence – Pamela's "vellum-book of white paper," Clarissa's "Will," and *Sir Charles Grandison*'s collaboratively written and read letters. These documentary inheritances substitute for the presence of the women whose experiences have occupied the novel proper.

In substantiating the interpretative authority of masculine modes of writing and reading, these concluding episodes with their summary "texts" appear to accord with the account of the "rise of the novel" offered by critics from Ian Watt to Nancy Armstrong. But in the novels considered under the rubric of pastoral in Part II the progressivism implicit in this model, along with the authority it grants masculine modes, is challenged. In the work of Henry Mackenzie, Laurence Sterne, and Thomas Cogan, pastoral stands for the integrity of a past order whose separation from the corruptions of history and of women has in each novel a spatial equivalent: the farm Harley establishes for old Edwards, uncle Toby's bowling green, the more generalized motif of retirement that takes the hero from city to country in Cogan's satire of sentimentalism.

Colonial narratives of the period, in contrast, problematize the fundamental assumptions of pastoral and georgic by invoking a sense of the "otherness" of place in the presumed *absence* of history. Scottish

Enlightenment historiography had made current a reading of property
relations that tied possession to the advance of civility. In Edward
Bancroft's *Charles Wentworth* and the anonymous *The Female American*, the
protagonists' responses to the women encountered in the colonies test
such conceptualizations. The positive connotations of the hero's georgic
enterprise in *Charles Wentworth* are massively qualified by his confronta-
tions with women identified with the extremes of slavery and communal
ownership. *The Female American* constructs a matrilineal plot that undermines hierarchical property relations as part of its celebration of
women's power. Both colonial narratives envision an existing, dehis-
toricized pastoral order invigorated by georgic industriousness. But the
protagonists' gender finally proves significant to the resolutions of the
two novels: in *Charles Wentworth*, agrarian capitalism and a renewed
domestic economy reinscribe hierarchical relations with the hero's
return to England; *The Female American* similarly ends with the achievement of domestic order, but it is one that substantiates, rather than
subordinating, female authority in the "new world."

Part III turns to a number of texts that examine the problem of
community within England. These novels again counterpoint pastoral
and georgic, identifying each genre with a range of assumptions about
gender, discourse, and politics. In the novels of Sarah Scott and Clara
Reeve, pastoralism is associated with the received conventions of a male
discourse that trivializes women's achievements by codifying them as
aesthetic. The community of women that both novels underwrite at
once resists and reproduces these associations by suggesting that
women's labor should be valued because it contributes to the maintenance of existing social hierarchies. As a result, these novels finally
endorse, rather than controvert, the status quo. "Confederacy" narratives, on the other hand, which I consider in the second section of this
part (chapter 8), focus on women's function as a cipher of cultural
alienation and disorder. This function is linked to their capacities as
story-tellers, fabricators of narratives that testify to the rewards of
self-making. Here we see most clearly the challenge to masculine modes
of reading and writing posed by distinctively female forms of labor –
ways of making both ideas and things – that retain a continued and
vigorous presence in eighteenth-century narrative.

Part IV focuses on the more narrowly political meaning attached to
plot in the closing decade of the century and on the correlative attention
to questions of audience. From mid-century, pastoral had been stigma-
tized by its opponents for its perceived relation to the luxury and

effeminacy associated with the culture of sensibility. But in the radical writing of the 1790s, pastoral comes to be figured in terms nearly opposite to those that had prevailed earlier. For these writers, it stands not for a past culture of inherited privilege, but for a future golden age. With the radical appropriation of pastoral, conservative writers similarly re-define their generic allegiances. They respond to the radical novelists' arguments for political change with satires that expose the "fictive" status of their opponents' political and literary plots. But as parodies of radicalism, anti-Jacobin novels remain subject to the limitations of polemic. The concluding chapter 12 focuses on the work of a conservative author, Jane West, whose challenge to radicalism is integrated within a politics of reading that goes beyond derivative satire. In her novels, georgic self-making becomes the vehicle for the articulation of a fully realized middle-class consciousness. In granting to fiction a reformative agency for strengthening the individual's commitment to a national identity, West's novels bring together the issues of gender, genre, and plot in ways that anticipate the controlling terms of the historical novel.

The Epilogue briefly considers the transformations of georgic and pastoral within the new genre's defining fiction, Walter Scott's *Waverley*. As the two modes are adapted by the historical novel from signifiers of identity to markers of temporality, their relation to the spheres of gender and of labor becomes atrophied. The concurrent emergence of the historical novel and virtual disappearance of georgic and pastoral as distinct modes raises interesting questions about the place of women and their capacity for self-making as represented within early nineteenth-century fiction. To consider patriarchal formulations in the romantic novel from the vantage of eighteenth-century understandings of women and property is to see how revolution and resistance to it worked to circumscribe the plotting of female identity. What happens to Rose Bradwardine and Flora MacIvor at the moment when Edward Waverley's "romance" so famously ends and the "real history" of his life begins?

PART I

Section one: Samuel Richardson and georgic

Introduction

The relations of property to personality are as fundamental to *Clarissa* as they were to the culture in which the novel was written. They are also as varied. Richardson testifies to the centrality of property by having the inheritance of an estate precipitate the plot of his novel. But with Clarissa as legatee, it is gender that becomes the key complication around which the issue of possession revolves. Conventionally a conduit for property, woman here acquires the means by which she can become an agent in her own right. But the contemporary strictures that define female behavior make impossible Clarissa's translation of private virtue into public action. Hence her female confirmation of the traditional link between ethical disinterestedness and land ownership comes to be disallowed.

In narrating the matter of the inheritance retrospectively, Richardson further casts the bequest as a symbol of a past order whose efficacy the novel will then contest. The terms of the grandfather's will which provoke the novel's initial struggle thus problematize the governing assumptions of the civic humanist discourse that served as "the dominant paradigm for the individual inhabiting the world of value" in early eighteenth-century Britain.[1] The symmetrical balancing of his bequest at the novel's beginning with Clarissa's at its end encourages a comparative reading of the two.

The terms of Clarissa's own will represent a significantly different understanding of the relation of self to property. This understanding emerges over the course of the novel by means of an attention to labor as a creator of value and hence as a vehicle for bourgeois consciousness. Contemporary poetry, as many critics have noted, drew extensively on Virgil's *Georgics* as precedent for their explorations of labor in a nascent commercial culture. I shall argue that Richardson's *Clarissa* also adapts the classical genre in ways appropriate to a post-Augustan age, as the novel balances the claims of inwardness against the countervailing pulls of an old aristocratic and new materialist order. In its eighteenth-century novelistic incarnation, the georgic mode continues to accord property the central importance it holds in the civic humanist tradition. But it makes its possession the reward of those who labor constructively to restore order. For both Richardson and his successors, the georgic mode affords a powerful means of tailoring an emergent individualism to the need for consensus and social stability.

CHAPTER I

"Clarissa" and the georgic mode

From the beginning of the novel, Clarissa's relation to property is represented figuratively, in the sense of those qualities she possesses as an individual, and literally, in the estate she has inherited from her grandfather. The terms of the grandfather's bequest make clear his commitment to a conservative understanding of property; for him, land confers dignity on and grants agency to its possessor. The will establishes that she may at eighteen leave the "great part of his estate to whom she pleases of the family, and the rest of it (if she die single) at her own discretion." His motive is "to create respect for her" as a shield against the envy that her goodness may attract.[1] His action expresses faith in her possession of a virtue that is not compelled or expedient, but innate and constructive. The note detailing the events leading to the inheritance suggests, moreover, that during his lifetime the grandfather secured his title to her time by publicly expressing the value of her labor: "in order to invite her to him as often as her other friends would spare her, [he] indulged her in erecting and fitting-up a dairy-house in her own taste. When finished, it was so much admired for its elegant simplicity and convenience that the whole seat, before of old time from its situation called *The Grove*, was generally known by the name of *The Dairy-house*" (41).

Clarissa's acts of possession can be seen as doubly metonymic. They change from the figurative ownership implicit in her "erecting and fitting-up [the] dairy-house in her own taste" to the literal inheritance of the entire estate. The name change which testifies to her constructive powers confirms that process of association on which metonymy depends. It also takes us out of the world of nature (The Grove) and "places us in the historical world of events and situations."[2] Here, as Margaret Anne Doody writes, the "man-made" is privileged over the "natural." Doody reads this as an "anti-romantic, anti-pastoral" gesture.[3] More constructively, we can see that the change of name sanctions the value of labor as conferring meaning on both person and place.

The process by which The Grove becomes The Dairy-house, in which pastoral place name becomes a site of productivity, thus realizes the terms of Locke's famous discussion of property in chapter 5 of the *Two Treatises of Government*: "Whatsoever, then, [man] removes out of the State that Nature hath provided, and left it in, he hath mixed his *Labour* with, and joyned to it something that is his own, and thereby makes it his *Property*." That "which is his own" is the property each man possesses uniquely in his individual self. To illustrate his point, Locke invokes the analogy of gathering acorns and apples "from the Trees in the Wood," asking: "Was it a Robbery thus to assume to himself what belonged to all in Common?" To return a negative is to admit "that 'tis the taking any part of what is common, and removing it out of the state Nature leaves it in, which *begins the Property* . . ."[4] In Joyce Appleby's reading of the passage, Locke refutes the central tenets of Filmer's *Patriarcha* by establishing as privileged the inalienable right of self-possession: "Our property in ourselves is not shared in common, and through our own exertions – our labor – we make from common property private property."[5]

For the Harlowe family, the natural rights argument that "the labour . . . *made* his *Property* who takes that pains about it"[6] is secondary to the imperatives of primogeniture and "family-aggrandizement" (152). From their perspective, Clarissa's claim to independent selfhood must yield to the more customary Lockean argument for male domination over women.[7] This strain of natural rights theorizing about property reads the female body as itself a kind of property. Accordingly, Clarissa's utility will be realized in a marriage that secures the coherence of the family estates. This sense is endorsed by the anonymous author of *Critical Remarks on "Sir Charles Grandison," "Clarissa," and "Pamela,"* who contends that Clarissa's value rests unconditionally on her physical intactness:

This chastity, this delicacy, &c. may probably enough be termed political; some people have reckoned it the meer invention of the statesman or politician; but . . . its fitness and propriety are founded on the nature of things and of human society. In all societies there are families, inheritances, and distinctions of ranks and orders. To keep these separate and distinct, to prevent them from falling into confusion, on all which the good oeconomy and internal happiness of the state much depend, the chastity and continence of women are absolutely and indispensably necessary. Therefore it has been universally agreed, to educate the sex in the principles leading to that continence, and to make their honour and reputation consist in adhering to them. In women of condition, in short in all above a certain rank, the inconveniencies of deviating from these principles are always very observable, and sensibly felt; particular families are hurt, orders are confused, inheritances are uncertain, the example is bad, and the scandal great. Therefore in all such we perceive this political chastity strongly to prevail; but in the rank below them we find it, for obvious reasons, exerting no great influence.[8]

As this passage makes clear in its closing reference to those of the "rank below" women of "condition," it is extrinsic political circumstance that compels chastity and its more visible correlative, delicacy. The constitutive power of female sexuality within the "nature of things" threatens to disable the higher good of the "internal happiness of the state." The defense of this higher good, enabled by the rule of property, requires woman's internalization of propriety as a check against her innate sexuality. By this reckoning, Clarissa becomes an outcast from the order of both her family and the state itself.

The terms of her grandfather's settlement speak to a contrary relation between female self and social good, in which women have a more active power to do good. Before his death, his view apparently prevailed within Clarissa's immediate family. The Harlowes seemed also to acknowledge her claim to a distinct identity based on the pleasures of continuous and actively engaged labor, and not just on the mere fulfillment of her role as daughter, niece, and granddaughter. In her superintendence of the household, as her mother described it, Clarissa's attention to "family cares" was "richly repaid in the reputation your skill and management have given you" (94).

But the inheritance of the estate (which appears to Clarissa the true object of Solmes's "love") alters her place within the family economy. In attaching a palpable reward to "reputation," the grandfather's bequest grants her potential agency as a property owner. The transformative and civilizing capacity of individual effort formalized in the name change (from The Grove to the Dairy-house) has also, and more dangerously, led to Clarissa's own change of status. The Harlowes respond with a narrowly prescriptive assertion of her subordinate role as daughter and of her moral obligation to defer to their wish that she marry Solmes. Her resistance ultimately brings to bear on her the force of what the anonymous author calls the system of "political chastity." The inheritance of the Dairy-house, intended as a tribute to individual integrity, in fact sets in motion the plot of exile that leads inexorably to her rape, and to her final entry into her spiritual "father's house."

Surprisingly, twentieth-century commentary has echoed the terms of "political chastity" in assigning to Clarissa an instrumental function. Since in her world property serves as "a metaphor for woman and a synecdoche for male hegemony over her," the bequest renders the heroine a "man–woman, an adult–child, a propertied property."[9] The legal synonymy between the terms "woman" and "property" enables a web of affiliations in which the seemingly opposed interests of a James Harlowe or a Robert Lovelace become one; this has the effect, as Terry Eagleton has written, of making Clarissa the "discourse" of the text, "magically unchanging in itself yet source of 'magical' transformations in others."[10] She is thus represented as object of others' acts of self-construction, rather than as agent in her own right. But it is only partly the case that Clarissa is enmeshed by her antagonists' desires.

Richardson also establishes for Clarissa a prior history in which her identity is achieved by a methodical and productive use of time. The "erecting and fitting-up [the] dairy-house" and the terms of her grandfather's will are of a piece with her attentiveness to the poor as well as her "particular distribution of her time," by which, "had she calculated according to the practice of *too many*, she had actually lived more years at *sixteen*, than *they* had at *twenty-six*" (1469–70). The paralysis induced by the crisis of "courtship" is bracketed in the novel by a more purposive construction of labor, embodied most perfectly in Clarissa herself.

Analysis of *Clarissa* through reference to the eighteenth-century understanding of property was pioneered by Christopher Hill, whose approach was subsequently developed by Ian Watt and Terry Eagleton. More recently, J. G. A. Pocock's civic humanist discourse has afforded critics such as John Barrell and John Zomchick a more sophisticated paradigm for the relation of property to civic identity.[11] Pocock's model describes eighteenth-century thought as organized by a dialectical relation of ancient to modern conceptions of property in which the citizen patriot's virtue, secured by the leisure and impartiality granted by the possession of land, defines itself in opposition to the "[s]pecialized, acquisitive, and post-civic" man of commerce, feminized by his passionate enthrallment to mobile or "imaginary" property.[12] The residual aristocratic code with which Lovelace is aligned – and the near-parodic emulation of it that drives the Harlowes' acquisitiveness – functions in the text as a corruption of this patriot ideal.

We understand the qualities of such corruption by contrast with Clarissa's exemplary expression of her inward virtue in the form of purposive labor. This location of her integrity in the practice of an industriousness, externalized in the caring for her poor and internalized in scrupulous self-questioning, recalls the "modern identity" anatomized by Charles Taylor. The "punctual self," developed through the writings of Locke, follows from the period's "affirmation of ordinary life" and of the "powers of disengaged reason – with its associated ideals of self-responsible freedom and dignity – of self-exploration, and of personal commitment." In its capacity for self-making, it exists in fundamental opposition to the civic humanist circumscription of personality by antecedent notions of disinterested virtue. And in its participation in the embourgeoisement of eighteenth-century culture, it reveals the dynamic reciprocity between real property, on the one hand, and consciousness, on the other.[13]

The central importance accorded Locke in the story of the eighteenth century told by Taylor is consistent with that of another skeptical reader of civic humanism, Joyce Appleby. Her study of seventeenth-century economic writing leads her to conclude that while arguments between court and country dominated political discourse in the early eighteenth century "fragments of the liberal paradigm found lodging in other inquiries." The Machiavellian moment of historical consciousness that defined the experience of the English ruling class, and that led to the affirmation of the "patriot citizen," did not speak to those "outside the political nation." For them, the classical paradigm of a revived republicanism was secondary to the individualist model of society propounded by Locke and his successors. Reacting against the limitations of Whig historiography, revisionist critics like Pocock have, according to Appleby, employed an unnecessarily narrow definition of political thought that depresses the significance of the "originators of liberal ideas" who began with a "critical stance toward government regulation of the economy, [and] ended up with propositions subversive to traditional authority and those privileged to exercise that authority both at court and in the country."[14]

Historians of the middle class – the class most aware of its status "outside the political nation" – provide further evidence for the emergence by mid-century of a distinctive mentality for which the construct of civic humanism proves inadequate. As Paul Langford has recently noted, while the "respect which attended property was a striking feature of the mental landscape of the eighteenth century," the battle waged between the defenders of the landed and the moneyed interest was principally confined to the decades of the 1690s and 1700s and had essentially ceased by the mid-Georgian period.[15] Thereafter the emphasis fell less on divisions between kinds of property and more on its capacity to civilize, a capacity voiced most eloquently by the Scottish Enlightenment thinkers for whom property is, in the words of Adam Ferguson, "a matter of progress" and a "principal distinction of nations in the advanced state of mechanic and commercial arts."[16]

Historians have given little attention, however, to the ways in which the georgic mode provided the eighteenth century with a vocabulary that inscribed this "progress" within the terms of a continuous tradition. Virgil's representation of man as "a hard laborious Kind" (line 95), envisioned his fall from a state of pastoral ease to unremitting effort as at once loss and gain. The ending of the Golden Age was the necessary condition for the emergence of human inventiveness:

> The Sire of Gods and Men, with hard Decrees,
> Forbids our Plenty to be bought with Ease:
> And wills that Mortal Men, inur'd to toil,
> Shou'd exercise, with pains, the grudging Soil.
> Himself invented first the shining Share,
> And whetted Humane Industry by Care:
> Himself did Handy-Crafts and Arts ordain;
> Nor suffer'd Sloath to rust his active Reign.
> E're this, no Peasant vex'd the peaceful Ground;
> Which only Turfs and Greens for Altars found:
> No Fences parted Fields, nor Marks nor Bounds
> Distinguish'd Acres of litigious Grounds:
> But all was common, and the fruitful Earth
> Was free to give her unexacted Birth.
> *Jove* added Venom to the Viper's Brood,
> And swell'd, with raging Storms, the peaceful Flood:
> Commission'd hungry Wolves t'infest the Fold,
> And shook from Oaken Leaves the liquid Gold:
> Remov'd from Humane reach the chearful Fire,
> And from the Rivers bade the Wine retire:
> That studious Need might useful Arts explore;
> From furrow'd Fields to reap the foodful Store:
> And force the Veins of clashing Flints t'expire
> The lurking Seeds of their Coelestial Fire.
>   ...
> And various Arts in order did succeed,
> (What cannot endless Labour urg'd by need?)
>
> (II.183–218)

Embracing the progressivist implications of this model, the eighteenth century adapted the classical theme of labor as a civilizing agent. In response to the imperatives of capitalist enterprise, labor was accorded the capacity to regenerate both the citizen and the state. Spenser, Jonson, and Milton, encouraged by the spirit of the New Science and religious reform, had earlier depreciated pastoral and epic relative to alternative models of "virtuous and heroic behaviour" that anticipated Augustan interpretations of *Georgics*.[17] Thomson, Pope, Dyer, Grainger, and Gay, in turn, variously develop the possibilities of the Virgilian ideal of moderation in order to stigmatize acquisitive excess and defend the right uses of wealth. Critical attention has, in the main, focused on poetry as the period's chosen vehicle for expressing the Virgilian ethos.[18] But georgic is, as Anthony Low comments, "primarily a mode rather than a genre. It is an informing spirit, an attitude toward life, and a set of themes and images rather than anything so definite, say, as a four-book didactic poem of two thousand lines on the subject of agriculture."[19] And as such, it appears pervasively in the novel as well as poetry.

In *Clarissa*, the only direct allusion to *Georgics* occurs in the opening pages as James Harlowe and Clarissa debate the limits of his authority over her. At issue is the existence of female integrity and its sufficiency as a guide to action. Clarissa's refusal to meet with Roger Solmes, the Harlowes' chosen suitor for their daughter, has provoked from James an account of the family's plan to overcome her resistance. "[I]t is resolved that you shall go to your uncle Anthony's," he writes:

If after one fortnight's conversation with Mr. Solmes, and after you have heard what your friends shall further urge in his behalf, unhardened by clandestine correspondence, you shall convince them that Virgil's *amor omnibus idem* (for the application of which I refer you to the Georgic, as translated by Dryden) is verified in you, as well as in the rest of the animal creation; and that you cannot, or will not, forego your prepossession in favour of the moral, the virtuous, the pious Lovelace (I would please you if I could!), it will then be considered, whether to humour you, or to renounce you for ever. (218)

James's allusion to a universal sexual appetite refers to Virgil's description of the "Force of Love" in Book III of *Georgics*. In the influential 1697 translation, to which James refers, Dryden renders the passage as:

> Thus every Creature, and of every Kind,
> The secret Joys of sweet Coition find:
> Not only Man's Imperial Race; but they
> That wing the liquid Air, or swim the Sea,
> Or haunt the Desart, rush into the flame:
> For Love is Lord of all; and is in all the same.
>
> (III.375–80)

Clarissa responds to James's insult in two distinct registers, each rhetorically consistent with her sense of her correspondents. To her friend and
confidante, Anna Howe, she voices sharp anger, but adds her recognition that James's imprudent comment has allowed her to seize the
offensive. Emphasizing her politic recognition of the advantage to be
garnered from his deviousness, she declares her intention to use "a piece
of the art they accuse me of" to foil the "master-stroke of my brother's
policy." She intends deliberately to take umbrage at "his vile hint from
the Georgic" in order "to palliate the refusal of obeying" the demand
that she prepare to leave for her uncle Anthony's. To James himself she
levels the charge of puerile cleverness; his sexual allusion functions
merely "to display your pedantry" and breaches that "*humanity*" that
was supposed to be "a branch of your studies at the university" (218–19).

Contemporary commentary on Dryden's translations of Virgil reinforces the eccentricity of James's choice of tag, and justifies both
Clarissa's response to James's misapplied learning and her resistance to
his use of sexuality as a master trope.[20] But, in practice, her tactical
maneuvers depend on her family's compliance with the idea of a
distinctive female "delicacy" (220). To affirm her own participation in
the culture of politeness, she must thus construe James's reading of
human nature as a form of misogyny. In declaring herself "entitled to
resent [the] infamous hint ... for the sake of my sex as for my own"
(219), she locates her claim to individual integrity in the context of what
he believes to be an entirely factitious "delicacy," "purity," and "virgin
modesty" (223).[21]

But the affective terms of discussion prove to be property, not politeness. James's denial of an inwardly defined female virtue is peripheral to
his overriding concern with the material benefits of chastity. Clarissa's
investment of "matrimonial duty" with the concerns of the "*soul*" seems
to him irrelevant to "the light in which this whole debate ought to be
taken." And so, with a great flourish, he closes down the debate, by
declaring the definitive terms that govern her meaning to be those of
"PROPERTY" (220).

The Harlowes and Lovelace unite in their common reliance on a
rhetoric that at once conflates women and property and justifies their
actions. From the Harlowes' perspective, Lovelace's declaration that
Clarissa is "*his*, and *shall* be *his*, and he will be the death of any man who
robs him of his PROPERTY," must be met by the "absolutely determined"
counter-claim of "the right of a father in his child."[22] If "Love is Lord of
all" and if Clarissa has proven her susceptibility by "prefer[ing] the rake

to a father," then the father is justified in taking whatever measures necessary to prove his superior title to the property of his daughter.

From the start, however, an alternate interpretation of property relations centered on conditional rather than absolute or prescribed rights has defined Clarissa's sense of her place within the family. In the energetic cultivation of property, real and personal, Clarissa affirms the value of her labor. This recalls the emphasis within the georgic mode on the capacity of individuals to invest the quotidian with meaning. Her affirmation acquires additional power from the tenacity with which she defends such precepts. Even at the end of her life, she resists the lure of expedient compromise and asserts the primary value of her integrity. Justifying to Anna Howe her decision "never to have Mr. Lovelace," she thus declares:

> Had I been his but a *month*, he must have possessed the estate on which my relations had set their hearts; the more to their regret, as they hated *him* as much as he hated *them*.
>
> Had I not reason, these things considered, to think myself happier without Mr. Lovelace than with him? My will too unviolated; and very little, nay, not anything as to him, to reproach myself with? (1161–2)

The consolations of the unviolated will and the unalienated estate remind the reader again of the appropriateness of the "principal device" of the design Clarissa has etched on her coffin: "a crowned serpent, with its tail in its mouth, forming a ring, the emblem of eternity," circling the inscription of her name, her age, and the date, April 10th, on which she left "her father's house" (1305–6). Clarissa marks her end by returning us to the context of the novel's beginning: the daughter who claims her integrity in opposition to the familial demand that she yield to their desire to consolidate estates.

Richardson's exploration of the power of making through the experiences of a female protagonist is a recurrent feature of eighteenth-century narrative. As Fielding's Sophia Western and Amelia Booth, Radcliffe's Emily St. Aubert, and Holcroft's Anna St. Ives suggest, women consistently serve as the vehicle for testing the possibilities of an individualist ethic. But their purposiveness and verity are finally made subordinate to their narrative function, either as agents of the hero's transformation into a member of the landed gentry or as foil to his failure to discharge the range of responsibilities such membership entails. In the first instance, marriage marks the heroine's end; in the second, death and apotheosis. Nancy Miller, in a paradigmatic reading of *Pamela* and *Clarissa*, encodes these alternate plots as euphoric and dysphoric, as structures signaling social advancement in the one case and alienation in the other.[23] But in the eighteenth-century novel, gender and genre are mutually informing and also expressive of wider cultural practices unified by a fundamental concern with property.

Such practices allow us to contextualize *Clarissa*'s depiction of property relations through a plot centered on an eminently marriageable eighteen-year old woman. The juridical equation of wives and property offers one perspective; in Blackstone's famous phrase, "By marriage, the husband and wife are one person in law; that is, the very being or legal existence of the woman is suspended during the marriage, or at least is incorporated and consolidated into that of the husband."[24] On the threshold of legal extinction, Clarissa claims title to an inwardness that she believes licenses her participation in the choice of a husband. The "mixing of her labour" with the things of this world seems to her to affirm the prerogatives of both self-possession and individual agency. Juxtaposed against this subjectivity is the imminent fact of her status as object, dependent on the determining power of her spouse. To put this in the terms of the recurring double plot of the eighteenth-century novel: the range of possibilities opened up by the experience of "courtship" will be closed down by the subordination of the heroine in a concluding marriage or death. Or, to adapt a more abstract frame: the body of the novel engages a Lockean understanding of property as an active process of making, and does so by locating the heroine's experiences within the context of the georgic mode. The ending of the novel offers instead an obverse, civic humanist reading of property as denominating selfhood, and as therefore granting exclusive authority to confer meaning to the male character.

We may then propose that woman textualizes male anxiety about social and economic change. The emergent order construes woman as possessed of distinctive qualities that originate in continuous negotiation with experience. The residual order defines her as a form of property whose meaning reflects the need to secure patterns of inheritance. In incorporating both of these paradigms, the novel enables "woman" to express many of the ambivalences common to a bourgeois culture marked by the wish to accommodate stability and continuity to the imperatives of aspiration and emulation.

Virgilian georgic, Anthony Low maintains, is centrally "a poetry that reflects on the making of history."[25] The generic transliteration that enabled georgic's appropriation by the "new manner of writing" is in a very particular way bound up with the cultural history of the eighteenth century, the period that saw the "rise of the novel." Many recent critics – Nancy Armstrong and John Bender among them – press the notion of an altered literary field into the service of a much larger claim: they ascribe to the novel a remarkable capacity to effect historical change. I hesitate before that claim. The terms of the argument sketched above do suggest significant conjunctions of fiction and history. These can best be explored, however, not through totalizing assertion but through close readings that show how and why the eighteenth-century novel so consistently envisions the labor of women in relation to their value as property.

CHAPTER 2

Making meaning as constructive labor

Those labors consonant with the georgic mode which were Clarissa's in the period before the moment of the novel's opening scene are bound up with the powers conferred on her by her loving grandfather. Such powers reflect his sense of the qualities that will later be impressed upon the reader as distinctive of Clarissa in her role as heroine: her dazzling virtue, her moral scrupulousness, her attention to social duties. But in this novel Richardson pursues a double strategy, isolating and idealizing the heroine's virtue to the point that she becomes "all mind" (555), while gradually transferring to Belford the associations with georgic that had at first been represented as unique to Clarissa. As a result of this transference, the meaning of the georgic mode itself and the narrative and cultural ends it can serve also undergo change.

As it is retrospectively invoked, Clarissa's status as heroine depends on her knowledge of her own worth and her dedication to labors that confirm her individual virtuosity. The pressure of events in the novel transmutes this artist figure possessed of "reputation" and "taste" into a tragic heroine whose preparations for death (especially the elaborately decorated coffin) nonetheless continue to speak to her aesthetic sensibility. Belford's labors, on the other hand, can be seen as self-denying rather than self-defining. As one of his duties as executor of her will, he compiles the text that justifies her title to consideration as "not only an ornament to her sex, but to human nature" (1363), even as it lays bare his own frailties. Yet, paradoxically, in the very anonymity of his work, he discovers a way to speak to the community at large. Despite Clarissa's central role, it is Belford's apparently peripheral identity that seems finally to be more compatible with georgic as a mode concerned with the socially constructive and enabling impetus of labor. Her labor, played out in the context of her relation to and status as property, comes finally to stand as emblem of a residual order. Its limitations are subsumed by the emergent order epitomized by Belford, who in his role as bourgeois hero engages in modes of production centered on the building of a text. With the shift of attention from real property (the Dairy-house, the Harlowe estate, the woman's body) to portable (the letters, "The History of a Young Lady"), the georgic emphasis on labor finds expression especially in the labor of making meaning. This chapter will consider how the equation of woman and property, and the correlative associations of gender and genre, allow this meaning to communicate so distinctly the informing principles of a newly powerful middle class.

Shortly after Belford first meets Clarissa, at a party designed by Lovelace to make her appear publicly as his wife, he writes to Lovelace entreating him to spare her. His appeal rests on the assertion of her "striking difference" from other women and on the implication of Lovelace's individual and family "honour" in the preservation of her exemplary virtue (710, 713). But Lovelace refuses to rise to the bait of either the personal claim of distinctive innocence or of the social one of aristocratic mores. Instead, he draws on a narrowly legalistic interpretation of relationship in order to justify his predatory actions:

And whose property, I pray thee, shall I invade, if I pursue my schemes of love and vengeance? – Have not those who have a right in her, renounced that right? – Have they not wilfully exposed her to dangers? – yet must know that such a woman would be considered a lawful prize by as many as could have the opportunity to attempt her? (717)[1]

As so often in Richardson's novel, the terrible ironies of Lovelace's speech depend on its unintentional echoes. James Harlowe's denomination of his sister as "PROPERTY" is clearly recalled here. More insidious is Clarissa's own use of a complementary vocabulary to convey her recognition that to others she has little more than object status. Likening her alienation from her family to being lost in a wilderness, Clarissa early figures her position as that of a "poor estray [with] not one kind friend" (566). Later, when she escapes to Hampstead and contemplates departure for America, she again defines herself in a letter to Anna as one of those stray animals whose legal status Blackstone would tie to their being "by nature tame or reclaimable": "[T]he man who has had the assurance to think me, and to endeavour to make me, his *property*, [she writes to Anna] will hunt me from place to place, and search after me as an estray: and he knows he may do so with impunity; for whom have I to protect me from him?" (754).[2] The metaphoric elaborations surrounding the first allusion yield in the second to the bald recognition that she is considered simply as property, as a being with no claim to self-possession or to protection from the family that has renounced her. Lovelace's rhetorical questions assume that the "rights" to Clarissa are vested in external agents; Clarissa's comments acknowledge both the juridical truth of such a reading and its emotional cost.[3]

As Clarissa continues to enumerate in the letter to Anna the reasons behind her proposed emigration, she returns to the novel's recurring theme of the right uses of wealth. Now, however, she construes the estate bequeathed to her in recognition of her enactment of the georgic ideals of moderation and productive labor in terms of pain rather than pleasure. Its possession has encouraged Lovelace and her family to act on their common assumption of a transparent equivalency between the meanings of woman and property. In the process, she has been stripped of the agency that allowed her to exercise her impulses toward improvement. Yet even as she renounces the possibility of litigating for the estate, Clarissa exhibits the sensibility that first prompted her grandfather to bequeath it to her: "Then as to my estate, the enviable estate which has been the original cause of all my misfortunes, it shall never be mine upon litigated terms. What is there in being enabled to boast that I am worth more than *I can use*, or *wish to use*? – And if my power is circumscribed, I shall not have that to answer for, which I should have if I did not use it as I ought: which very few do" (754).

Clarissa's sense of herself as an accountable being leads her to define power as a moral obligation to act in constructive and responsible ways. The reiteration of "use" in the passage underlines the social purpose that attaches to the fact of possession.[4] For Lovelace, on the other hand, power operates in distinctly self-referential terms. As Belford recounts, "from the cradle, as I have heard thee [Lovelace] own, thou ever delightedst to sport with and torment the animal ... that thou lovedst, and hadst a power over" (710). The contrast of utility and sportiveness here speaks to a recurring difference in their modes of representation. Clarissa tends to render experience in the form of causally structured narratives with strong endings, while Lovelace takes delight in the elliptical pleasures of change and indeterminacy.

Responses to property in terms both of self-possession and of control over external objects thus function paradigmatically for Clarissa and Lovelace. Her sense of accountability encourages an acceptance of authority and a scrupulous attention to the uses to which she puts her talents. His sense that resistance serves as a catalyst for inventive self-display leads him repeatedly to test the integrity of others. Deconstructionist critics following William Warner have tended to read these opposed notions of agency as the axis around which the formal and ethical issues of the novel cohere. The limitations of such interpretations follow from their exclusion of the historically crucial (and inter-related) terms of class and gender, and of the key role played by Belford in enunciating them.

The contrast of Clarissa and Lovelace is often represented in the light of structural oppositions generated from the meanings first assigned the principals, whether these be psychoanalytic, archetypal, or informed by a deconstruction of the "humanist sublime."5 But questions relating to gender disturb such categorization and transform the opposition of Clarissa and Lovelace into parity. In the gender politics that underscore Richardson's novels, independent female action consistently appears as at once necessary and suspect. Initially, the heroine is invested with the capacity to articulate the ideal order that each novel advances. Clarissa may thus in the past, with the sanction of her grandfather's encouragement, have realized the right uses of wealth, but the conditional voice in which she speaks before the rape ("if my power is circumscribed, I shall not have that to answer for, which I should have if I did not use it as I ought") marks the degree to which her agency is compromised by the loss of male protection. Only when she recovers a form of protection in Belford's promise to serve as her executor can she again assume a purposive role in relation to her property. And at this point, of course, she is very nearly dead and Belford is firmly installed as the bourgeois hero, with a special mandate to do for her what she has been unable to do for herself.

Lovelace's responses to Clarissa are, in turn, doubly determined by gender. On the one hand, he asserts his proprietorial rights to her in terms that echo the Harlowes' denial of her inwardness and claims to self-possession. On the other, he admits that one of the impediments to formalizing that ownership through marriage is his recognition of her integrity. Marriage would give him only legal title to a self that in its completeness would make him perpetually feel his own limitations: "To tell me of my acquisition in her, and that she, with all her excellencies, shall be *mine* in full property, is a mistake – it cannot be so – For shall I not be *hers*; and not *my own*? Will not every act of her duty (as I cannot deserve it) be a condescension, and a triumph over me?" (734).

Richardson's comic novels acknowledge that the "*irrevocable* destiny" of marriage, as Lady G. in *Sir Charles Grandison* says, demands that a woman's name be "sunk, and lost! [and that she become the] property, person and will, of another, excellent as the man is; obliged to go to a new house; to be ingrafted into a new family; to leave her own, who so dearly love her."[6] In neither *Pamela* nor *Sir Charles Grandison* does the imminent denial of female selfhood appear to trouble the prospective husband. But in *Clarissa*, Lovelace clearly finds the legal fiction of his own preeminence an insufficient shield against what he assumes will be a continual and disturbing awareness of his spouse's excellence.

The codes of gendered behavior that determine both Clarissa's inability to pursue independent action and Lovelace's ambivalent response to her superior virtue mesh with generic conventions adapted from the Restoration stage. These are implicitly associated with a departure from the more mundane concerns of the "new manner of writing." In a 1748 letter to Aaron Hill, Richardson thus describes his work as "more than a Novel or Romance . . . it is of the Tragic Kind."[7] The Preface to *Sir Charles Grandison* similarly describes the "melancholy Scene" of his previous novel as one in which a "truly *Christian Heroine*, proves superior to her Trials; and her Heart, always excellent, refined and exalted by every one of them, rejoices in the Approach of a happy Eternity"; Lovelace, "in the Bloom of Life," possessed of "Wit and Youth, of Rank and Fortune, and of every outward Accomplishment" (i. 3–4) effects her apotheosis and his own destruction. The mutual intransigence of the principals, the paralysis of action induced by the fierce sense of the threat represented by the other, the waste of excellence conveyed by their deaths: each of these speaks to Richardson's sense that tragedy has a higher stake than novel or romance to artistic and moral seriousness.

The particular use made of tragedy in *Clarissa*, however, works to reinforce a very novelistic dedication to the middle ground between the high cultural claims of tragedy and what Richardson himself seems to assume are the lower ones of novel and romance. Tragedy provides him with a formal structure for distinguishing between the attractive but ultimately self-destructive absolutism of a Clarissa or a Lovelace and the consensual authority Belford achieves in his accession to full maturity in the novel's denouement. But Belford's preeminence as narrator in the period following Clarissa's death disrupts our ability to read the novel as tragedy.

The expiatory deaths of the principals usher in a period of lengthy negotiations overseen by Belford in his sometime role as possessive individualist. His tempering of the claims to ownership of Clarissa's body and effects, made equally and aggressively by the Harlowes and Lovelace after her death, consolidates the mediatory function of property law in the fallen world of the novel's ending. In the "Conclusion" to the novel written by Belford, such law acquires providential agency: the scourge of James, who finds himself "obliged at a very great expense to support [the] claim to estates" (1491) of his termagant wife, and the indirect benefactor of Belford himself, whose son through Lord M's "devise" (1493) (his "testamentary disposition of real property"[8]) will inherit the Hertfordshire estate once intended for Lovelace.

The novel's deployment of tragic conventions also invites consideration in terms of gender. Tragedy affords Richardson a structure through which he can not only vindicate consensus but also depict its agents as necessarily male. Clarissa's heroic virtue is represented in the novel as at once radically her own and intrinsic to her sex. Although she is exemplary as a tragic heroine, her sex allows Richardson to question the efficacy of her virtue on the grounds that being a woman limits the independent pursuit and realization of her principles. The first adjustment in Clarissa's affiliation with an ideal of self-affirming labor thus occurs with the death of her grandfather; after his death she may invoke but not enact the conditions of the georgic mode. The logic of the novel in fact suggests that Clarissa's inheritance of her grandfather's estate precipitates a literalized enforcement of the equation between woman and property, an equation implicit in the drugged body Lovelace rapes, and fully realized in the corpse over which all wrangle.

The double structure of tragedy – its movement toward catastrophe and the recognition effected in the denouement – works in concert with a parallel shift from the representation of Clarissa's virtue to the enactment of Belford's. The inheritance, paradoxically, renders Clarissa's commitment to integrity (both literal and figurative) increasingly abstract and without agency. Her death, in turn, frees Belford to realize through his industriousness a qualified form of her ideals. Francis Bacon's commendation of genuinely purposive reading seems appropriate to this discussion of Clarissa's commitment to the ennobling capabilities of the active life which is denied her: "And surely, if the purpose be in good earnest, not to write at leisure that which men may read at leisure, but really to instruct and suborn action and active life, these Georgics of the mind, concerning the husbandry and tillage thereof, are no less worthy than the heroical descriptions of virtue, duty, and felicity."[9] *Clarissa* advances a female exemplar of virtue and duty whose sensibility is fully attuned to the value of instruction. It is Clarissa's experience that provides the matter of the novel and the making of her self into a saint that provides Belford with his life's work. But at the end of the novel, he effects the negotiations and compromises necessary for the georgics of the mind to engage the complexities of civic society.[10]

Belford's executorship includes amassing and arranging for the publication of the letters; this becomes the project of the narrative itself. Within the fiction sustained by epistolary correspondence, his is the disembodied voice which alerts readers to inconsistencies in characters' representations and instructs us in editorial practices of excision and abbreviation. His shadowy presence also affords a textual correlative to our own alternations between absorption in and detachment from the letters. In this distancing capacity, the editorial voice secures for itself something approaching omniscience. The conclusion to this chapter will argue that this adjustment from engagement to judgment allows Belford to assume the role of historian, not in the classical mode of one who describes public events, but in the sentimental mode that informs the philosophical histories of the Scottish Enlightenment writers. With them, as well, he shares a distinctive response to property as a civilizing agent and gauge of cultural progress. But first, I would like to consider how in *Pamela* the idea of contract substantiates the link between civility and property that will be so important to Richardson's later fiction.

The progressivist edge in narratives which take issues relating to property as their originating point can be seen in their reliance on the principle of contract. This is especially evident in novels like *Pamela* where the hero's final assimilation of the heroine's virtue proceeds by reference to scenes in which Pamela either accedes to or resists compacts proffered by Mr. B. Ann Louise Kibbie has suggested that the novel sets in tension two ideas of female character and two models of property: a mercurial personality whose relationships are transactional is played off against a fixed self whose constancy exhibits a rejection of the marketplace for the stability of landed property.[11] A detailed look at a pair of early letters – numbers one and eleven – suggests the ways in which "the conflict between a current and a fixed self" (561), which Kibbie sees as central to the period's understanding of women, is in fact experienced equally (if dischronically) by Mr. B and Pamela. Such conflict produces a contractual vocabulary through which B will understand the interdependence of the literal and figurative connotations of self as property, first in relation to Pamela and then himself.

In the novel's opening pages, the two male arbiters of Pamela's plot concur in their evaluation of the female body as a form of property. Mr. Andrews's response to the "four golden guineas, and some silver" that Mr. B gives Pamela after his mother's death alerts us to their shared reading of woman in material terms: "we *fear*," writes her father, " – yes, my dear child, we *fear*, – you should be *too* grateful, and reward him with that jewel, your virtue, which no riches, nor favour, nor any thing in this life, can make up to you" (3).[12] Within the conventions of a seduction narrative, "that jewel" of chastity appears the sum of Pamela's worth, both to the would-be rake Mr. B and to her parents who wish her death before dishonor.

But Pamela's initial ingenuous account of her acceptance of the guineas is soon followed by a letter that reveals she has exchanged the passive role assigned women in the seduction scenes of early amatory novels for a more active and vocal resistance.[13] Her claims to integrity depend on a self-possession that, typically of a nascent commercial society, acquires authority from the perceived failure of B's *noblesse*. Excusing the impropriety of her language, she maintains that it is "his own fault" that "I *he* and *him* him too much" in her letters, since his familiarity with her has caused him to "lose all his dignity" (11). The connection here between class and genre – the leveling "he" and "him," the medium of epistolary exchange – emerges quickly in the novel. While letter one makes brief reference to Pamela's status change – her lady's "goodness ... qualified [me] above my degree" (1) – and while her father's response reads her status change as a manifestation of seduction, the pendant letter eleven, in keeping with the emergent ideology of commerce, is at once more overt and less precise about the class implications of B's and Pamela's encounter.

This ambivalence is heightened by Richardson's initial attention to the customary double connotations of "place" as physical site and hierarchical marker. Mr. B attempts his seduction "in the summer house in the little garden," standard *locus amoris* of contemporary fiction.[14] But when Pamela excuses her attempted exit by declaring, "It does not become your poor servant to stay in your presence, Sir, without your business required it; and I hope I shall always know my place" (11), the figurative usage of "place" appears distinctly problematic. Our suspicion that Pamela speaks ironically to B's transgression of social place is confirmed by their dialogue as recounted in the remainder of letter eleven. Richardson has invoked received conventions of plot and place only to allow Pamela to skew them with her reliance on a reciprocally binding contract, a contract that comes into play when B willfully violates the existing terms of class hierarchy.[15]

Michael McKeon's account of Pamela and B as "transitional" figures, "equally and symmetrically representative of that complex social phenomenon which their posterity learned to call the rise of the middle class," plots the narrative convergence of the principals "from the opposite corners of industrious 'virtue' and corrupt aristocratic 'honour'."[16] Letter eleven suggests that Richardson in fact uses the virtue/ honor complex, as he does seduction narratives and pastoral romance, as ironic counters to his own privileged terms of labor and contract. Conveying the authority of the latter, however, poses distinctive representational problems since in Richardson's novel their vehicle is a relationship – that between master and servant – whose meaning is socially and economically prescribed. Richardson addresses this difficulty in part by according gesture a powerfully expressive role in the dialogue between Pamela and Mr. B in letter eleven. But he also structures their encounter in ways that reveal the principals casting off the exclusive languages of their distinct classes in favor of a shared vocabulary dominated by personal and fiscal exchange.

In marking out a discursive realm that is neither that of privilege nor of subordination, this vocabulary also establishes a social space that supersedes the conventional markers of place – literal and figurative – of the letter's opening. In rejecting B's claim that he has done no "harm" to her with the "frightful eagerness" of the kisses that accompany his offer to make a "gentlewoman" of her, Pamela maintains that, on the contrary: "you have taught me to forget myself, and what belongs to me, and have lessened that distance that fortune has made between us, by demeaning yourself, to be so free to a poor servant" (12). Rather than asserting his class right to seduce servants, Mr. B concurs with the charge, echoing its language in "own[ing] [he has] demeaned" himself. He then invokes the principle of utility and exchange to justify and compensate. His attempt was "only to try [her]," he declares, and then, "to make [her] amends for the fright," he puts some "gold in [her] hand."

In the novel's opening scene, B "gave [Pamela] with his own hand" the guineas which she accepted as due wages and which her father (after advice from widow Mumford) grudgingly acknowledged might be considered as a death-bed perquisite. For the "three or four years" previous to her lady's death, Pamela's remuneration took the form of "clothes and linen" (3); B's gesture, then, potentially defines Pamela in relation to what historians designate the initial stages of the wage system.[17] But while she accepts compensation for past labor, she refuses to engage her services in advance and in letter eleven rejects his placatory gift: "For to say truth I thought it looked like taking earnest, and so I put it upon the bench, and as he seemed vexed and confused at what he had done, I took the opportunity to open the door, and went out of the summer-house" (12). The literal and figurative meanings of "earnest" are nicely played out both in Pamela's immediate action and in her subsequent responses to B. Literally, "earnest" is money paid to secure a bargain or contract, and figuratively, "a foretaste, instalment, pledge, of anything afterward to be received in greater abundance" (*OED*). In refusing this sexual contract, Pamela makes possible the plot of the novel itself, a plot dedicated to securing "in greater abundance" the rewards of consummate virtue. What is necessary for the completion of the plot is B's conversion to the supreme value of the figurative rather than the simply literal properties of Pamela.

His comments on her dowry reveal his final acquiescence to the terms of this inner worth. She brings to the marriage, he tells her,

> an experienced truth and well-tried virtue, and a wit and behaviour more than equal to the station you will be placed in; to say nothing of this sweet person, that itself might captivate a monarch; and of the meekness of temper, and sweetness of disposition, which makes you superior to all the women I ever saw. (301)

Despite his deference to her integrity, virtue still appears here as a commodity, something which B's labor has invested with a value that the contract of marriage will allow him continuously to reap. Moreover, his commendation of her "experienced truth and well-tried virtue" grants to himself a responsibility for her qualities which the structure of the novel in fact contests. Fielding's *Shamela* made comic capital of this assumption, setting up Booby as the gull of his scheming servant's intention to obtain "a settled settlement, for me, and all my heirs, all my whole lifetime . . . or else crosslegged is the word."[18] In the original, Pamela's plots are not represented as fiscally self-serving, nor is B the dunce he appears in Fielding's text. But B's understanding does repeatedly lag behind Pamela's. Richardson directs our attention to this discrepancy (and tacitly to her precocity) by constructing scenes in which B recapitulates an experience formerly hers. Such repetition tends to work in terms that confirm an adjustment in B's understanding of Pamela first as literal and then as figurative property. Through his involvement with Pamela, then, B acquires full knowledge of the complexities of bourgeois modes of commodification and exchange.

The most densely realized account of the transfer of her knowledge to him by way of his enactment of her inwardness occurs after Pamela's departure from the Lincolnshire estate. Her absence and a now acute awareness of her exalted virtue paradoxically provoke a markedly physical response from B, a "severe illness" (237) that lifts only when she returns and symbolically restores the balance of physical and spiritual. As so often in *Pamela*, he marks the significance of the occasion by offering a summary account of the novel's plot. But in this instance, he gives equal play to beauty and virtue as provocation for a seduction he finally realized would "make *you* miserable, and me not happy" (239). With that conclusion in mind, he "resolved to overcome [him]self" (239). His struggle to master her by enacting the derivative terms of a seduction plot ends with the achievement of self-discipline and the declaration that he will endeavor to be "[his] own original" (240). Just as Belford realizes the terms of Clarissa's meshing of inwardness and socially responsible labor, so too in the comic mode of *Pamela* does B.

The plot of *Pamela Volume II* suggests that, paradoxically, for B to "be [his] own original," he must continuously defer to his wife's greater virtue. "I shall behold you with awe," he tells her after she confronts him about his possible adultery with the Countess, "and implicitly give myself up to all your dictates: for what you *say*, and what you *do*, must be ever right."[19] Yet even as B's recognition of Pamela as his "tutelary angel" grants narrative priority to her influence, his moral reformation is not represented exclusively as the outgrowth of deference to an idealized female sensibility realized in disinterested labor (*Pamela Volume II*.314). It is also a response to the obverse of that order, a virtual counter-world that appears in both *Pamela* and *Clarissa* in the form of a female confederacy.

CHAPTER 3

Wicked confederacies

Clarissa's father responded to her elopement from Harlowe Place by leveling a curse at her. Toward the end of her life, she returns repeatedly to the accuracy of his prediction "that [she] may meet [her] punishment, both *here* and *hereafter*, by means of that very wretch in whom [she has] chosen to place [her] wicked confidence" (509). In fact, her punishment is effected by Lovelace not alone but in concert with Sinclair and her women, that "wicked confederacy" (825) that Clarissa envisions as dedicated to her destruction and whom Judith Wilt argues participate actively in the rape.[1] The collaborative rape also confirms James Harlowe's *Georgics* allusion, *amor omnibus idem*, in two complementary ways. In the first place, the complicity of both sexes in the working out of the curse speaks to the accuracy of his assertion of a universal sexuality. In the second, it serves to conflate those who foretell her fate – father and son – with those who enact it. Clarissa will later strengthen the Harlowe/harlot link by extending the notion of confederacy beyond its earlier exclusive denomination of the Sinclair group. Writing to Mrs. Norton, she condemns in similar terms the collective leaguing against her evident in the Harlowes' "strong confederacy . . . (a strong confederacy indeed!), against a poor girl, their daughter, sister, niece" (1168).

Clarissa's final willingness to indict her family for reneging on their given relationships with her as daughter, sister, and niece marks her release from the guilty sense that she in her own person affords proof of James's allusion to sexual appetite as "in all the same." In refusing to offer herself as "harlot-niece" (909) to Lovelace's family after the rape, she initially accepted her identity with the women at Sinclair's house, an identity displaced only by her subsequent attention to the complicated business of dying. The women themselves persist in "vouch[ing] for the inclinations and hypocrisy of the whole sex" (940), viewing Clarissa's modesty as at best fragile self-delusion. In their attempts to degrade her, they enact "so vile a confederacy" that their victim wonders whether it is the result of a "compact with the grand deceiver, in the person of his horrid agent" (900), Mrs. Sinclair. The suspicion of demonic influence expresses her sense of the terrible unnaturalness of women preying on members of their own sex – "can there be any woman so vile to woman?" – and a correlative faith in an inherent sympathy and protectiveness that binds women together in a community of shared interests.

This latter ideal predominates in *Sir Charles Grandison*. In Richardson's final novel, the focus is on groups of women dedicated not to seduction but to securing marriages. Yet the structure and disposition of these groups are curiously allied with their negative incarnations in *Clarissa*. As in *Clarissa*, their relationship with the heroine is complex, largely because these secondary female characters are granted a forthrightness denied the protagonist. But in both novels an unsentimental manipulation of courtship rituals allows these subordinate women to consolidate (at least temporarily) an independent authority. And in both novels, such authority comes with the recognition of a clear distinction between an outward compliance with the forms of "female" behavior whose terms are mandated by men, and a more fundamental solidarity experienced by women whose language with each other is shaped by a candor that specifically excludes male participation. Lady D's conversation with Harriet Byron, whom she wishes to see marry her son, affirms the compact of interests women must pursue independent of male knowledge:

Remember that I value you for the frankness you are praised for – A little female trifling to my *son*, if you will, in order to be assured of his value for you (and men love not all halcyon courtships) but none to *me*, my love. I'll assist you, and keep your counsel, in the first case, if it be necessary. He shall love you above all the women on earth, and convince you that he does, or he shall not call you his – But no female trifling to his mother, child! We women should always understand one another. (1.278)

Harriet Byron's status as Richardson's heroine demands that she be slightly distanced from the kind of knowingness the Countess here expresses. It is left to Charlotte Grandison to make explicit the terms on which "women of superior talents" secure authority in marriage. "[A] fool and a wit are the extreme points, and equally unmanageable," she maintains; between the two is the appropriate husband, one who accepts his wife's "will [as] a law to him" (1.274) as long as publicly he appears the ascendent partner.

The necessary complicity of the husband in his own private subordination points to the limitations of this benign female authority. These limitations prove crucial in *Pamela* and *Clarissa*, where the maternal figures of Mrs. Jervis and Mrs. Harlowe reveal themselves unable or unwilling to contain their master's and husband's wilful treatment of women as property. But Richardson somewhat obscures the culpability both of these women and, more interestingly, of the predatory men, by directing the reader's attention to the "evil" women who symmetrically counterbalance the "good" ones: *Pamela*'s Mrs. Jewkes and Mrs. Jervis and *Clarissa*'s Mother Sinclair and Mrs. Harlowe. There are strong narrative reasons for this in *Pamela*: with the division of responsibility for Pamela's suffering, B's eventual reformation to *paterfamilias* gains in credibility. In *Clarissa*, the parallel fates of Sinclair and Lovelace allow elaboration of the deep suspicion attaching to the idea of female agency, which *Pamela* had conveyed through the confederacy of Jewkes and Mr. B.

The nature of this confederacy speaks to the greater capacity for wickedness assigned women over men in Richardson's fiction. Mrs. Jewkes, in her supervision of Pamela at the Lincolnshire estate, consistently outdoes B in his role as aristocratic debaucher. When Pamela declares that B's claim to her as his "property" is only "such as a thief may plead to stolen goods," Mrs. Jewkes responds with a spirited defense of a gentleman's right to consider women as found property. To her, assertions of individual integrity on the part of female servants constitute "downright rebellion"; the only form of possession for which the young and the pretty ones may petition is the remuneration that follows their seduction. His "shill-I shall-I" hesitations consequently seem to Mrs. Jewkes an unnecessary niceness: "if I was in his place, he should not have his property in you long questionable" (108), she tells Pamela. Her assumption of masculine identity here anticipates her later appearance as surrogate rapist in the scene in which B, disguised as Nan, enters the bed shared by Pamela and Mrs. Jewkes. When he interrupts "the dreadful time of reckoning" to conciliate the shrieking Pamela, a clearly exasperated Mrs. Jewkes eggs him on: "'What you do, Sir, do: don't stand, dilly dallying. She cannot exclaim worse than she has done: and she'll be quieter when she knows the worst'" (178–9).

In the event, of course, B is quelled by Pamela's exemplary virtue and his confederacy with Jewkes dissolved. The distance between B and his former agent now serves as one measure of his internalized probity, for, as Pamela notes, while Mrs. Jewkes's "talk and actions are entirely different from what they used to be, quite circumspect and decent"

(339), it is still "all *say* from her, and goes no further than the ear" (303). In the novel's postscript, where her "odious character" casts into relief the "amiableness of Mrs. Jervis" (451), Mrs. Jewkes's ties to B are further attenuated. No longer does she serve as seducer *manqué*, her sexual threat vividly realized in Pamela's initial description of her "huge hand, and an arm as thick as my waist... She has a hoarse, man-like voice, and is as thick as she's long" (97). She is now invoked as a lesson to the "UPPER SERVANTS of great families" on "what to avoid" if they wish "to make themselves valued and esteemed by all who know them" (451).

In *Clarissa*, such minimizing of female agency by reversion to issues of role rather than personality is jettisoned for an extravagantly detailed death-bed scene in which the "spectacle" of the "huge quaggy carcase" (1388) of the unrepentant Sinclair provides an occasion for Belford's extended peroration against "the miry wallowers the generality of men of our class are in themselves and generally trough and sty with" (1393). The self-loathing hyperbole here is designed at once to establish Belford's revulsion from his former libertine ways and to reinforce the bestial imagery used to define Sinclair at the novel's end. As with most of Richardson's bad women, she has throughout been characterized as masculine. But the comic capital made from the confusion of sexual signals in *Pamela* – Mrs. Jewkes responds to Pamela in terms that are not, as the latter primly observes, appropriate to "two persons of one sex" (91) – is largely absent here. Mrs. Sinclair is instead cast as a consummate performer, able perniciously to exploit those forms of authority to which Lady D's speech (quoted above) referred in *Sir Charles Grandison*. She uses the distinction of "female" and "woman" to practice her trade in the divided house, observes the conventions of a decorous public language in the presence of Clarissa and a private, complicitously "frank" one with Lovelace and her confederates, and manipulates courtship ritual in the prostitution of desire.

But just as Mrs. Jewkes offers a displaced version of B's role as seducer, so too does Mrs. Sinclair exaggerate in her person Lovelace's faults by rendering in exclusively carnal terms the social and sexual ambivalences inherent in his character. After the rape, he goes so far as to suggest that she bears primary responsibility for the act: "Oh that cursed, cursed house! But for the women of that! – Then their damned potions! But for *those*, had [Clarissa's] *unimpaired* intellects and *the majesty of her virtue* saved her, as it once did by her humble eloquence, another time by her terrifying menaces against her own life" (1183). Sinclair's "vile associate," Sally Martin, later concurs with this judgement, "acknowledg[ing] that [Clarissa's] ruin was owing more to their instigations than even ... to [Lovelace's] own vileness" (1378).

The female confederacy's capacity for evil is tied to the women's offenses against the strictures of both gender and class. In place of that natural sympathy which consolidates women's friendship as a defense against an alien male world, they enact a counter order epitomized by a self-serving aggression the novel deems the special province of predatory men. As Lovelace observes, their deviance from the norms of feminine sensibility compounds their threat: "A bad woman is certainly, Jack, more terrible to her own sex, than even a bad man" (935). In his summary account of the Sinclair entourage, they come to incorporate a radical misogyny, more frightening than that expressed by men because collectively voiced and enacted by women who are all educated and of "parentage not contemptible" (Sinclair is even a "woman of family" [940]).

Its wilful repudiation of both social advantage and the "natural" distinctions of gender in the interests of business means that the female confederacy finally stands as the novel's nightmare vision of a fully realized commodity culture. The social leveling that underwrites the vigorous expansion of the market thus has the effect of making persons property and investing property itself with consummate value. Within this new order, the terms of patronage and deference which once shaped class relations yield, as Lovelace himself recognizes, to a system of universal clientage. By this reckoning, Lovelace's role relative to the Sinclair entourage shifts from sponsor to dependent, one as vulnerable to their authority as Clarissa herself. He unwittingly has served as their procurer, affording them the opportunity to impose on this "perverse lady" a "humility and passiveness" that will make her "draw in their traces" (940) and so secure the continued viability of their commerce.

Their trade in flesh thus makes them at once horribly parodic versions of the masters they nominally serve and, paradoxically, more powerful than those masters. The terms of sexual difference that make a Lovelace intermittently susceptible to Clarissa's assertion of a distinctive feminine virtue fail to disturb their relentless acquisitiveness. James Harlowe's *Georgics* allusion, like Lovelace's attempted seduction, assumes that the proof of equal sexual appetite removes from women any claim to an inherent female morality. In its absence, they suppose that women will defer to the terms of class and gender as established by male judgment. But the confederacy headed by Sinclair suggests both that such terms are more imagined than real and that women manipulate male desire in order to further their own fundamental attachment to power.

The attribution of power to women here invites scrutiny of the relation between the terms of gender and class, since in the eighteenth-century novel the former so often affords the vocabulary for exploring the latter. *Clarissa* suggests that a culture which fails to secure consensus about the need for all-embracing distinctions of masculine from feminine liberates an energy that the novel genders as destructively female. But the life histories that epitomize this female energy refer to the terms of class as well as sex. Sinclair's confederates, Sally Martin and Polly Horton, we are told in the Conclusion, betrayed their "sense ... and good modern education" through indulgence "in the fashionable follies and luxuries of an age given up to those amusements and pleasures which are so apt to set people of but *middle fortunes* above all the useful employments of life" (1491). The two women here figure the dangerous squandering of bourgeois prudence in the emulation of aristocratic excess.[2]

The novel, which opens with a celebration of one form of female labor in Clarissa's industriousness, thus ends with a lamentation on its willful repudiation by those women of "*middle fortunes*," whose best interests, the Conclusion asserts, properly lie in their pursuit of the "useful employments of life." This chapter began with the argument that the novel's intervening seven volumes mark out the curtailing of Clarissa's usefulness as social agent, but allow her glorious example to effect Belford's reform and enactment of what is finally coded as masculine labor. I would like now to turn to consider the narrative implications of that labor, and, more specifically, the ways in which Richardson's gendering of reading and writing comes to stand for the relative capabilities of men and women.

CHAPTER 4

"The work of bodies": reading, writing, and documents

The interest of Belford's role in the book lies less in his distinct attributes as a character and more in the function he serves as purported editor of the correspondence we read. The source of the published text and the design behind its production are revealed to us only as Clarissa readies herself for death. Intent on having "justice" done to her character by securing a "protector of [her] memory," she requests that Belford, "the *only* gentleman possessed of materials that will enable him to do [her] character justice" (1176), serve as her executor. *Clarissa's* testamentory origins give an additional ironic twist to its status as property: it is both a material object, "The History of a Young Lady," and an extended prologue to "The Will" through which the heroine orders her worldly goods and her vindication. From her perspective, the publication of the correspondence affords strong evidence that she is "well satisfied of [her] innocence" and marks the relinquishment of her ties to the world of the living. In sparing her "the necessity of writing her own story" (1178), Belford thus releases her from the thrall of the past: "I shall also be freed from the pain of recollecting things that my soul is vexed at; and this at a time when its tumults should be allayed in order to make way for the most important preparation" (1176–7).

Yet despite this turn inward, Clarissa retains an acute sense of audience. She anticipates in highly characteristic moral terms the reception of her text. She hopes that "when [Lovelace] comes to revolve the whole story placed before him in one strong light, and when he shall have the catastrophe likewise before him; and shall become in a manner interested in it: who knows but that from a still higher principle, he may so regulate his future actions as to find his own reward in the everlasting welfare which is wished him by his obliged servant, Clarissa Harlowe?" (1177). The "one strong light" provided by the gathering of the scattered correspondence into a coherent text will allow "interest" to provoke conversion. Clarissa's faith in the reformative agency of her "whole story" rests on the assumption that her death will give an irresistible moral point to the plot of innocence reviled.

Belford's account of the authority her narrative possesses depends upon a quite different view of the reader's relation to the text:

You cannot imagine how proud I am of this trust [he writes to Lovelace] . . . As she is always writing, what a melancholy pleasure will the perusal and disposition of her papers afford me! Such a sweetness of temper, so much patience and resignation, as she seems to be mistress of; yet writing of and in the midst of *present* distresses! How much more lively and affecting, for that reason, must her style be, than all that can be read in the dry, narrative, unanimated style of persons relating dangers and difficulties surmounted! The minds of such not labouring in suspense, not tortured by the pangs of uncertainty about events still hidden in the womb of fate; but on the contrary perfectly at ease; the relator unmoved by his own story, how then able to move the hearer or reader? (1178)

If Clarissa's version of narratorial success takes as its measure Lovelace's capitulation to her edifying "whole story" and subsequent "regulat[ion of] his future actions," Belford's involves a more complex novelistic tension between participation and detachment. He emphasizes how reading what has been written to the moment invites an emotional engagement that both heightens and deflects readerly self-consciousness. The oxymoronic "melancholy pleasure" produced by the "lively and affecting style" depends on the playing of this vicarious emotion against the distance created by retrospective knowledge. Clarissa has believed that narrative authority derives from the text's expression of objective moral truths to which readers, once drawn by "interest", must defer. This gives way in Belford's reckoning to a diffuse sensationalism that privileges crisis and indeterminacy and aims to make the reader recapitulate the writer's experience of being "in the midst of *present* distresses."

In these accounts of reading, Belford and Clarissa exemplify a wide-ranging distinction within the period between sentimental and didactic discourses. As the eighteenth-century novel engages more fully with the culture of sensibility, the distinction becomes at once increasingly problematic and less clearly oppositional.[1] With the limited narrative techniques available for shaping readers' responses indirectly, authors needed to negotiate carefully between their desire to sustain the illusion of their created worlds and the dangers implicit in allowing readers unmediated access to them.[2] The negative associations of sentimentalism with effeminacy and vicarious emotion compound the difficulties inherent in a spectatorial aesthetic that aims to be at once affective and definitive.

These difficulties might seem magnified in *Clarissa* where the epistolary mode limits narratorial intrusion. The lack of a controlling voice has invited critics to invest individual characters with authority, a tactic that in fact reduces the scope of authority. If we consider the novel from the perspective not of particular fully realized characters but from that of the character who effectively makes the text (and who so achieves something approaching to the quality of omniscience) a quite different understanding emerges. In the anonymity of his labor as editor, Belford makes the substantial issue of the novel the authority of language itself. By deflecting attention away from Belford as personality, Richardson is able to exploit the metatextual possibilities implicit in his characters' status as readers and writers. In the contrast of Belford and Clarissa as readers, for instance, one discerns Richardson's own divided sense of both his authorial mandate and his relation to his audience. One of the consequences of the feminized paradigms of reading advocated by Belford is its confirmation of a subjectivity that may function independent of authorial intentions. As the complicated history of revisions to the novel reveals, Richardson strenuously resisted such gestures toward readerly autonomy. But his attempts at control invariably conflict with the equally powerful desire to retain his readers' sentimental engagement with the plight of his characters. In the Postcript, he thus voices the contrast of didactic and sentimental in terms of a distinction between guide and story that devalues the significance of affective involvement: "And it will, moreover, be remembered, that the author, at his first setting out, apprised the reader, that the story was to be looked upon as the vehicle only to the instruction" (1499).

Richardson's language here recalls that of Clarissa's letter to Belford, quoted above, in which she details her hope for Lovelace's reformation through reading. But this assertion of a prescriptive over a provisional hermeneutic need not necessarily discredit Belford's sentimental, "interesting" mode. As reader, Belford testifies to the absorbing pleasures of female suffering. But it is his role as an editor who engages in feats of ordering and excising that comes to constitute a privileged form of masculine labor. In fact, the novel construes the relation between the two activities of reading and editing in such rigorously causal terms that they can only artificially be distinguished. Belford's susceptibility as reader is thematically represented as a necessary prelude to his role as editor. To Clarissa, his "courage, independence, and ability to oblige"

(1176) sanction her choice of him as executor. More importantly, his maleness endows his feminized sensibility with a capacity to realize virtue through his labors in ways that are denied Clarissa.

In Belford's account to Lovelace of his first meeting with Clarissa, this gendering of labor leads to an irreconcilable opposition between woman as "all mind" and woman as "mere body":

> You may think what I am going to write too flighty; but, by my faith, I have conceived such a profound reverence for her sense and judgment that, far from thinking the man excusable who should treat her basely, I am ready to regret that such an angel of a lady should even marry. She is, in my eye, all mind: and were she to meet with a man all mind likewise, why should the charming qualities she is mistress of, be endangered? Why should such an angel be plunged so low as into the vulgar offices of domestic life? Were she mine, I should hardly wish to see her a mother unless there were a kind of moral certainty that minds like hers could be propagated. For why, in short, should not the work of bodies be left to *mere* bodies? (555)

This is an extraordinarily rich passage in its representation of Belford's understanding of female labor as the "work of bodies" – the childbirth that would "see Clarissa a mother." Her "sense and judgment," evident to the reader both in the voluminous correspondence which precedes this comment and in the georgic industry to which she dedicated herself at her grandfather's estate, cannot be accommodated within the frame of such a limited and literalized interpretation of woman's labor. Only by denying her gender and invoking the transcendent category, "all mind," can he testify to her worth.

The novel wavers in considering his central question – "why should such an angel be plunged so low as into the vulgar offices of domestic life?" – as a genuinely open or a rhetorically closed one. In the retrospective moments before the crisis of courtship forces the issue of Clarissa's right to her own person, "the vulgar offices of domestic life" appear fulfilling and constructive. They afford the means by which her exemplary virtue can be both realized and acknowledged in ways that confirm her worth as an individual and as an active participant in her community. But in the novel's present, the activities of reading and writing come to displace other kinds of labor. Thus questions of ownership come to be textualized and gendered through epistolary exchange.

In using the medium of letters to explore questions relating to self-possession and material value, Richardson carefully distinguishes between the characteristic modes of Clarissa and Lovelace. He also measures the qualities of inwardness expressed through their mutual involutions against Belford's constitutive powers as editor. Curiously, the value attached to Belford's editorial function exists in inverse proportion to his actual participation in the novel's epistolary exchanges. This emerges in the discrepancy between the relative infrequency with which his own letters occur and his status as primary recipient of Lovelace's correspondence. In this, he resembles Anna Howe, who also appears more often as occasion for the text than as material contributor to it. The connection between these characters' survival and final prosperity and their limited textual presence is not arbitrary. It is both consistent with and revelatory of the reverse conditions under which Lovelace and Clarissa are represented.

Their failures of communication suggest that Richardson maintains in *Clarissa* a resolutely ironic view of those forms of self-expression that aspire to absolute coherence or impermeability. In Leo Braudy's powerful rendering of the novel's central contest, the prevailing figure of penetration signifies the principals' obsessive concern with the exclusionary authority that comes with intactness: "both Lovelace and Clarissa act out of fear that they will themselves disintegrate if they do not first annihilate or by dying obviate the existence of others." The countervailing impulse to this struggle between the "impenetrable penetrators" occurs in the novel's representation of reading as a potential vehicle for the progress that the exchange of ideas makes possible.[3]

It is a peculiarly modern idea that reading represents a "mixing of one's labour" with another's thought in a way that permits individuals to claim not only ownership of those ideas but also community with other like-minded persons. As a number of critics have recently argued, intellectual property emerged as a key issue early in the eighteenth century, after the Copyright Act of 1710 initiated a debate that contested the respective merits of limited as opposed to perpetual copyright and that was resolved in favor of the former only in 1774. In Trevor Ross's formulation of the terms of this debate, the proponents of perpetual copyright express a patrician understanding of literature as remote from the corruptions of the marketplace. For them, intellectual property could thus be afforded the same protection as real estate since, according to William Enfield, writing in 1774: "Literary property . . . is indeed a kind of property invisible and untangible; but it is not on that account less real." The more modern view (implicit in the premises of the defenders of limited copyright) held that the circulation of a literary work allowed its ideas to become communal property: "the very matter and contents of . . . books," records Justice Yates in his dissenting opinion on *Millar* v. *Taylor* in 1769, "are by the author's publication of them, irrevocably given to the public; they become common; all the sentiments contained therein, rendered universally common; and when the sentiments are made common by the author's own act, every use of those sentiments must be equally common."[4]

As a London bookseller, Richardson might reasonably be expected to conform to his peers' advocacy of perpetual copyright as a hedge against the incursions of the provincial book trade. The activities of Belford, however, are in keeping with that complex of responses associated with the opposite side of the literary property debate. It is he, as the eponymous title emphasizes, who allows "Clarissa" to circulate within the public sphere, to become the property of readers, each one of whom by his purchase effectively imitates Lovelace's claim to ownership of her by an act of literal possession: rape or reading. Belford's motives, of course, are not Lovelace's. Lovelace wishes to shore up the rake's code by proving Clarissa a "mere body"; Belford to vindicate her memory and his own reformation by subjecting both to a disinterested communal judgment. The model of exchange implicit in the circulation of *Clarissa* as text has, moreover, powerful antecedents within the novel itself. There the edifying possibilities of the commerce of ideas are explored by means of a distinction between Clarissa and Lovelace, on the one hand, and Belford and Anna, on the other, not only as readers, but also as writers. In the cluster of associations informing their characteristic modes of writing, Richardson again enforces the preeminent value of Belford's editorial labors.

Lovelace's activities as writer are shaped by what William Warner calls "parodic displacements."[5] Lacking a coherent self, he appears an accretion of responses to the various and contingent actions of others, a "perfect Proteus" (1243) in his dazzling capacity to adjust appearances. As a number of critics have suggested, Lovelace paradoxically embodies the "feminine" mode of writing, "a more inward, bodily relationship to script."[6] For him, writing cannot formalize his status as unified subject, nor can correspondence involve an implicitly contractual relation between individuals. Consequently, he reads Clarissa's letters without her permission and writes forged ones, delighting in his capacity to be absorbed by the identity of another and refusing to grant that identity anything more than a highly conditional verity.

If Lovelace takes pleasure in the multiform possibilities language affords, Clarissa is no less compulsive in her enthrallment to the written word. As she writes to Anna:

And indeed, my dear, I know not how to forbear writing. I have now no other employment or diversion. I must write on, although I were not to send it to anybody. You have often heard me own the advantages I have found from writing down everything of moment that befalls me; and of all I *think* and of all I *do* that may be of future use to me – for, besides that this helps to form one to a style, and opens and expands the ductile mind, everyone will find that many a good thought evaporates in thinking; many a good resolution goes off, driven out of memory, perhaps, by some other not so good. But when I set down what I *will* do, or what I *have* done on this or that occasion; the resolution or action is before me, either to be adhered to, withdrawn or amended; and I have entered into *compact* with myself, as I may say; having given it under my own hand, to *improve* rather than go *backward*, as I live longer. (483)

Clarissa expresses here two reasons for writing: the first, an obsessive response to the absence of alternative "employment or diversion," the second, a constitutive act that recalls the terms of Charles Taylor's "punctual self" in its assumption that the self may be anchored in history by means of a documentary "compact." But, as Anna Howe realizes, in a variable world such compacts can be dangerously limiting in their constriction of the possibilities for exchange or arbitration. In urging Clarissa to come to some agreement with Lovelace about the settlements for their marriage, she advocates writing only if Clarissa finds herself unable to speak: "But speaking is certainly best: for words leave no traces; they pass as breath; and mingle with air, and may be explained with latitude. But the pen is a witness on record" (588).

Anna's advocacy of "latitude" in negotiation provides a context for reading the inflexibility of Lovelace and Clarissa. Lovelace's flouting of the contractual norms of letter writing and reading in his interceptions and forgeries affords one version of a self-aggrandizement that refuses regulation. Clarissa's self-reflexive "compact" with the written word involves an equal resistance to any broadening engagement. Their mutually intransigent languages offer textualized instances of their denial of "the idea of contract," which in John Zomchick's summary account of legal historiography serves as the dominant framework for "the development of new forms of social intercourse" in the eighteenth century.[7]

The ideal of contract as according "the individual both a sense of freedom and a means of establishing relations with others" is refused by Lovelace and Clarissa, both individually and collectively.[8] The novel represents their self-willed exclusion from the possibilities of contract by its reproduction of a limited number of letters between the principals.

And when they do correspond, the exchanges are paltry and mutually frustrating, more often than not begging requests for answers to which obdurate silence is returned. The most notable exception to this is the letter in which Clarissa secures a brief respite from Lovelace's attentions by claiming that she is "setting out with all diligence for [her] father's house" (1233), a reference which he interprets literally as Harlowe Place, but which to her signifies heaven. The differences between the terms of this letter and the norm in their correspondence are highly revealing. Its apparently conciliatory tone depends upon a double linguistic deceit which, once revealed, emphasizes Clarissa's removal of herself from the complex of property relations which shape the meaning of character in the novel. As she explains to Belford, a "*religious* meaning is couched under it," a meaning which substitutes a divine for an earthly father, heaven for Harlowe Place, and an allegorical for a novelistic her-meneutic. Firm in her conviction that Lovelace "had [no right] to invade [her]" (1274), Clarissa plays with the literal and figurative signifi-cations of property. In the process, what appears to Lovelace an authen-tic gesture of forgiveness and a prelude to marriage is revealed to be a summary rejection both of him and the things of this world. Her transformed vocabulary thus definitively marks her translation of herself from the context of "mere bodies" to that of "all mind."

At different points in the narrative, the complementary displacements of Lovelace and Clarissa exclude both from the possibility of genuine correspondence – epistolary, sexual, or social. Yet Lovelace's ability to articulate the novel's ideal – "mutual obligation is the very essence and soul of the social and commercial life" (760) – Clarissa's earlier realiz-ation of its terms in the remaking of her grandfather's estate, and Belford's anticipated pursuit of it as detailed in the novel's Postcript reinforce its centrality. For Belford, the terms of "mutual obligation" are met in his dedication to the editing of a text whose circulation will affirm the interdependence of "the social and commercial life." The conjunc-tion of the individual, the textual, and the social under the sign of conversion allows Belford to stand as positive type of the new economic man, one whose inner resources have enabled him to master the effeminacy traditionally associated with mobile forms of property.

In his history, we thus see mapped out a series of changes in which the achievement of authority depends on the assimilation and subordina-tion of what the novel variously construes as feminine: a sentimental reader, he becomes a judicious editor; a libertine dedicated to consump-tion, he becomes a *pater familias* with a strong commitment to the reform of those to whose corruption he once contributed; a confidant, he becomes an historian. Throughout this process, Belford consolidates his status as a coherent bourgeois subject, one who defines himself *through* but not *as* property.

In both *Clarissa* and *Pamela*, women enable these changes. Belford and B paradoxically achieve comprehensive control only after their equation of women and property has been shaken by the vicarious experience of female subjectivity each acquires through reading: Belford of Clarissa's letters, and B of Pamela's journal. I will return at the end of the next section to the transmutation of woman to text which both novels effect. I would like now to focus on *Pamela*'s use of the activities of reading and writing figuratively to render the feminization of the hero.

In *Pamela*, the configuration of woman, property, and text is initially detailed from the separate points of view of master and servant. To B, Pamela appears a form of property whose meaning is defined by the social and literary conventions of the seducible servant. To Pamela, claims to ownership of self justify her resistance to B's depredations, resistance memorialized first in her epistolary correspondence and then in her journal. But when the exchange of letters abruptly ends and Pamela is forced to conceal her journal account of events by stitching it into her clothes, the metaphoric significance of her writing changes. As a purely private document, the journal carries negatively self-reflexive connotations. Unlike letters, it serves no mediatory function and so must be considered apart from the modes of exchange central to "social and commercial life." It substitutes for the amendments implicit in a commitment to "mutual obligation" an unvarying accretion which has no necessary terminus.

The journal expresses the limiting characteristics of private property as understood by those Adam Ferguson deems "the interested." As "the great storemaster among animals," man instinctively, Ferguson maintains, "apprehends a relation between his person and his property, which renders what he calls his own in a manner a part of himself." For the interested, this relation is entirely sufficient. In their ceaseless accumulations, "the interested find the object of their ordinary cares . . . and, when extremely corrupted, the price of their prostitutions."[9] The circularity of the process described by Ferguson demands that such an individual read the "relation between his person and his property" as one of effective identity. It is just this reading, of course, that prevails in the conventional elision of women and property. Pamela's journal thus literally and metaphorically signifies property: it is both an alienable text recounting events and her responses to them, and, as an object, a metaphor for the female body as property. The closeness of the two terms means that she herself as property is unable to translate the textually constructed private self into a publicly acknowledged and active social being.

The difficulties attaching to this shift from private to public help us to understand the significance of the occasion of B's conversion to Pamela's virtue. Only after he has read her account of their relationship and acknowledged it a "very moving tale" (213) can he begin to contemplate the possibility that he might "defy the world and its censures, and make my Pamela amends" (214) through marriage. Only when the written female self becomes the read one, in other words, can it begin to participate in the contract made possible through the masculine power to make meaning. Through B's reading, the text and Pamela together acquire a value that is both intellectual and material. He vicariously experiences the trial of her virtue through the commerce of ideas that his reading of the journal makes possible. Once convinced of her exemplary qualities, he materially enacts the principle of conversion by altering her status from servant to wife.

The narrative representation of the scene of reading also directs our attention to the ways in which *Pamela*, like *Clarissa*, uses textual experience to figure other forms of relationship, most particularly those that align fictive and "real" readers. Both works summon through the act of reading a double contractual relationship. Within the text, male reading of female writing regulates the meaning of woman as property by subjecting her reflexive text to public scrutiny. The contextualizing nature of this scrutiny in turn allows the particular male character to stand as a figure for the educable "real" reader outside the text. B and Belford thus serve as narrative hinges, characters through whom the metaphoric significance of woman as property is revealed to and internalized by "real" readers.

We are further directed in this interpretative exercise by the meanings attaching to the physical site of B's reading. In his earlier encounters with Pamela, the garden served the standard function of the *locus amoris*: backdrop to a programmatically rendered seduction. Here, the garden becomes an integral part of the narrative of conversion. The scene begins with B meeting Pamela in the garden. Having received from her two more parcels of letters as supplement to those seized by Mrs. Jewkes, he proposes that she sit by the pond with him. We know from an earlier entry in her journal that for Pamela the pond provokes discomfitting memories of the suicide she contemplated after her failed attempt to escape from the Lincolnshire estate: "for want of grace, and through a sinful despondence, [the pond] had like to have been so fatal to me; and the sight of which, ever since, has been a trouble and reproach to me" (187). B has, in fact, reached the point in her journal where she records this experience and for him the coincidence of plot and place seems felicitous: "'Come,' said he, 'this being the scene of part of your project, where you so artfully threw in some of your clothes, I will just look upon that part of your relation.' '– Sir,' said I. 'let me, then, walk about at a little distance; for I cannot bear the thought of it.' – 'Don't go far,' said he" (213). Reading, however, soon becomes enactment as B paces out the setting of her attempted suicide: "When he came, as I suppose, to the place where I mentioned the bricks falling upon me, he got up, and walked to the door, and looked upon the broken part of the wall... 'Why this,' said he, 'my girl, is a very moving tale'" (213). The conflations here – of literal bricks and emotional response, of external and internal experience – invite analysis.

From one perspective, B is simply remaining true to form in his recapitulation of an earlier experience of Pamela's. Over the course of the novel, Pamela's responses have acquired a predictive force, leading the reader to expect that her claims to self-ownership and productive labor will ultimately be absorbed by B and made his own. In this scene, however, it is more specifically Pamela's *text* that works conversion. And as he mixes his labor with it through his reading, B demonstrates the supersessionary power available to men who are able to construe relations in property terms. He not only makes the text his own by acting out her experiences, he also, in doing so, proleptically signals the possession of her self which will come to him through marriage. This scene, then, marks a turning point: B's mastery of Pamela's words, confirmed by the supererogation of his physically enacting her brush with suicide, gives him powers of definition, socially if not morally, which he will exercise in the remainder of the novel.

That B should seek out those places Pamela's narrative has invested with affective and spiritual significance also signals the peculiar quality of the status change he experiences. The distinctive features of the exemplary civic humanist to which B is entitled by birth – a disinterestedness that attunes him to public virtue and makes him fit for office – are not the ones recuperated in his rejection of libertinism. B instead enacts the terms of that material culture with which Pamela has throughout been associated, a culture that renders personality as responsiveness to change and possession as the reward of direct labor. In pacing out the places to which Pamela's story refers as he reads it, B makes vivid the connection between experience and reformation. His experiential recuperation of her ordeal effects his own enlightenment and confirms his status as bourgeois hero.

By mixing his own labor, physically and intellectually, with her story, he also transforms it from a circumstantial narrative of virtue persistently challenged to a sequential one whose coherence depends, as the running title announces, on the motif of "virtue rewarded" through marriage. The transference of her labor to him – the capacity for self-scrutiny he acquires through his reading of her journal – thus attests at once to her reformative agency and to her redundancy. As Ann Louise Kibbie has argued, "what happens after the wedding is not so much a *continuation* of the plot as an *undoing* of it."[10] But in the process of "undoing" Pamela's claims to self-possession, Richardson carefully re-channels her reforming energy in ways that are intended to be both ethically and narratively satisfying.

In all three of Richardson's novels, the displacement of female energy is registered through a double process. The moral consolidation of the hero represents the more obvious form of transference. Equally important, however, is the concluding emphasis on documents which privilege social over sentimental expression. The conclusions of *Pamela* (and *Pamela Volume II*), *Clarissa*, and *Sir Charles Grandison* each feature documents which substitute for the actual, physical presence of the women who have dominated the narrative proper. At the end of *Pamela*, the hastily written and carefully secreted journal in which she records her distress is supplanted by "a vellum-book of white paper, some sides of which I hope soon to fill with the names of proper objects" on the cover of which she writes "*Humble* RETURNS *for* DIVINE MERCIES" (427). In *Pamela Volume II*, her "little book upon education" (435) conveys her understanding of Locke to the interested, and complements the depersonalizing impulse that lies behind her rendering herself as "PRUDENTIA" in the concluding letter's allegorical micro-narrative. In *Clarissa*, "The WILL" both expresses Clarissa's final wishes and provides the subject for the letters following in which her survivors testify to her exemplary virtue. And in *Sir Charles Grandison*, epistolary exchange between individuals gives way to a collaborative writing of letters which are then destined not for single but multiple recipients.

What we witness in this final displacement of female energy, then, is the substitution of the literal property of the text (now focused in a single document) for the body of the woman. The nature of the hero's reformation suggests one explanation for this transfer of meaning. His fallen state in both *Pamela* and *Clarissa* is marked by a possessive desire that construes the female body literally as a form of property. The reformation of both B and Belford involves their assimilating those qualities of female inwardness that further their ability to function as self-regulating participants in a bourgeois social order. Here the contribution of reading is crucial since it allows Richardson to make coterminous the awareness of fictive and "real" readers. Within the novel, the male reader has his turn toward virtue confirmed by a textual encounter with the female exemplar's experience.[11] Correspondingly, the attention of the real reader is directed away from the heroine's body as object of desire to her writing as agent of change. As she becomes less susceptible to interpretations which literalize her as property, the text itself comes to embody meaning. The concluding document serves as a peculiarly concentrated version of this process. It is literally a portable form of property, whose inscribed meaning formalizes the consensual nature of the relationship between the individual and the social order that sustains him.

Sustains *him* because this shift from physical presence to document also marks the orientation of the narrative away from a sentimental rendering of female experience and toward the socially authoritative model of consensus represented by the community of readers at the novels' endings. Given the ideas of female labor and property explored in this chapter, such a maneuver answers the challenges to male hegemony implicit in a Pamela or Clarissa, on the one hand, and a Mrs. Jewkes or Mother Sinclair, on the other. Exemplary women in these novels seem to have a near perfect sense of the ideal community sustainable by their virtuous labor. In relation to such perfection, men are invested with the capacity to compromise and so to engage productively in the public sphere. As social mediators, they also check the rapaciously individualistic excesses of those confederacies of women whose understanding of the body as literal property potentially sanctions a radical materialism.

With the displacement of the female exemplar by a textual variant of herself comes a concluding emphasis on the circulation of ideas made possible by a community of readers. Richardson thus signals to his real readers that the essentially private nature of their activity has public and social implications. What one might term the objective correlatives to

Pamela's status as B's wife – the "*Humble* RETURNS" volume in which people are entered as "proper objects" for her to consider in her new role as "accomptant" (427) and the "newly presented closet" (425) in which she keeps it locked – together speak to this conjunction of private space and public efficacy.[12] In *Sir Charles Grandison* we have another version of this in the communal reading with which the novel ends: letters are sent unsealed in order that they may circulate freely among distinct groups of people.[13]

Reading here serves to consolidate a community in which inter-pretive authority is ultimately invested in men: Belford, B, and Sir Charles all in turn mandate the conditions and significance of corre-spondence. The masculine modes of reading and writing Richardson proposes have come to be accepted as normative. They are the ones in which, as Ian Watt describes them, realist techniques enable the repre-sentation of middle-class experience, representations which in turn, as Terry Eagleton and Nancy Armstrong have argued, participate directly in "the English bourgeoisie's attempt to wrest a degree of ideological hegemony from the aristocracy in the decades which follow the political settlement of 1688."[14]

Two reservations concerning this model need to be considered. The first, which I will elaborate in subsequent chapters, turns on the con-tinued and vigorous presence of distinctively female forms of labor – intellectual and actual – in contemporary novels. The second involves the tangled relationship between masculine consciousness and female paradigm in eighteenth-century discourse. For two of the period's most compelling emergent discourses – the novel and philosophical history – the conjunctions of past and present, of individual and culture are best imagined by invoking the intersecting terms of woman and property. Writers of widely various political affiliations testify to the centrality and interconnections of these terms by their habitual reference to them. The Whiggish John Millar with his leanings toward a bourgeois rendering of progress here joins company with Adam Ferguson with his civic human-ist bent. If we consider Belford as a micro-historian rendering a culture through the details of a single life, he has much in common with these Scottish Enlightenment thinkers who with a much wider historical view explore the relations of mind to situation. As Part II will suggest, this convergence grows out of their shared pursuit of questions of inward-ness and of change. To this end, they use the metaphorical properties traditionally ascribed to women in order to understand the civilizing capacity of real property.

Among the difficulties encountered in constructing a coherent and properly affecting narrative of the past, Adam Ferguson writes, is the disjunction between the "sublime and intelligent" classical historians who "understood human nature" and their successors who abandoned the "productions of genius" for the "record[ing] what they were pleased to denominate facts":

> With them ["the early historians of modern Europe"] a narration was supposed to constitute history, whilst it did not convey any knowledge of men; and history itself was allowed to be complete, while, amidst the events and succession of princes that are recorded in the order of time, we are left to look in vain for those characteristics of the understanding and the heart, which alone, in every human transaction, render the story engaging or useful. (78–9)

From an historiographical perspective, the representation of early modern Europe failed to achieve affective power because it allowed the "order of time" to take precedence over that of the "understanding and the heart." One of the solutions favored by Scottish Enlightenment thinkers intent on repairing this lack involved augmenting the received narrative of factitious history with parallel accounts "Of the Rank and Condition of Women in Different Ages" or the "Progress of the Female Sex."[5] These supplementary records of women helped to secure two distinct but complementary objectives. On the one hand, feminocentric narratives subverted the authority of narrowly political history by advancing the claims of a sex imagined to have a specially privileged relation to qualities of inwardness, "those characteristics of the understanding and the heart." Yet, on the other, the intrinsic claims of women's historical agency were subordinated to their explanatory function as index to the progress of civil society, a progress that was seen to confirm the doctrine of separate spheres and "different talents."[16] As John Millar writes in 1779,

> When we examine the circumstances which occasion the depression of the women, and the low estimation in which they are held, in a simple and barbarous age, we may easily imagine in what manner their condition is varied and improved in the subsequent periods of society. Their condition is naturally improved by every circumstance which tends to create more attention to the pleasures of sex, and to increase the value of those occupations that are suited to the female character; by the cultivation of the arts of life; by the advancement of opulence; and by the gradual refinement of taste and manners. From a view of the progress of society, in these respects, we may, in a great measure, account for the diversity that occurs among different nations, in relation to the rank of

the sexes, their dispositions and sentiments towards each other, and the regulations which they have established in the several branches of their domestic economy.[17]

The indexical understanding of women that shapes Millar's account is a product not only of the imperatives of Enlightenment historiography but also of the constitution of civil society itself. With the "cultivation of the arts of life" and "the gradual refinement of taste and manners" – those benchmarks of progress – come the risks of effeminacy. One means of limiting its corruption of the body politic, as the "culture of sensibility" suggests, is to localize "weakness" in women, and especially in the female body.[18] Another is to counter what Ferguson calls the dangers of "a growing attention to interest, or of effeminacy, contracted in the enjoyment of ease and conveniency" by advocating a georgic industriousness capable of mediating between the public and the private spheres:

The habits of a vigorous mind are formed in contending with difficulties, not in enjoying the repose of a pacific station; penetration and wisdom are the fruits of experience, not the lessons of retirement and leisure; ardour and generosity are the qualities of a mind roused and animated in the conduct of scenes that engage the heart, not the gifts of reflection or knowledge. (255–6)

The emphasis here on active engagement returns us to the larger world of "national and political efforts" (256), the realm in which a "disinterested love of the public" (258) provides a corrective to the attractions of "private interest, and animal pleasure" (256). For conjectural history, as for the novel, the contemporary turn to feminized qualities of inwardness, delicacy, and refinement of taste and manners marks out the border at which civic progress intersects with national decline.

The sexual politics implicit here are not, however, straightforwardly oppositional. Woman is not simply the "other" against which enlightened culture defines its commitment to "the classical order of things."[19] The voices which we now identify as central to the civic humanist tradition do in the main imagine women's discursive role as dedicated to endorsing an order in which landed property is the source of power. But in these two recognizably new "manners of writing," the novel and philosophical history, one detects a more complex interrelation between the masculine authority projected through the narratorial voice and the female exemplars through whom the "story" is conveyed. In both genres, this is evidenced by a characteristic and revealing attention to the rhetorical and formal possibilities opened up by the slippage between the supposedly transparent terms of "woman" and "property." Such slippage speaks to the constitutive role both play in the underwriting of bourgeois culture in the eighteenth century.

The affiliations between women and property – extending from near equation to ironic counterpointing – are in part a function of the literal and figurative values each possesses. Women can be depicted through reference to both sex and gender: according to the imperatives of objective biological distinction or of the more amorphous categories of the "feminine." Property, likewise, denotes both real estate and liquid assets, on the one hand, and inward (although socially determined) qualities, on the other. Literal and figurative can also be expressed in the light of such complementary distinctions as extrinsic and intrinsic or form and meaning: in each instance there appears a fruitful tension between a seemingly stable designation – the female sex, real property – and the less determinate meanings made accessible by metaphorical usage. In both novel and philosophical history, such tension serves valuable rhetorical and ideological functions. In the process of analyzing these functions, we come to recognize more clearly the connections between the large grid of historical explanation offered by the master narratives of Ferguson and Millar and the hugely expanded (and yet concentrated) version afforded by the micro-history of a single woman like Clarissa.

In accounting for the advances of civil society and the preeminence it accords the rule of property, Kames, Millar, and Ferguson thus construct a narrative "Progress of the Female Sex" as paradigmatic of an inward "refinement of taste and manners" which they gender female. But the distinction between the female sex and an innate sensibility is complicated by the seemingly inevitable progression of society from refinement to effeminacy. When effeminacy threatens the survival of the "arduous virtues," sexual difference is re-invoked to argue for a renewed dedication to the public sphere and to "national and political efforts." The historian who has "render[ed] the story either engaging or useful" by allowing the status of women to map cultural progress and also show its potential decay confirms his judicious intelligence by urging the corrective powers of "manly occupation."[20]

Clarissa too grants final authority to a male character who selectively realizes qualities which the novel at first advanced as the matter of the heroine's plot. Belford's emergence as custodian of a newly rationalized order depends on his internalization of the forces which shaped the heroine's plot: probity, self-possession, familial integrity. Once absorbed, such qualities are re-directed outward in those reforming activities that define his eventual responses to a much expanded world. Significantly, in both novel and history, the conjunction of women and property serves as both agent and expression of a new order. Property provides the materials from which these stories of cultural advance are assembled. Woman, as a form of property whose utility is realized by man's labor and capacity for internalizing otherness, both enables and represents this civilizing process.

PART II

Pastoral

Introduction

In their distinctive representations of personal and civic identity, georgic and pastoral reveal the complex affiliations between literary form and social and economic process. As the previous chapter argued, the georgic understanding of individual enterprise as an agent of a progressive social order underwrites that mode's centrality to numbers of eighteenth-century novels. For authors aligned with the emergent middle class, the georgic mode enables the representation of change within the context of an authoritative and continuous tradition alert to the redemptive possibilities of labor. For those writers, however, whose response to the burgeoning commodity culture was more skeptical, georgic's involvement with the forces of reformation signals its inadmissibility as a principle of narrative organization. Accordingly, numbers of conservative writers turned to pastoral as an alternate structure. In doing so, they confirm the political implications attaching to generic preference – whether for pastoral or georgic.

For the conservative writer, the attractions of pastoral derive in large part from its high cultural associations. As a classically sanctioned genre directed toward a privileged audience, pastoral acquired additional appeal to the hierarchically minded by virtue of its decline in literary fashionability over the previous fifty years. In its later eighteenth-century incarnations, it comes to stand for an elite ideal of male communion made possible by withdrawal from an interested world. When contemporary novels, then, adapt the formal and thematic conventions of pastoral, they demarcate a masculine realm that sets itself apart from the emergent order, an order they identify with women and their propensity for change and novelty.

While this division of masculine from feminine, residual from emergent, and stricter from more relaxed configurations of hierarchy, sets pastoral and georgic in oppositional terms, they are not, this chapter will argue, categorical absolutes. Even in *The Man of Feeling*, the novel with which I begin, pastoral is at once privileged through direct allusion and more generalized thematic affiliations and exposed as ineffectual in its efforts to explain (or compensate for) things as they are.[1] The second section will explore the ways in which this ambivalent positioning of pastoral as both political ideal and failed paradigm follows from uncertainties of audience, uncertainties heightened by Mackenzie's awareness of the imperfect mesh between the elite values to which pastoral appeals and the parvenu form of the novel itself. Such disjunctions, however, Mackenzie attempts to make purposive by deliberately counterpointing the high cultural pastoral and the vulgar "wretched offspring of circulating libraries" in order to argue that the novel if reformed could speak to "men of genius and of knowledge."[2] Laurence Sterne's *Tristram Shandy* and Thomas Cogan's *John Buncle, Junior, Gentleman* reinforce the centrality of this reformative impulse to the "culture of sensibility" even as it marks out its connection to anxieties about effeminacy (for which reading recurrently serves as synecdoche). The third and final section will explore these relations between genre and gender in the more pointedly political context of two novels whose articulation of a colonial discourse devoted to rationalizing acquisitiveness brings clearly into focus the instrumental functions of pastoral and georgic. In Edward Bancroft's *Charles Wentworth* and the anonymous *Female American*, the characteristic features of pastoral and georgic are transposed on to settings whose exoticism licenses a demystifying of the relation between women and property. Through the whole of chapter six, this link between women and property will be seen as fundamental to the ways in which georgic and pastoral as distinctive genres substantiate their claims to represent an ideal order.

CHAPTER 5

"The Man of Feeling"

PASTORAL AND "THE MAN OF FEELING"

Sentimental fiction's refusal to engage with the progressivism variously endorsed by contemporary writers such as Fielding and Richardson has consistently been read as the expression of a highly conventional set of gendered oppositions in which the Man of Feeling's passive effeminacy implicitly contrasts with the realist hero's confrontational masculinity. G. A. Starr thus argues that sentimental narrative substitutes for the *Bildungsroman*'s emphasis on education and process a regressive or static protagonist, whose behavior his culture "associates with infancy or femininity, but not with masculine adulthood."[1] More recently, Michael McKeon has historicized this hero, suggesting that the Man of Feeling needs to be understood in terms of a double strategy: seventeenth-century aristocratic honor internalized in the early decades of the eighteenth as feminine virtue is in turn at mid-century claimed by the hero as a "distinctively male possession."[2] When this gendered reading is supplemented by one that invokes what are for Henry Mackenzie the complementary terms of genre, however, a more sceptical understanding of "feminine virtue" emerges. At key moments in *The Man of Feeling*, pastoral is used in ways that signal not the internalization, but rather the displacement of the feminine.

In *The Man of Feeling*, pastoral stands for the consolations of an exclusively male communion that can be discovered only by repressing awareness of present exigencies and focusing on the past. I will argue that these affiliations between pastoral, male communion, and the elite culture of the past prove to be crucial to the working out of the narrative reflexiveness that is so consistent a feature of sentimental literature. In adapting pastoral to a critique of the novel form (and of those aspects of contemporary culture for which it stands as type), Mackenzie also identifies women with all that he finds suspect. In a series of contrasts in which the first term is gendered female, the second male, he sets reading against writing, mobile property against permanent property, and present and future against the past. Such divisions allow us to understand more precisely the constitutive role played by gender and genre in the politics of sentimental narrative.[3]

We can see the ways in which the genre underwrites a politically conservative reading of the past in the scene when Harley, accompanied by the discharged soldier old Edwards, pauses on his return home after his unsuccessful sojourn in London:

When they had arrived within a little way of the village they journeyed to, Harley stopped short, and looked stedfastly on the mouldering walls of a ruined house that stood on the roadside: "Oh heavens!" he cried, "what do I see: silent, unroofed, and desolate! Are all the gay tenants gone? do I hear their hum no more? Edwards, look there, look there! the scene of my infant joys, my earliest friendships, laid waste and ruinous! That was the very school where I was boarded ... 'tis but a twelvemonth since I saw it standing, and its benches filled with cherubs: that opposite side of the road was the green on which they sported; see it now ploughed up! I would have given fifty times its value to have saved it from the sacrilege of that plough."

"Dear Sir," replied Edwards, "perhaps they have left it from choice, and may have got another spot as good." "They cannot," said Harley, "they cannot! I shall never see the sward covered with its daisies, nor pressed by the dance of the dear innocents: I shall never see that stump decked with the garlands which their little hands had gathered." (95–6)

The proscribed terms of georgic, signaled here by the slighting reference to the "sacrilege of that plough," confirm the scene's commitment to the contrary ideal of pastoral. The elegiac tone of the passage is established through a verbal repetition that superficially resembles Goldsmith's lament to "Sweet Auburn, loveliest village of the plain." But while *The Deserted Village* contrasts the "barren splendour" of the present with a georgic past "[w]hen every rood of ground maintained its man," Mackenzie's daisy-covered sward upon which garlanded innocents dance instead recalls the high artifice conventional to pastoral.[4]

Pastoral imagery proves especially congenial to *The Man of Feeling*'s conservative values in part because, as Andrew Ettin has suggested, the genre typically evokes a predominantly masculine world which, with its focus on sexually unfulfilled relationships, also emphasizes containment and resistance to change.[5] The inflection of genre by gender is heightened by Mackenzie's recurring references throughout the novel to standard misogynist claims about the link between women and social corruption. Virtue is, consequently, represented as recoverable only in exclusively masculine contexts, of which the small farm granted to old Edwards stands as a type, a miniature Arcadia undisturbed by intrusive women. The description of the farm as "a scene of tranquil virtue to have stopped an angel on his errands of mercy!" typically focuses on the representational and aesthetic rather than the functional:

Harley had contrived to lead a little bubbling brook through a green walk in the middle of the ground, upon which he had erected a mill in miniature for the diversion of Edwards's infant-grandson, and made a shift in its construction to introduce a pliant bit of wood, that answered with its fairy clack to the murmuring of the rill that turned it. I have seen him stand, listening to these mingled sounds, with his eyes fixed on the boy, and the smile of conscious satisfaction on his cheek; while the old man with a look half-turned to Harley, and half to Heaven, breathed an ejaculation of gratitude and piety. (101–2)

Edwards's granddaughter makes no appearance in this insistently pictorial rendering of affective and temporal relationships. The compositional alignment of the figures and the carefully detailed visual connections between them work both to imply a divinely sanctioned, recessive world and to suggest that the order of grandfather, substitute father, and child establishes an ideal patrilineal pattern to which women appear unnecessary.

Harley's verbal exercises – specifically, "Lavinia. A Pastoral" – tend, in turn, to be prompted by female duplicity and to be shaped by highly conventional structures. The news of Miss Walton's imminent marriage to Sir Harry Benson prompts the writing of this poem (in the form of Shenstone's famous pastoral verses) in which he declares that his feeling for her, "could never rely" on words – "It reign'd in the throb of my heart, / It gleam'd in the glance of my eye." But she, he now suspects, participated in the falsifying language of social exchange:

> Oh fool! in the circle to shine
>   That fashion's gay daughters approve,
> You must speak as the fashions incline; –
>   Alas! are there fashions in love?
>
> Yet sure they are simple who prize
>   The tongue that is smooth to deceive;
> Yet sure she had sense to despise
>   The tinsel that folly may weave.

Having entertained the possibility that she never differentiated between his authentic voice and the duplicitous ones of others, Harley draws on the conventional misogynist association of verbal and sexual susceptibility and speculates that "Perhaps, when she smil'd upon all, / I have thought that she smil'd upon me." Such promiscuousness leaves him "undone," fit only to anticipate "the peaceable womb" of the grave. Most bizarre is the concluding fantasy of the poem, in which Harley imagines that after his death he will return to watch over Miss Walton: "Perhaps, if [she is] with sorrow oppress'd, / Her sorrow with patience to arm." But as the final stanza of the poem suggests, his notion of patience is complicated by overtones of vengeance, by the desire to inflict upon her a pain commensurate with his own: "Then! then! in the tenderest part / May I whisper, 'Poor COLIN was true'; / And mark if a heave of her heart / The thought of her COLIN pursue" (115–17).

Both the miniature Arcadia Harley constructs and the poem he writes align the received conventions of pastoral against the unreadability of the modern world, whose quintessential human cipher appears to be the duplicitous woman. Only through the exclusion of women, it is implied, can the pastoral conditions of innocent male communion be achieved. But even as Mackenzie draws on pastoral to denominate contemporary iniquities, he carefully limits its reformative agency. In this novel, the turn toward the past that pastoral necessarily involves dislocates its representative figures from the present, leading each of them finally to death or madness. Throughout, the failure of individuals to survive and prosper is thus linked to a focus on the past. When Harley visits Bedlam, a tacit parallel is established between the mad mathematician, stock-jobber, schoolmaster, and bereft lover who monotonously recount their stories and Harley's own withdrawal from an unbearably interested world through the construction of an alternate order. The Bedlam prison, in other words, in a manner familiar from Augustan poetry, serves as a displaced image of the pastoral. Conversely, the beggar Harley encounters on the road to London makes the necessary compromises that ensure his relative prosperity. Unable to find a settlement or to acquire sufficient money by detailing the woes of his past life, he turns to fortune-telling and discovers that trading on the future yields impressive dividends.

Harley's pastoral and the beggar's fortune-telling function paradigmatically in the novel. The prescriptive structures on which Harley relies to detail his love for Miss Walton in "Lavinia. A Pastoral" contrast with the beggar's novelistic strategies as projector, fabricator, and interpreter of his listeners' fantasies. But these representational differences extend beyond authorial choice of form. They also engage with questions of reception and of audience, questions that prove central to Mackenzie's sense of what, potentially, the novel can accomplish.

The opportunistic narratives spun by the beggar for monetary reward represent one extreme of a spectrum whose opposite is found in the received conventions that govern Harley's pastoral composition. The limitations attaching to the novel as a parvenu mode are made explicit in *The Man of Feeling* through various representations of female reading discussed below. Those associated with pastoral are, as the conflicting modern interpretations of *The Man of Feeling* as sentimental or satiric suggest, more complicated and are best understood in the context of the changing status of pastoral in the hierarchy of eighteenth-century genres.

Late eighteenth-century conservative estimations of pastoral's appropriateness as a vehicle for social criticism within the novel follow, paradoxically, from pastoral's increasingly attenuated connections in both form and meaning to contemporary notions of historical process. In terms of content, the idealizing version of pastoral championed by Pope in his debate with Philips at the beginning of the century centered on a timeless Golden World. Classical pastoral was prized, then, for the aesthetic possibilities produced by its high artifice and for its detachment from the particular and mundane – qualities that run exactly counter to those that underpin the realist novel. In formal terms, the genre's discursive functions had been steadily assumed by georgic over the course of the century.[6] A "high and serious kind" in the Renaissance and seventeenth century, pastoral had diminished in prestige and expressive range in the eighteenth. Crabbe's stigmatizing of it as the "Mechanic echoes of the Mantuan song" points to the widely held view that the genre voiced the literary and social concerns of a previous aristocratic age.[7]

But it is this very failure to engage actively with contemporary culture that makes pastoral so useful to conservative late eighteenth-century novelists. Pastoral – manifestly classical in origin, possessed of a distinct vocabulary, directed to a privileged, male readership – helps to register authorial suspicion of the present and bleakness about the future. Its attractions are not limited to this capacity to offer indirect appraisal of things as they are, but extend also into an evocative (if often uneasy) rendering of an hierarchically ordered past. And, as with the georgic mode discussed in the previous chapter, pastoral derives its explanatory power from its ability to function as the organizing term for a range of key cultural issues.

We can see very clearly the capacity of pastoral to serve as focus when we consider it in relation to the question of audience, where generic and socio-political issues intersect. As the previous chapter revealed in its discussion of *Clarissa*, Belford's extension of personal conversion into the realm of public reform epitomizes georgic's purposive orientation toward the future. The publication of the correspondence that allows this shift from the private to the social appears constructive because enlargement of audience is tacitly equated in Richardson's novel with augmentation of meaning. By contrast, pastoral's retrospective vision carries with it a correlative skepticism about the benefits of widening participation in the public sphere. In the internal critique of novel writing and reading that is so conspicuously a feature of *The Man of Feeling*, Mackenzie questions the assumption that access to print encourages the consolidation of a newly virtuous community. Ultimately, his correlation of gender and genre leads him to identify print culture as a perniciously effeminizing force that has made the "Frivolous and the Interested . . . the characteristical features of the age" (82).

His own novels, which he describes in the later *Julia de Roubigné* as "memoirs of sentiment, and suffering," work both formally and thematically to emphasize the virtues of readerly isolation (as opposed to the community of readers celebrated in the conclusions of Richardson's novels).[8] In *The Man of Feeling*, he refuses to make a continuous story from the surviving fragments, providing us with nothing more than a "bundle of little episodes" (5) accidentally rescued from use as gun-wadding. Textual authenticity is assured here not by reference to a standard of coherence, but of contingency, not through the direction provided by an authoritative voice, but by a narratorial unwillingness to mediate the reader's experience of the partial manuscript. As the footnote to the opening chapter eleven declares, "the Editor is accountable only for scattered chapters, and fragments of chapters" (7).

This refusal to subordinate the episodic to the imperatives of plot or to a controlling narratorial presence represents the formal realization of Mackenzie's claim that "narrative would destroy" the reader's "sentiment[al]" engagement with his work.[9] The conditions of the manuscript's recovery direct our attention to another of his skeptical responses to notions of progress. In its changed status from testamentary private memoir, to functional gun-wadding, to circulating public text, *The Man of Feeling*, it is implied, has diminished rather than grown in meaning. As a result, the difference of past from present appears as a fall from intimacy to anonymity.[10]

Considered from the vantage of audience response, the complementary but antithetical relationship between pastoral and the "common herd of novels" that informs *The Man of Feeling* acquires particular significance. On the one hand, pastoral and novel each have limitations which the narrative proximity of the other within the single text of *The Man of Feeling* makes apparent. Pastoral, in its cultivated timelessness, is limited in its capacity to promote that "certain refinement of mind" which distinguishes "works of genius and feeling." And the "debasement" of the contemporary novel in turn precludes its fulfilling its potential, as Mackenzie's 1785 *Lounger* essay describes it, to offer "an interesting relation of events, illustrative of the manners and characters of mankind."[11] But, on the other hand, using each as corrective to the other allows Mackenzie to convert narrative reflexiveness into a form of commentary that balances the inward and private against the social and public.

This concern with achieving parity between the inward and particular and the public and exemplary surfaces repeatedly in prefatorial declarations of intent. Frances Burney's *Evelina* (1778) is entirely typical of contemporary fiction in its gesture toward this double orientation: "To draw characters from nature, though not from life, and to mark the manners of the times, is the attempted plan of the following letters."[12] But deprived of the authority that established genres like history give to such attempts to chart the relation of inner nature to social institutions, Burney must hedge her claim to social commentary with an opening admission that "[i]n the republic of letters, there is no member of such inferior rank, or who is so much disdained by his brethren of the quill, as the humble Novelist" (7). For her, as for Mackenzie, this depressed status has more to do with audience than with author. Directed toward "young ladies in general, and boarding-school damsels in particular," novels typically spread "contagion" and "distemper" by invoking "the fantastic regions of Romance ... coloured by all the gay tints of luxurious Imagination." Faced with the vulgar expectations of an audience at once female and bourgeois, an author like Burney limits her defense of the novel to the rather limp declaration that hers at least "may be read, if not with advantage, at least without injury" (8).

Numbers of Burney's contemporaries, however, including Mackenzie, were prepared to assume a more interrogative relation to the stigma
associated with novels. One could speculate that this was especially true
of educated, male writers whose familiarity with classical genres enabled
a posture of ironic detachment from, rather than apologetic acceptance
of, the taint attaching to the novel. They counter the perceived lowness
of the chosen form by summoning within their novels the terms of these
more prestigious genres. Popular fiction and the female reader continue
to provide the negative point of reference. But allusions to pastoral
establish a positive standard through their affiliations with elite culture
and the masculine, public domain.

Mackenzie signals this intent to write against the grain of contemporary fiction in the "Introduction" to *The Man of Feeling*. In the editor's
account of how he came to possess the manuscript of Harley's life, the
tone is conversational, the activity framing it the quintessentially male
one of shooting. Disappointed, he tells us, by the loss of the quarry
which he and his hunting partner, the local curate, had pursued "in a
breathless state of expectation" (3), the editor stops and registers in
precise detail the peculiar features of the scene before him. It is very
much a literary landscape. Such features as the carving on the trees are
standard to Renaissance pastoral, others ("a single crow, that perched
on an old tree by the side of the gate") anticipate Wordsworthian
revisions of it. But it is the sight of a woman walking by with a book in
her hand that prompts conversation between the two men:

> "Some time ago," said he, "one HARLEY lived there, a whimsical sort of man
> I am told, but I was not then in the cure; though, if I had a turn for those things,
> I might know a good deal of his history, for the greatest part of it is still in my
> possession."
> "His history!" said I. "Nay, you may call it what you please," said the curate;
> "for indeed it is no more a history than it is a sermon" . . . "I should be glad to
> see this medley," said I. (4–5)

As a "medley" – a heterogeneous mixture – the manuscript incites the
kind of curiosity and engagement disallowed by programmatic reading.
When he comes to inspect the "bundle of little episodes," the editor thus
finds himself "a good deal affected" and speculates that had the "name
of a Marmontel, or a Richardson, been on the title page – 'tis odds that I
should have wept" (5).

The significance of these teasingly incomplete observations and of the
distinction between the reading woman and the conversing men will

only later become apparent when Miss Walton's ties to Harley are more fully detailed. The effect at present of withholding information is to dramatize the uncertainties of the reader's relation to the text. In denying us the regulatory conditions of genre or literary reputation – this is not a history, a sermon, or a novel whose famous authorship underwrites our attention – the editor enforces an awareness of the contingencies of reading when the conventional directive signposts are withheld. Mackenzie will later enlarge on this contrast between discretionary and prescriptive reading by aligning it with the oppositional terms that structure the novel proper: on the one hand, the new order, verbal prowess, a feminized corrupt present, and an emotional investment in the siren lure of the future; on the other, the countervailing virtues of a civilization shaped by an authentic masculine consciousness, itself secured by lineage and broad acres. In this novel, to put it more bluntly, woman and especially woman reading (Miss Walton, Emily Atkins), emblematize cultural decay and prove the bane of all that is upright and true. Such a designation of literacy as degenerate is clearly fraught with difficulties for an author who wishes to redefine without alienating his audience. By incorporating within the novel monitory instances of "female reading" and by counterpointing these against the conservative values expressed in Harley's pastoral writing, Mackenzie attempts the reformation of both his audience and the novel form.

READING WOMEN

Harley's encounter on the road to London with the fortune-telling beggar ends with his bestowing a shilling on the story-teller, contrary to the dictates of "Virtue." The action is prompted by the impulses of "a younger sister of virtue's, not so severe as virtue, nor so serious as pity" (22). It speaks to Harley's compassion, but also rehearses his experiences in the city, where cunning and dishonesty consistently result in monetary reward. Harley has gone to London to secure a lease to crown lands lying contiguous to his "little paternal estate" (13). His attempts to win an "interest with the great" fail when the lease is granted to a footman, now gauger (i.e. exciseman), as reward for the pimping of his sister to the baronet in whose power the grant lay; the point of this episode, as with so many in the novel, can be found in the alignment of money, upward mobility, and self-making.

The episode is also typical in its equation of woman and property: the baronet accepts the prostitution of the gauger's sister as payment in kind for the conferring of the lease. In this model of exchange, Mackenzie implies, status distinctions are hopelessly contaminated, and with them, social and personal identity. Correspondingly, the narrative of the seduction of Emily Atkins offers, in effect, the plot of the gauger's sister recounted from the woman's point of view. Here, the seducer's success depends on his insidious use of reading. While "inflaming" texts had long been part of the libertine arsenal, Winbrooke's technique is more insidious. He breaks down his victim's adherence to traditional hierarchies by suggesting that judgments may be based on entirely personal, rather than social, criteria; as Emily says, he "asked my opinion of every author, of every sentiment, with that submissive diffidence, which shewed an unlimited confidence in my understanding" (57). Emily's susceptibility to such rhetoric has been conditioned by her reading of "plays, novels, and those poetical descriptions of the beauty of virtue and honour, which the circulating libraries easily afforded" (55) – those "swarms of foolish and of worthless novels" as James Fordyce caustically labels them in *The Character and Conduct of the Female Sex* (1776), "incessantly spawned by dull and by dissolute scribblers, and with unwearied industry disseminated from our Circulating Libraries."[3]

The relation, implicit in Fordyce's language, of novel writing and reading to sexuality is confirmed in Emily's subsequent history. Winbrooke proposes that Mr. Atkins's anger at the seduction of his daughter be softened by a cash payment: "'Honour, my dear Emily,' said he, 'is the word of fools, or of those wiser men who cheat them. 'Tis a fantastic bauble that does not suit the gravity of your father's age; but, whatever it is, I am afraid it can never be perfectly restored to you: exchange the word then, and let pleasure be your object now'" (61–2). Linguistic, sexual, and social structures are here represented as negotiable, once the measure of value has been established in terms of exchange, rather than worth fixed in accordance with long-established convention.

Emily's re-definition by the plot of seduction disallows her adherence to the alternate female plot of marriage. Her father has briefly concealed from her the inheritance of a sum which would remove the inequality of "rank and fortune" (59) that precludes her marriage to Winbrooke; in the interval, she is seduced and enters into a different transactional world in which her person commands a steadily diminishing cash value. But *The Man of Feeling* does not finally invite a sympathetic reading of Emily's plight. Instead, our attention is deflected toward the suffering father: "'my Emily was the joy of my age, and the pride of my soul! – Those things are now no more! they are lost for ever! Her death I could have born! but the death of her honour has added obloquy and shame to the sorrow which bends my grey hairs to the dust'" (73).[14] The elegiac cadences of this complaint align his mourning with Harley's lament on the vanished landscape of his childhood, "laid waste and ruinous" (95) by the depredations of the nouveau riche squire. And Harley's advice to Mr. Atkins, that he should "look beyond [the world]" (73) for solace, anticipates the conditions of his own death, suggesting in turn that for both men relationships with women have proven fatal.

Harley's death is precipitated in part by his inability to voice his love for Miss Walton, an inability originating in his relative poverty in the face of her fortune of 4000 pounds a year. His final words confess his feeling for her: "'To love Miss Walton could not be a crime; – if to declare it is one – the expiation will be made.'" She responds: "'I know your worth – I have known it long – I have esteemed it – What would you have me say? – I have loved it as it deserved.' – He seized her hand – a languid colour reddened his cheek – a smile brightened faintly in his eye. As he gazed on her, it grew dim, it fixed, it closed – He sighed, and fell back on his seat, – " (130). The logic of this scene suggests that when he contravenes class boundaries with a declaration of love (boundaries defined by the new order through reference to commodification rather than lineage), he commits a "crime" that demands the "expiation" of his own death.[15] In the process, Miss Walton mysteriously emerges as the agent of his destruction, a role for which we have been prepared by her engagement, willed or passive, with the forces of the new order. She is, like Emily Atkins, a reader, first appearing in the "Introduction" as a figure "pass[ing] between the trees ... with a book in her hand" (4); she is rumored to be engaged to Sir Harry Benson, and she survives this novel to appear in *The Man of the World* as the executrix of Harley's will who has made his philanthropy, "the business of [her] life."[16] If Harley's death is, as Patricia Meyer Spacks suggests, "surely the most dramatic example of sexual avoidance in western literature," the sexuality which he resists functions as a trope for other contractual relations (literal and figurative) to which significantly Miss Walton consents.[17] The intersection in her person of verbal, sexual, legal, and fiscal affiliations rehearses terms familiar from contemporary conduct books. John Brown's hugely successful *An Estimate of the Manners and Principles of the Time* (1757) traces what he sees as the present "*Crisis* so important and alarming" to a pervasive "'*vain, luxurious* and *selfish EFFEMINACY*'," itself a consequence, in part, of "weekly essays, amatory Plays and Novels, political Pamphlets and Books that revile Religion." This latter mode of consumption in turn implicates commerce in the feminizing of culture: "The Passion for Money, being founded, not in Sense, but Imagination, admits of no Satiety."[18]

The terms upon which Brown's analysis draws – women, money, reading, imagination, the confounding of distinctions, and the confusions of gender which will ultimately precipitate social collapse – figure prominently in fiction of the period. As Samuel Jackson Pratt's *Liberal Opinions* (1775) and *Shenstone-Green* (1779) and George Walker's *The Vagabond* (1799) attest, the destabilizing effects of reading were seen as especially noteworthy. While these three novels center on the temporary madnesses suffered by male readers who respond uncritically to a particular text, female readers are more often presented as permanently compromised, even contaminated, by the very act of reading. James Fordyce thus inveighs against "certain books, which we are assured ... are in their nature so shameful, in their tendency so pestiferous, and contain such rank treason against the royalty of Virtue, that she who can bear to peruse them must in her soul be a prostitute, let her reputation in life be what it will." Interpretation and judgment, the saving distance from textual infatuation that the male protagonists recover at the end of Pratt's and Walker's novels, are here denied the female reader. Her malleability ultimately depends upon the absence of a coherent identity, an absence which Fordyce would preserve by advocating attention to a living as opposed to a dead "text": "Your business chiefly is to read Men, in order to make yourselves agreeable and useful. It is not the argumentative but the sentimental talents, which give you that insight and those openings into the human heart, that lead to your principal ends as women."[19] By limiting women's "reading" to the interpretation of male will and desire, Fordyce suggests that "natural" subordination is externally mandated rather than inherent. The reading of actual texts encourages the illusion of authority over an imagined world, an authority that might well serve as precedent to demands for real power.

The cultural assumptions about the nature and capacities of women that underlie these notions of reading also inform the relation of Miss Atkins to Miss Walton and of both to the novel as a whole. The prostitution of the woman reader depends upon the ability of words to penetrate her "soul" unimpeded by the moral consciousness which presumably mediates between the male reader and his potential contamination. Women must therefore be defined sentimentally, in relation to the heart and not the soul, to feeling and not intellect, to social compliance and not individual cultivation. Miss Atkins errs in her preference for the latter of each of these terms, while Miss Walton's actions accord with the former. That Miss Walton is, despite her exemplary behavior, tacitly held accountable for Harley's death, reflects the peculiar double bind of her gender. As ciphers defined by their context, women become in this novel both type and agent of the mutability that is seen to inform the larger social world. From this perspective, there is finally a negligible difference between the two women, a commonality reinforced by their financially determined relations with men. Miss Walton, indeed, can no more escape entanglement by others' intentions, be they Sir Harry Benson's amorous or Harley's testamentary ones, than can Miss Atkins. She is bound to the enactment of a future whose terms are set by the conflicting desires of men to define her in their own images.[20]

Mackenzie's identification of women with mobile property (including the books they read) exemplifies his antipathy towards the momentous cultural shift signaled by the increasing prominence of Lockean notions of property. As *The Man of Feeling* witnesses, to consider personal worth as separable from the possession of broad acres is necessarily to unsettle the traditional bond between individual and polity.[21] For Harley, identity is inextricably allied with real property; patrilineal inheritance gives the sanction of time and the promise of continuity to the political relations which follow from the connection of the two. For the new order, the attractions of property depend on its alienation from the past. After amassing a fortune by manipulating "imaginary" money, the (significantly unnamed) parvenu who remakes the landscape of Harley's childhood extends his sway from city to country. Those features of the landscape, like the school-house, which testify to an established communal order, are erased, and in their stead emerges a purely economic understanding of land as yet another projection of the self-created personality. As the conduct literature of the period tirelessly asserts, the instability and openness to the future characteristic of such a personality mark him as essentially feminine. In this novel, he is, in a parallel manner, linked to the coupled figures of Miss Walton and Emily Atkins, figures whose baleful influence can only finally be evaded by the sacrificial death of the suffering male.

The reader in turn grasps the oppositions of masculine worth and feminine insubstantiality as they impinge upon the act of interpretation. Harley's understanding of world and text expresses itself in literary form through his pastoral compositions; the stylized, masculine mode made accessible by a privileged education connects him to the more austere virtues of the classical past. The women in the novel, conversely, read rather than write, and in doing so open themselves to the uncertainties implicit in their attraction to the imagined over the known. They also suggest the equivocal status of the reader of Mackenzie's text, whose surrogate they are.

When such regressions are pursued to their logical end, *The Man of Feeling* must itself become the object of critical scrutiny. As a form of public property, the novel is apparently bound to the system of values Mackenzie deplores; as a construct which plays with the reader's imagination and anxieties about the future, the novel elicits those emotions which he wishes to suppress. But, as his 1785 *Lounger* essay on fiction suggests, it is possible for novels at least potentially to stand apart both from those "young" and "indolent" readers for whom "the labour of thought is irksome" and from those authors "whose necessities or vanity prompted them to write." "Considered in the abstract," he maintains, "as containing an interesting relation of events, illustrative of the manners and characters 'of mankind, it [the novel] surely merits a higher station in the world of letters than is generally assigned it."[22]

The position he imagines, as his descriptive language implies, is the one currently occupied by the work of his Edinburgh peers, Ferguson, Kames, and Blair: philosophical historians who complicate political narrative by their introduction of conjectural accounts of the "manners and characters of mankind." Mackenzie's familiarity with the circle of Scottish Enlightenment philosophers and historians suggests that he recognized the challenge posed by historiography to novelistic representations of individual identity and its relation to the larger culture.[23] In this light, the intimations in *The Man of Feeling* of the need to reform reading practices assume a double function: metanarrational references at once enforce the topicality of the novel and deflect criticism of it as an expedient or vulgar form by stressing the novel's capacity for self-analysis and correction. When such metanarrational commentary alludes to classically sanctioned genres – as it does in Mackenzie – the corrective impulse becomes allied with an exclusionary one that defines as privileged the presumed reader.

"THE MAN OF FEELING" IN CONTEXT: STERNE'S "TRISTRAM SHANDY" AND COGAN'S "JOHN BUNCLE, JUNIOR, GENTLEMAN"

Mackenzie's attempt to reinscribe the novel's status by defining the form as ideally masculine is consistent with the practice of numbers of his contemporaries. The appeal to a male audience, the alignment with traditionally sanctioned genres, and the identification of women with the corruptions of the present and uncertainties about the future are recurring features. When Mackenzie's novel is situated in the larger context of the "culture of sensibility" between two representative texts like Sterne's *Tristram Shandy* (1760) and Thomas Cogan's *John Buncle, Junior, Gentleman* (1776–8), these anxieties about novel-reading as effeminizing can be seen to become progressively more acute. Each of the three works responds either by invoking an existing literary tradition with which they claim a family resemblance – pastoral and historiography, for instance – or by inventing a spurious one, a pseudo-tradition that works ironically to cast into relief the loss of a continuous literary heritage.

Such appeals to an authoritative corpus evidence once again the complicated process by which class and gender issues are so often elided in eighteenth-century novels, by which effeminacy and women come to stand for the perceived threat of an emergent order. When the three works are considered sequentially, however, it is possible to discern a growing self-consciousness about the distinction of the terms of class from those of gender and a correspondent need to argue their relation. Cogan thus establishes connections between the "depraved taste of a grovelling Citizen" and the extension of women's influence through reading far more explicitly than do his predecessors.[24] But even in *Tristram Shandy* where, as Tristram says, his uncle Toby's "life was put in jeopardy by words," it is the volubility and desires of women that threaten male order.[25]

In *Tristram Shandy*, pastoral and classical history together serve as foils to the principles of change and corruption that are gendered female. The timeless world of pastoral meshes with the potential certainties of history-as-event in uncle Toby's bowling green, the carefully bounded terrain against which the highly acquisitive and mutable world of the novel is set.[26] As Tristram suggests in qualifying his judgment on "this vile, dirty planet of ours," it is "not but that the planet is well enough, provided a man could be born in it to a great title or to a great estate" (9). Without these public markers of status, the Shandy family establishes hedges against uncertainty through eccentrically individual forms of accumulation.

Walter's haphazard covetousness verges on the parodic. He acquires not things, but ideas, although the analogy Tristram employs to exemplify his father's possessions establishes that, like Toby's, Walter's approach to the abstract is entirely concrete: he "pick'd up an opinion, Sir, as a man in a state of nature picks up an apple. – It becomes his own, – and if he is a man of spirit, he would lose his life rather than give it up" (176). Walter, in accordance with the conjectures of Locke's *Second Treatise*, owns the idea by virtue of mixing his labor with it. But the double allusion to knowledge conveyed by ideas and apples implies the potential for corruption inherent in such desire, a potential realized in the Widow Wadman, "a daughter of Eve," who, when she sees uncle Toby among her things, "[foists him] into her inventory" (440, 441). The conventional aggression of concupiscent widows acquires additional masculine overtones by the allusiveness of her entry into uncle Toby's paradisaical garden, an entry that echoes that of the seducer in the early amatory novel (through to Lovelace in *Clarissa*), whose approach through the garden to the heroine's house figures his ultimate penetration of her body.

The masculinity of the Widow depends for much of its comic effect on the converse feminization of uncle Toby. His modesty, we are told, "arose to such a height in him, as almost to equal, if such a thing could be, even the modesty of a woman: That female nicety, Madam, and inward cleanliness of mind and fancy, in your sex, which makes you so much the envy of ours" (54). The ironic tone here and conspicuous absence elsewhere of any women approaching this exemplary status, give additional point to those other gendered qualities possessed by uncle Toby which innumerable conduct books recommend to their receptive female audience. Uncle Toby, for instance, finds his characteristic modesty offended by the language of the Widow Wadman, a response Tristram anticipates in his exploration of his uncle's frustrated attempts to render intelligible the history of his wound. John Gregory's sententious description of the ideal woman in his 1774 *A Father's Legacy to his Daughter* could easily stand for Toby's defining characteristics: "One of the chief beauties in a female character, is that modest *reserve*, that retiring *delicacy*, which avoids the public eye, and is disconcerted even at the gaze of admiration ... This modesty, which I think is so essential to your sex, will naturally dispose you to be rather silent in company."[27] But while uncle Toby's more endearing qualities are explained by reference to a feminine ideal of silent recessiveness, the point is quite clearly not a defense of women but a demonstration of their redundancy. In this novel, as in *The Man of Feeling*, idyllic communion is possible only in exclusively male contexts. Once again, it is the detailing of the sensible male's relationship to property that conveys his blend of archaic honour (martial or amatory) and emotionalism.

The place with which Toby is most closely identified, the bowling-green, echoes in its smoothness and circumscription, the feminine qualities which Burke's *Enquiry* associates with beauty rather than sublimity. In his proprietorial responses to this "feminine" place, Toby reveals a distinctly erotic pleasure: "Never did lover post down," Tristram tells us,

> to a belov'd mistress with more heat and expectation, than my uncle *Toby* did, to enjoy this self-same thing in private; – I say in private; – for it was sheltered from the house, as I told you, by a tall yew hedge, and was covered on the other three sides, from mortal sight, by rough holly and thickset flowering shrubs; – so that the idea of not being seen, did not a little contribute to the idea of pleasure preconceived in my uncle *Toby*'s mind. (80)

The image of the bowling-green as "mistress" supposes that property can function as an extension of its owner ("this self-same thing") and, potentially, as a means of explaining uncle Toby to himself and others. Such definition of person through place plays adroitly with conventions that sentimental narratives more usually dedicate to specifying the stages of women's experience.[28]

Toby's obsessive enactment in the bowling green of the siege of Namur underlines his disengagement from time (a disengagement that bears an intriguing relation to that achieved by sentimental heroines when a concluding fictional sleight of hand secures their summary marriage and consequent detachment from the mundane). William Ray interprets uncle Toby as a parody of naive historicism and realism, a figure bent on "creating for his public a rendition of the past that will bear no trace of subjective manipulation according to personal motive, but merely reflect objective reality."[29] But uncle Toby's naive historicism is complicated by the terms of gender and genre, women and pastoral. As with Harley's "miniature Arcadia" – the farm he constructs with Edwards and his grandson – masculine communion is achieved here by denying temporal processes (and the women who are represented as their agent) and retreating into a circumscribed Golden World where past experience can be repetitively enacted. In *Tristram Shandy*, this retreat is at once inconclusive, absurd, and deeply affecting, since the progress of the war dictates the inevitable failure of Toby's attempts to stay the passage of time. In *The Man of Feeling*, Harley's withdrawal, sanctioned as it is by belief in an antecedent world of value, is treated more solemnly.

Yet despite these tonal and conceptual differences, both texts juxtapose women, present corruption, and future anxiety against a solitary figure whose authentic male consciousness can apparently only be substantiated in contexts that preserve intact the behavioral codes of the past. Thomas Cogan's *John Buncle, Junior, Gentleman* (1776–8) draws into tantalizing proximity a sequence of ideas that centers on a vision of contemporary life as an amalgam of forms of substitution, principally "external show" for "intrinsic value" (II.135). Not surprisingly, the governing figure for this state of moral absence is woman herself, for whom, "*gayness* of apparel is often made to atone for its [value's] poverty" (II.135).[30] This near universal willingness to accept the superficial in lieu of the substantial follows from the predominance of the "fancy" (II.131), a faculty whose effects are felt both in the behavior of women and in the current degeneration of language from its former pristine reflection of meaning. Language, Cogan suggests in terms reminiscent of Harley's "Lavinia. A Pastoral," has detached itself from meaning to the point that "expressions, which were at first dictated by a feeling heart and refinement of thought, are now thrown away upon the most trivial occasion" (II.132).

This process of attenuation, by which society moves progressively away from the authentic and toward the counterfeit, although everywhere evident in conversation, finds its true origins in habits of reading. Cogan supposes that "writers and readers have a reciprocal influence upon each other," that there were originally "[m]en of distinguished genius [who] often possess[ed] the power of leading the taste of an age," and that their profundities are diluted and made vapid by each subsequent generation of readers-become-writers to the point of general inanity. "[P]ublications in the sentimental stile" have proven especially susceptible to this process of rarefaction since they "neither require deep attention to investigate them, nor recollection to fix them in the mind" (II.131).

Yet, even as it attacks sentimentalism, Cogan's text formally replicates many of the features of the genre in its paratactic structure, its denial of a coherent narrative consciousness, its abrupt ending.[31] The novel lacks the sustained irony which would allow us to interpret this as a Sternean undermining of sentimentalism through a conscious play with sentimental absurdities. But its failure to recapitulate Sterne's brilliant achievement is itself interesting. The novel evokes, as *The Man of Feeling* does, an author baffled by his awareness that his desire to represent corruption must itself be corrupted by his chosen medium.

Language can only function as a scourge of vice, in other words, if it can disentangle itself from prevailing mores.

Cogan's perception of the rift between thought and expression is embodied in the actual lack of connection between his novel and its supposed progenitor, Thomas Amory's *The Life of John Buncle, Esq; Containing Various Observations and Reflections, Made in several Parts of the World, and Many Extraordinary Relations* (1766). Amory's "whimsical and *outré* story," as Clara Reeve describes it, bears no relation in subject or style to *John Buncle, Junior, Gentleman*'s entirely unexceptional and rambling plot.[32] Cogan's ironic gesture toward a nominal affiliation, in other words, works to call attention to an anxiety about the lack in contemporary culture of a tradition of either great texts or responsive readers. Cogan addresses these issues directly in the novel's opening pages which, in a variation of *Tristram Shandy*'s inability to get its protagonist born, offer a mass of prefatorial material centered on the metaphor of the birth of the book. While the bookseller searches among his "virgin titles" for one to affix to this text, the author rejects any including the word "sentiment": "Though to profess genuine sentiment, said I, be the characteristic of every virtuous and sensible heart, yet at this delicate aera of British refinement, when every *Cook-maid* talks sentiment, and every Porter boasts of his sensibility, the word is become so wretchedly prostituted to subjects *void* of sentiment, that it must be thrown off amongst the exploded phrases" (1.16). This conflation of gender, class, and genre depends on readers being made the index of the book's worth, to the point that the novel is finally designated as "prostitute" or "virgin" according to its accessibility to the cook-maid or porter.

How does an author, then, define an audience which excludes those who cannot, in terms of class or gender, be denominated authentically "delicate"? In this novel, Cogan relies on the traditional distinction of real from personal property which he illustrates through a contrast of country and city. The former offers to the gentleman "the blessings . . . which God benevolently intended to be the inheritance of man"; the latter is designated the province of the "grovelling Citizen" with his "effeminate manners, and a depraved taste" (1.144–6). The relation of the depraved and feminized citizen to reading is governed by the terms of a mutually contaminating prostitution, that of the gentleman by a providentially ordained possession of the "virgin" text.[33]

CHAPTER 6

Colonial narratives: "Charles Wentworth" and "The Female American"

Within much eighteenth-century fiction, the previous chapter has suggested, the trope of reading represents the relation of gender to genre as complementary. Conservative novelists like Mackenzie in part construct a sense of the corruptions of the present by investing the past with a pastoral innocence and wholeness from which is excluded everything that presently vexes. It is not accidental that this past is shaped in accordance with a traditionally masculine literary form: by this means it acquires a narrative wholeness and explanatory power that also empowers the present narrative and its author. If pastoral figures coherence, then a novel which recapitulates its terms may through its allusive structures recover the authority of the past. As we have seen, the coherence of the form allows the novelist obliquely to assert a parallel integrity at the level of meaning. In the work of elite male writers like Mackenzie and Sterne, the possibility of translating the desire for order into its achievement, however, is arrested by the inescapable pressure of history. Both novelists represent the opposition of private desire to public history in spatial terms. Harley in the farm he establishes for Edwards and uncle Toby in his bowling green carve out a territory from which women and the change which they signify are willfully excluded. Although Cogan's novel appears a virtual "repository of commonplace middle-class sentiments," he too finally advocates withdrawal. The interested, feminized city is rejected in favor of the country, that symbolic realm where the gentlemanly communion of the past may be recovered through denial of the present.[1]

This spatial rendering of the "flight from history" in Mackenzie, Sterne, and Cogan is complicated in colonial narratives by the assumption on the part of the metropolitan culture that the colonized lands have no actual history.[2] To enter the colonial domain is thus to engage actively in the present with an order imagined as fully potential because untrammeled by any of the constraints of a past. According to Locke's famous phrase, "in the beginning all the World was *America*."3 For the eighteenth-century novel, America continues in many ways to represent the possibilities of this latent meaning. In the nineteenth century, a systematic and coherent imperial discourse will use the absence of history to rationalize in moral terms various forms of exploitation. But in the eighteenth, which has not yet consolidated such a rhetoric of dominion, the relation of "civilized" to "uncivilized nations" is often elaborated in the terms of mutual critique.4 The vantage each affords of the other is, nonetheless, finally nullified by the reassertion at the end of the text of the anxieties attaching to the new bourgeois order within the home culture. As the novels considered in the next two sections reveal, the tendency to think through the new by feminizing it leads Edward Bancroft in *Charles Wentworth* and the anonymous author of *The Female American* to focus on women and property as the organizing figures for understanding the new world and its relation to the old. Here again, gender and genre prove mutually informing frames of reference. These novels set in the Americas adapt pastoral to the colonial context of primitivism, contrast it with the modern extension of georgic – that is, agrarian capitalism – and in the process reinscribe the fundamental relation of women to property and to the potential for self-making.

MEN AND THE COLONIAL ADAPTATION OF PASTORAL: EDWARD BANCROFT'S "HISTORY OF CHARLES WENTWORTH"

The details of Edward Bancroft's biography direct our attention to his active involvement in a range of distinctively modern forms of knowledge: medicine, science, revolutionary politics, capitalism, journalism, natural history, colonialism. Born in Westfield, Massachusetts, he was a spy for Franklin in London and (at the same time) for the English, a medical doctor and member of the Royal Society and of the College of Physicians, an entrepreneur who secured patents for dyes to be used in the manufacture of textiles, a political analyst in his *Remarks on the Review of the Controversy between Great Britain and Her Colonies* (1769), a writer on American subjects for the *Monthly Review*, a natural historian who detailed his experiences of Dutch Guiana in *Essay on the Natural History of Guiana* (1769), and a novelist, author of *The History of Charles Wentworth* (1770).5 His Guianan narratives, the *Natural History* and *Charles Wentworth* (whose second volume is set in Guiana), mark him as an exemplary commentator on the eighteenth-century "contact zones," described by Mary Louise Pratt as "social spaces where disparate cultures meet,

clash, and grapple with each other, often in highly asymmetrical relations of domination and subordination."[6]

Guiana was one of the most volatile of such "contact zones." John
Nicholl, following earlier voyages by Raleigh, Keymis, and Berrie,
pictured it in 1607 as "a pleasant, rich and golden Countrey."[7] But the
actual borders of this "countrey" remained undefined: located between
the Orinoco and the Amazon (Spanish and Portuguese spheres of
influence), the "Wild Coast" was throughout the century the contested
site of imperial expansion on the part of the Dutch, French, and English.
The first European settlers had farmed cotton and tobacco, but the
competition provided by the superior Virginia product finally precipitated what D. A. G. Waddell describes as a "sugar revolution." The
revolution was in large part a function of the peculiar conditions of sugar
production which dictate that the crop be processed on cutting; sugar,
then, "is necessarily an industrial as well as an agricultural operation."[8]
Since the indigenous Amerindian population was both necessary to the
Europeans' survival and resisted enslavement, African slaves provided
the manual labor for both field and factory.[9] By mid-eighteenth century,
Guiana had instituted a carefully graduated hierarchical system in
which Amerindians were regarded as trading partners and "free persons
of colour" (the children of slave women and their European owners)
maintained control over the slaves.[10] To Edward Long, writing in his
1774 *History of Jamaica*, the consequent "racial hybridization" of the
South American settlements had produced "a vicious, brutal, and
degenerate breed of mongrels" whose imperfect regulation, attested to
by a number of slave rebellions (particularly the Berbice revolt in 1763),
demanded increased measures of repression.[11]

In his writings on Guiana, Bancroft refers only briefly to the "promiscuous intercourse of these different people [which] has ... generated
several intermediate casts."[12] Both the *Natural History* and *Charles Wentworth* deflect attention away from the complexities of the existing hierarchies by reducing them to a polarity of Amerindian and slave cultures
whose defining features are detailed through the contrastive vocabu-
laries of pastoral and georgic. For Mackenzie and Sterne, pastoral
functions as a form of denial, a means of representing the desired release
from the corruptions of the present. But in Bancroft's work, where the
public "history of actions and events" is "united with a series of melancholy accidents, and unamiable truths," pastoral signifies not the eva-
sion of history, but an achievable alternative to it.[13] In the Amerindians,
Bancroft discovers an order historically prior to civil society. This

culture is rendered as an embodied golden world, untouched by the divisions that follow the institution of property. It is a world, he writes, in which

... happily injuries are unfrequent, as they ever must be, in a state where luxury and inequality are unknown; where the inhabitants have no wants but are easily supplied; where every blessing of nature is the common undivided property of all; and where, of consequence, there can be no temptation to dishonesty and injustice. (318)

In this sociological rendering of pastoral as primitivism, the Amerindian "State of Nature" appears to Bancroft an "emblem of the fabled Elysian fields, where individuals need not the assistance of each other, but yet preserve a constant intercourse of love and friendship" (340–1).

Bancroft appends to this glowing tribute a Virgilian tag ("*O fortunati nimium, bona si sua norint*" ["oh, all too happy men, could they but know their blessedness"]) that works at once to provide classical authority and to establish an historical continuum between Virgil's literary imagination and his own "factual" representation.[14] His reasons for arguing such a continuum become apparent in his discussion of the Guianan slave society. In the fourth letter of the *Natural History* he turns from the Amerindian idyll which has provided his correspondent with "an idea of the state of *Guiana* before the *European* Nations visited ... [to consider] the subsequent changes which have been induced by *European* Policy, Industry, and Luxury" (349). The incursions of European history are predictably framed in the context of the georgic mode which is used to explain the benefits of metropolitan industriousness and appropriation. But the colonial slave economy makes imperative the distinction of the white settlers' enterprise from what Bancroft construes as the necesssary subservience of the black slaves. The georgic mode's representation of labor as self-affirming must thus be specified in racial terms. This division ultimately undermines the mode's explanatory coherence and, in conjunction with the implicit critique of European property relations central to the pastoral depiction of the Amerindians, works to interrogate the moral economy of the metropolitan culture itself.

Letter four of the *Natural History* incorporates two racially defined narratives that depend on a crucial distinction between white industry and black labor. In the first, Bancroft inscribes the colonialist as picaresque hero whose diligence is providentially rewarded:

Many of these [emigrants] are unfortunate persons, whom the unavoidable accidents of life, or frowns of fortune, have induced to seek an asylum in distant countries, where their industry is often so amply rewarded, that they are enabled to return with opulence and credit, and bless those accidents which reduced them to the necessity of abandoning their homes, and which they once esteemed the greatest misfortune. (366)

The second, which follows immediately upon this passage, opens with a qualification that confirms "industry" as an expression of mental discipline as opposed to actual work: "[a]griculture, and all other labour, in these Colonies, is almost wholly performed by Negroes ... as the White Inhabitants undertake no laborious employment" (366). The division of mind from body implicit in this representation of labor justifies, for Bancroft, the total subjugation of the slaves. He does not attempt, as many nineteenth-century imperialists would, the rhetorical strategy of negation in which the "other" appears, in David Spurr's formulation, as "absence, emptiness, nothingness, or death ... [so] clearing a space for the expansion of the colonial imagination and for the pursuit of desire."[15] Instead, the division of mind from body is represented as a necessary condition of the colonial economy:

In this state there is no medium; either the minds of the slaves must be depressed by abject slavery, or the lives of their masters are in imminent danger ... In this situation [the slaves] are subject to many complicated species of misery, exposed to the tyranny of the imperious, and lust of the libidinous, and to an incessant toil, which will have no period but with their lives. This treatment has the appearance of cruelty, and cannot be reconciled to the principles of justice and equity; many things, however, which are repugnant to humanity, may be excused on account of their necessity, for self-preservation. (367–8)

In this account, the black slaves, like the Amerindians previously considered, are excluded from history, their societies imagined as discontinuous with those "principles of justice and equity" on which the rule of property is founded. Despite their apparent opposition within the text, Amerindian and slave consequently appear at once as mirror images of each other and as a projection of the divisions that define the metropolitan culture. In this latter sense, they come to embody the dynamic of colonialism itself as Bancroft represents it: the emigrant who seeks "asylum in distant countries" is launched out of history to a "distant country" where he seizes the opportunity to exploit property in the debased form of slave labor. "Amply rewarded" he then "return[s] with opulence and credit" to assume his place in English society as a member of the propertied class and beneficiary of the "principles of justice and equity."

In the *Natural History*, generic conventions that privilege the informational over the experiential help to obscure the narrator's complicity in the systematic devaluing of human life that the colonial pursuit of property necessarily involves. But in *Charles Wentworth* the hero's sensibility, detailed through a plot of exile and triumphant return, provides a focal point for the exploration of "possessive individualism," the realization of selfhood in the accumulation of property. The novel's second volume probes the implications of such a rendering of personality through the hero's encounters with two women who represent contrary models of property: a black slave and the Amerindian wife of a European hermit.

Our understanding of these women as the medium for Charles's education in property relations is confirmed by a sudden turn in the novel's plot at the end of the first volume that leads to his generic redefinition from sentimental to picaresque hero. Desperate to escape England, Charles commits theft and forgery, acts which mark a radical break in the hitherto dominant sentimental plot of frustrated love. To him, the theft appears an "innocent deception" because the paper indentures which he has stolen have only an approximate or notional relation to real property.[16] His colonial activities, however, involve commerce in increasingly more palpable forms of property: driven by "[p]ride and ambition" (II.40), he is able successively to acquire a lucrative partnership with a Barbadian doctor, a share in a privateer which remains active until 1763 (when the Peace of Paris ends the Seven Years War) and, finally, two estates in Guiana, the purchase of which sets in motion the georgic sub-plot of the novel with Wentworth's determination to "augment by the arts of peace" the fortune acquired through war.

The ideological uncertainties characteristic of *Charles Wentworth* are a product of the novel's uneasy coupling of a celebratory vision of disinterested labor within a supposedly "natural order" and the various forms of exploitation that define colonial activity. Bancroft's own grasp of the issues is something less than uniform or assured, but the uncertainties become especially critical when he shifts from dramatic presentation to political commentary. The most striking instance of such disjunctions occurs shortly after the hero's arrival in Guiana. Here, Bancroft insists that we confront the political dimensions of property in their most debased form, that of master to slave. Initially, the hero, Charles,

appears as the happy husbandman in an imperial mode. But his purchase of the Guianan estates is contingent on an historic event, the
extraordinarily brutal suppression of the 1763 Berbice slave revolt. In a
graphic account of the punishments inflicted on the participants in the
rebellion sent to his brother in England, Charles describes his witnessing
to the burning alive of a female slave. She suffers, Charles informs his
correspondent, "with seeming insensibility, glorying in the part she
acted during the revolt, and declaring that she thought death, after the
few months liberty she had enjoyed, more eligible than ages of life in a
state of slavery; and incessantly exhorting her surrounding countrymen
to improve the first favourable occasion of renewing their attempts to
recover their natural freedom" (II.183).

Charles's testimony to the slave's triumphant resistance is made
ambivalent by the assumed vantage of spectacle and by the appropriation of her words implicit in his third-person rendering of them. As his
meditation on the meaning of this harrowing scene continues, he establishes another level of distance by probing the moral connotations of the
execution through allusions to two of the period's explanations of the
origins of society. He begins with the assertion that the "end of society,
and the basis of all its laws, are the preservation of life and property. To
the preservation of life we have a prior, unabrogable right, by the laws
of nature," a right which would invalidate capital punishment. But
when he returns to consider the slave revolt after this peroration on
natural justice, the categories just invoked are silently amended, as he
locates the source of the revolt in excessive lenity: "the master and
slaves are in a state of opposition somewhat like Hobbes's state of
nature" and only unremitting harshness and reminders of their status as
property can ensure the slaves' continued life and hence profit to their
owners (II.188).

The exclusion of the slaves from the natural law concepts suggests
that Bancroft sees Lockean and Hobbesian interpretations as culturally
specific, the products of political expedience, fiscal circumstance and
historical moment. Yet the rationalization of oppression through reference to political theory receives a severe check from the individualizing
question that Charles subsequently poses: have these slaves, he asks,
"justly been subjected to this state of slavery; if they have not, all the
severity which is necessary to preserve them in it, is but a repetition of
that injustice by which they were first reduced to subjection; and every
measure by which we oppose the recovery of their freedom, is tyranny
and oppression" (II.188–9). His answer – that there is no justification of

slavery whose end is simply the "gratification of luxurious, vitiated appetites" – cannot obscure, however, his own profiting from the trade and he can only conclude, rather lamely, "But, whatever may be the sentiments of others on this particular, I have resolved to make my stay as short as possible, *in a country where oppression and injustice are necessary for self-preservation*" (II.190).

Even as Charles attempts to evade the self-condemnation which his meditations on property must produce, the reader understands that a continuum has been established, an argument that binds apparently benign commercial activities to the most flagrant abuse of possession, slavery itself. The image of the immolated slave provides a focus for this periodically articulated critique of possessiveness and commodification. In her, gendered notions of the female body as property definitively mesh with political notions of class and race. Her contempt for these structures, pronounced in a dying speech whose power cannot be contained by Charles's re-framing of it in his own voice, resonates throughout the novel. While Charles, despite his reservations, acquiesces to proprietorial readings of selfhood, her impassioned defiance establishes them as inherently contaminated.

The sense conveyed in her attack on slavery that property necessarily generates tyranny and oppression is made explicit in the final stage of Charles's colonial excursion. Having left his plantations, Charles determines to visit the interior of Guiana, and discovers at the furthest point of his journey the European hermit, Mr. Gordon, and his Amerindian wife. On the way, he has visited a number of Indian settlements whose "abundant leisure . . . is usually employed either in indulging their constitutional disposition to indolence, social mirth, or the pursuit of rustic diversions" (II.248). A festival celebrating the successful cohabitation of a couple without benefit of "contracts, notaries, priests and witnesses" provokes a consideration of Thomas More's

Utopian republic [in which he advocates] not only cohabitation, but even a minute examination of the naked bodies of each other ... previous to the celebration of marriage; judging it unreasonable for those who will not even purchase a horse without the severest scrutiny, to conclude an engagement of so much consequence to their peace and happiness, without this circumstance; especially as their apparel is so apt for concealing their natural blemishes. But let me ask my heart whether I would wish to subject – but I have promised not to name her – to this scrutiny? No! there is a delicacy in the love of those whose sentiments have been refined by civilization, that is incompatible with a desire so gross –. (II.240–1)

While Charles here asserts that his sentimental education and delicacy preclude a response to women as property, his reaction to Gordon's wife makes it clear that "woman" in this novel is not a straightforward sexual category. It is instead a culturally specific notion that works to relativize male responses. Gordon's wife, he tells us, is a "perfect brown beauty, in the primitive state of her sex, being as naked as when delivered from the hand of nature ... I had leisure to survey her as she really was ... [and] her whole person, even in this natural, undisguised situation, necessarily obtained my entire approbation" (II.259–60). The topographical overtones of "survey" and "situation" emphasize the tacit parallel between this encounter and that with the executed slave. Both women have applied to them a vocabulary whose governing terms depersonalize and objectify.

The visual, even aesthetic, scrutiny of the female body merges with a reading of it as a text that generates political and moral disquisition. Bancroft's Rousseauian celebration of a "people not yet departed from the innocence, the ignorance, and the simplicity of a state of nature" thus meshes with the mode of commodification evidenced in the complementary figures of woman as slave and as wife to the "superior" European. In the process, the trope of woman as property, so central to the eighteenth-century novel, is briefly, but unequivocally, demystified.

Charles's "aesthetic" survey of his friend's wife proves especially interesting when seen in the context of Gordon as a displaced version of the younger man. Their early lives are remarkably similar, and the parallel is strengthened by Gordon's voicing of many of Charles's expressed beliefs. But Charles's discomfort with the slave trade pales beside the hermit's trenchant indictment of "social institutions" which he maintains operate under the "specious intent" of protecting property, while in fact "oppress[ing] ... subjects by that very wealth and power they gave for their preservation" (III.71). "Political society," he concludes, has "given being to property," the "cause of all social evils" (III.64, 79). Understanding this, he has elected to define himself in relation to the "natural society" of Guiana where "nothing ... [is] considered as a man's property, but the produce of his own labour" (III.80).

Charles's earlier response to the slave revolt was marked by the incipient recognition that slavery is not anomalous to a propertied culture, but a logical extension of that culture's intrinsic oppression. This acknowledgment, however, was no sooner registered than retreated from, as he determined to leave the colony as soon as his fortune was secured. Here too with Gordon, the critique of property remains oddly suspended, an impression underscored by the use of interpolated narrative to present his adventures. Gordon's arguments appear irrefutable, and Charles's failure either to challenge or assimilate them makes additionally perplexing his continued reversion to the imperatives of possession. Ultimately, the older man is rendered merely a curiosity, the defender of an anachronistic harmony between georgic energy and a pastoral innocence uninfected by profit or exploitation. The plot of his life – the retreat from Europe to the wilds of Guiana and then the construction of his own "natural society" – rehearses Wentworth's adventures to this point. But Wentworth's decision to return to England marks his tacit withdrawal from this plot. The relation of Gordon to Wentworth thus parallels that of the "new" new world (the one as yet uncorrupted by Europeans) to the old: the tantalizing possibilities of commitment to radical change, of rebellion against the norm, are entertained and then quietly abandoned. Gordon has played the role of the "informant," the insider–outsider who in James Clifford's ethnographic model is "made to speak for 'cultural' knowledge."[7] But ultimately, his narrative must be cast, as Wentworth's adventures on the journey home suggest, as eccentric rather than exemplary.

Wentworth's rejection of Gordon's primitivism is also cast, the return voyage suggests, as the product of an alternative explanatory structure. En route to England, Charles falls overboard, and is picked up by a ship bound for Philadelphia, a settlement on which he lavishes praise, envisioning "in these colonies the *embryo* of a mighty empire, which in some future century, by reducing those of other European states to its obedience, may give laws to European nations, til like them enervated by luxury and vice, it shall totter to its fall" (III.209). While Gordon saw his "natural society" as the ideal to which decadent societies should return, Wentworth's account of historical cycles finally casts such a vision as retrograde, and sees the future in terms of a vigorous American imperialism, which will ultimately suffer the present English fate of attrition through vice and luxury. His projection here of present conditions into the future is of a piece with the narrative's perspectival shifts, shifts which work consistently to construe political relations as both relative and corrupting. Gordon's paradisiacal settlement, when juxtaposed against the slave plantations, reveals the latter to be demonically fallen; the acquisitiveness that drives the colonial economy, emblematized in the executed slave and in the response to Gordon's wife, clarifies the more surreptitious but equally degrading embrace of commerce in England, imaged once more through the female body in the numerous prostitutes whose fates are traced in this novel. These ethical contrasts, generated in part by spatial ones – England and the colonies, domestic and foreign, exterior and interior – also work to confirm the novel's stadial representation of time. America in the future will follow England's course in the present, exercising imperial power and then losing it. Imperfectly and only intermittently articulated in the novel, this is, nevertheless, a significant historical insight in its awareness of both the constancy of the principle of power and the evanescence of its practice.

The novel's conclusion typically retreats from such perceptiveness. Bancroft, drawing on the fictional convention of the hero's movement away from engagement with historical change, marries Charles off and retires him to a country estate. Gordon's recognition that the iniquities of political society are sustained both by formal laws and by behavioral ones is repressed as the novel's conclusion works hard to efface his charge that "that refinement in our manners, which universally occasions a fallacious and servile conformity of character and conduct; introduces politeness, decorum, ceremony and fashion ... [which are] so many obstacles to a conformity with the dictates of reason and virtue" (III.65–6). Instead, we are treated to the spectacle of Charles's intended, Sophia, "led to the altar by the hand of love ... affected by the solemnity of the ceremony; so happily contrived to express the purity, dignity, and sanctity of marriage, and its chaste and important duties, so agreeable in themselves, and so necessary to the happiness and order of society" (III.212). As the recurring fulminations against urban chaos suggest, this vision of marital bliss is intended to serve as antidote to venality and lack of distinction. The public complement to such domestic integrity is found in the conversion of mobile to real property. Charles, his sister-in-law recounts, has "resolve[d] to lay out his fortune in lands, and apply his attention to agriculture, which he considers as the most useful employment of life, and the most deserving of encouragement; and all the profits he can gain by farming his own estate, he resolves to apply to relieve the honest industrious poor" (III.217). The georgic impulse is now yoked not to pastoral, as it is for Gordon, nor to colonial expansion, as it once was for Wentworth, but to agrarian capitalism, with the pursuit of profit softened by the rhetoric of benevolence. America has provided the means for this gentrified civility, but the novel must struggle hard to assimilate colonial wealth while repressing the complementary cargo of unpalatable truths which its pursuit has revealed.

WOMEN AND THE COLONIAL ADAPTATION OF PASTORAL: "THE FEMALE AMERICAN"

Charles Wentworth can be seen as representative of a number of contemporary novels centered on male experiences of colonial otherness. Typically, America offers Bancroft's hero indulgence in the disrupting and liberating energy of acquisitiveness; disrupting because it refuses the constraints on self-making that define the metropolitan culture, liberating because it entertains the promise that to be understood purely as a form of property releases the power of that self. In the more canonic eighteenth-century novels, such energy tends to be centered in virago figures (Evelina's grandmother, Mme. Duval, or Clarissa's persecutor, Mrs. Sinclair), women whose intercessions in the plot at once help to realize the extraordinary qualities of the heroine and to precipitate the novel's outcome. In colonial novels, where the imperial enterprise demands that the materially constituted self be gendered male, the ancillary women have a status as property which is so entirely definitive that they lack even the parodically acquisitive individualism allowed a Duval or Sinclair.

The purely functional role allowed women by Bancroft's rendering of them as commodity represents less a departure from the norm of male-centered contemporary fiction, than an extension and clarification of its organizing assumptions. The hero's return to England, retirement to a country estate, commitment to marriage as a form of possession which works to naturalize the subordination of female articulacy to male authority: all mark the conversion of the acquisitive into the proprietorial, and the figuring of the proprietorial in juridical and behavioral terms that at once reinforce and obscure the fact of ownership. The hero's adventures, originating in the picaresque conventions of exile and alienation, are given meaning by reference to the contrastive structures of georgic and pastoral, and are resolved by the suggestion that agrarian capitalism and a renewed domestic economy can establish complementarity between the individual and the social. This collaboration of gender and genre marks the hero's plot as an expression of the re-animated paternalist style that E. P. Thompson sees as central to the late eighteenth-century consolidation of the English gentry.[18]

When we turn to consider novels centred on women's colonial experience, however, significant differences emerge. In the anonymous *The Female American; or, The Adventures of Unca Eliza Winkfield* (1767), the female protagonist initially assumes the discursive functions assigned to men in novels like Bancroft's *Charles Wentworth*. But the final result of her achievement of authority (most especially linguistic authority) is not simply an inversion of power relations, but a more fundamental shift in the novel's focus of interest from questions of gender to those of culture. The disruption of the conventional opposition of female to male – and of the corollary contrasts of body to mind, oral to written, passive to active, subordinate to superior – deflects, in other words, the customary and highly regulated considerations of gender and hierarchy. Instead, the reader's attention is directed toward the heroine's relativizing interpretation of European and Indian cultures. In this comparative exercise, the traditional sources of male power are interrogated in terms that work at once to undermine them and to enforce a new understanding of women's potential authority.

This distinctively female authority, however, emerges only gradually within the novel. Initially, the heroine of *The Female American*, Unca Eliza Winkfield, structures her biography according to the plot (familiar from *Charles Wentworth*) of the male quest:

The lives of women being commonly domestick, the occurences of them are generally pretty nearly of the same kind; whilst those of men, frequently more vagrant, subject them often to experience greater vicissitudes, many times wonderful and strange. Though a woman, it has been my lot to have experienced much of the latter; for so wonderful, strange, and uncommon have been the events of my life, that true history, perhaps, never recorded any that were more so.[19]

The narrator here defines her uniqueness individually through her difference from the "lives of women" and generically through the construction of a plot stranger than "true history." But in the narrative proper, the oppositions of masculine and feminine, true history and private biography, are subordinated to a dialectical relationship of European to Indian, a relationship depicted as both complex and relatively unsusceptible to hierarchical categorization. This displacement of gendered by anthropological imperatives in turn allows for the representation of a specifically female power, a power for which Unca Eliza indirectly provides a genealogy in her account of her parents' relationship.

The account she offers turns on the assertion and then withdrawal of her Indian mother's power over her European father. The father, among a group taken captive by Indians, is saved from decapitation by the touch of the princess Unca's wand, functioning here as ministering alternative to the phallic axe. She then leads him by a halter to a beautiful bower where he is given drugs that induce a deep sleep, and when he awakens a highly ritualistic ceremony accompanies the removal of the halter and his release from bondage. In an exotic redaction of the Tom and Sophia courtship in Fielding's novel, he learns her language, and "[t]hough a complexion so different, as that of the princess from a European, cannot but at first disgust" (1.18), he finally loves her. The reversal of the original premises on which he first acceded to the terms of her culture now begins: he takes "extraordinary pains to instruct her" (1.19), she converts (and by doing so, makes his love complete), and they return to the colonists' plantation.

As the metonymy of her name with its conjunction of Indian and European indicates, Unca Eliza represents the potential merging of the two cultures. But as she details her own experiences, the repetition of the patterns established earlier in relation to her parents suggests that the new and old worlds are irreconcilably divided by their conflicting interpretations of gender. Female power is identified with pagan America and masculine repressiveness with Europe, a disjunction that is fully internalized by Unca Eliza only after she is cast on a desert island and, like a latter-day Robinson Crusoe, undergoes the trial of solitude. Despair at the approach of winter and the prospect of starvation ebb only when she speaks "in the imagined person of [her] uncle" (1.105), whose voice assures her that "[h]uman felicity or misery is confined to no place or circumstance of life" (1.109). In the absence of human society, in other words, moral injunctions still issue from a masculine center, even when, as here, that voice must be projected out of her own sense of absence.

The authorizing power of a male consciousness is reinforced by her first act after speaking her uncle's words: she begins only now to read consecutively the manuscript of the island's recently deceased hermit (having formerly consulted it unsystematically) and finds evidence there of the ruins of an ancient temple to the sun god whom the natives of a contiguous island worship on an annual visit. The hermit's writings counsel concealment for the duration of the visit, but Unca Eliza ignores his advice and determines to act on her own discovery of a network of underground corridors that provide access to the interior of the golden statue of the sun god. On the anniversary of the natives' visit she enters the cavity of the deity and with "more than female resolution" (1.156) addresses the assembled multitude. Masculine writing here gives way to female orality, and as subsequent events make clear, articulation is power. Afraid of confinement within the statue, she prognosticates her own rebirth as the deity's emissary on earth, and in doing so achieves an identity that, like her mother's before Unca's conversion to Christianity, remains untempered by European notions of decorum and self-effacement. Garbed in the high priest's golden vestments and jewels, and laden with weapons that blend the iconography of Aztec and Athena, she adapts the structures of religious patriarchy to secure veneration.

This assimilation of the discourses of linguistic and religious authority, as the recapitulation of her mother's early history confirms, locates her within the realm of the pagan or heretic. Unca Eliza's subsequent variation on her mother's plot suggests that it is only within these contexts that such autonomy can be imagined. The princess Unca's accession to the authority of her husband was signaled by her conversion to his religion. Here, Unca Eliza herself undertakes the conversion of the natives and in the process disallows her own divine status. The larger intent that informs this willing ceding of power can be inferred from the final twist on her mother's plot which occurs when Europeans arrive on the island three years later. Afraid that they intend to enslave the natives, Unca Eliza once more dons the high priest's garments and to the accompaniment of eery music advances toward the invading force, only to discover it headed by her cousin Winkfield. His men abandon him, convinced that he has consorted with a "she-devil" (II.95), and, indeed, the peculiarities of his subsequent courtship and marriage to Unca Eliza do suggest, in the context of the contemporary novel, a kind of bewitchment.

The subordination of the princess Unca to her husband's culture, made absolute in their removal from the Indian settlement, is nicely reversed here in Unca Eliza's relation to Winkfield. He learns the Indian tongue, and after "constant importunity" (II.127), convinces Unca Eliza to marry. Wakefield returns briefly to Europe, sells the golden treasure purloined from the island's subterranean caverns (which are subsequently, with the idol, blown up), "settle[s] his affairs, and [buys] a large library of books, and many kind of goods and linens" (II.170), and then returns to live out his life with Unca Eliza on the island. As with uncle Toby and Harley, the turn from "true history" is realized through the discovery of a separate place in which a transcendent pastoral vision can be realized. But the order of the pastoral island to which Winkfield returns is a product not of the exclusion of women, but of Unca Eliza's enactment of civility.

Although there is no direct invitation to read *The Female American* as a parable of colonial experience recounted from the point of view of one favorably disposed toward it, the novel easily accommodates such an interpretation. The two-generation pattern makes clear, in a period of mounting antagonisms, the kinds of amiable relations imagined as possible between old and new worlds. Contemporary letters enforce the appeal of the novel's vision of ordered plenty to Britons affected by the series of bad harvests in 1763 and 1764 and the high prices and riots which followed. "We have a very uncomfortable prospect," Sarah Osborn writes in October 1766, "the poor murmuring and rising in all parts, provisions at so exorbitant a rate, they must starve except the Parliament can find means to prevent the Forestallers who monopolize all things that ought to have been in common to the people." By December of the same year, her letters reach a new pitch of anxiety as she articulates the sense of a terrible novelty in this crisis: "No time or reign has ever produced events like the present. Surely some malignant star influences our conduct. All is Helter Skelter, sense and reason is fled to other climes."[20]

"Other climes" in *The Female American* provide a site for re-interpreting relationships between figures of authority and those they govern, in this novel rendered respectively as male and female, English and American. The construction of the new world as a female born from the conjunction of alien cultures, and as a force which attracts and then domesticates the questing male of the old world, offers a significant variation on Annette Kolodny's description of the American fantasy of land "as woman, the total female principle of gratification."[21] In *The Female American*, it is the woman's consciousness which possesses a transforming power, and the transformations effected depend, in large part, on the heroine's invigoration of pastoral with georgic notions of industry. The industry is dedicated, however, neither to the extension of commerce and imperialism, nor to their local correlative, the agrarian capitalism of a novel like *Charles Wentworth*. It is, instead, focused on Unca Eliza's renewal of a domestic order to which her husband willingly adheres. This perhaps explains the highly significant decision to end the novel not with a return to, but a retreat from, England. By this means, the religious, linguistic, and political authority attained by Unca Eliza over the course of the novel can be represented as intentionally relinquished in favor of a more completely satisfying domestic order. The exercise of integrity leads her not back to a culture that would deny her achievement, but forward, to the founding of a new vision of community.

PART III

Community and confederacy

Introduction

The conclusion to the *Female American* – specifically, its celebration of an ideal domestic order achieved not in England, but on the unnamed island where the heroine was shipwrecked – challenges many of the assumptions that condition the structure and meaning of eighteenth-century travel fiction. As the previous chapter's discussion of Bancroft's *Charles Wentworth* confirms, travel fiction's critique of the metropolitan culture through the contrasts provided by encounters with otherness is most often closed down by the hero's retirement to an English estate. There, the disruptive energies that precipitated his original quest are assimilated to existing hierarchical orders as territorial and acquisitive impulses, once directed outward toward the unknown, are reconstructed within the province of marriage and agrarian capitalism. *The Female American* resists this final recentering on England, and in so doing exempts its protagonists from definition by the customary forms of authority that prevail in novels like *Charles Wentworth*. *The Female American* is, in other words, a travel fiction that sustains to the end the utopian and feminist project asserted in its opening pages.

Its concluding gesture toward a sentimental ideal of relationship – a domestic order configured through affective bonds rather than exclusionary property relations – aligns *The Female American* with numbers of other late eighteenth-century fictions that draw on utopian themes to define their sense of community. Part III will focus on two particular versions of such collectivism, both defined by female membership. In the first group of texts I want to consider – William Dodd's *Account of the Rise, Progress, and Present State of the Magdalen Hospital*, Sarah Scott's *Journey Through Every Stage of Life* and *Millenium Hall*, and Clara Reeve's *School for Widows* – communities of women develop in specifically gendered terms the hierarchical principles that shape society as it presently exists. In the second group – Phebe Gibbes's *Mr. Francis Clive* and John Trusler's two novels, *Modern Times Or, The Adventures of Gabriel Outcast* and *Life; or, The Adventures of William Ramble* – confederacies of women work consciously and aggressively to exploit male-dominated structures. Whether these fictions adapt as paradigmatic a notion of community that complements the status quo, or a confederacy that undercuts it, the imagined spaces they create are mapped through reference to the determinants of class and gender. These books also, like the novels considered in chapters five and six, use a politically inflected vocabulary derived from pastoral and georgic to represent the work involved in constructing and sustaining such alternative orders. In short, the process of self-making that underpins these collectivities is enabled by the novelist's assumption that the terms of class, gender, and genre intersect.[1]

Part III begins with an account of two texts that for quite different reasons refuse to endorse the possibilities of self-making, William Dodd's *Account of the Rise, Progress, and Present State of the Magdalen Hospital* and Sarah Scott's *Journey Through Every Stage of Life*. Dodd's rendering of the "penitents" restored to the community from the dangerous confederacy of prostitution provides a particularly clear example of the ways in which a narrator's "paternal" understanding is used to limit women to designated roles as "useful and industrious members of the state."[2] Sarah Scott's *Journey* initially resists this prescriptive understanding, advocating instead the female confederacy's model of self-definition. But the attempt to imagine an alternative to the status quo is finally defeated by what the novel represents as the categorical regulation men exercise through their discursive authority. Both works depreciate the personal or social fulfillment of their individual characters by imagining community in terms that disallow the imperatives of change and continuity. In contrast, Sarah Scott's *Millenium Hall* and Clara Reeve's *School for Widows* reconstruct the economic bases of their imagined communities to allow the female protagonists a separate identity. Unlike the confederacy narratives, however, the communities within these novels stand in a parallel, rather than oppositional, relation to the existing masculine structures that would deny their integrity.

CHAPTER 7

Versions of community: William Dodd, Sarah Scott, Clara Reeve

WILLIAM DODD AND THE MAGDALEN HOSPITAL: REFORMING THE COMMUNITY

Eighteenth-century philanthropy gave institutional sanction to the imagined terms of female community first advanced in Mary Astell's *A Serious Proposal for the Ladies* (1696–7).[1] By mid-century, charitable foundations such as the Magdalen Hospital for Pentitent Prostitutes rationalized the need for such segregated orders by extending the argument made by Astell for an essential female virtue from moral into economic spheres.[2] We can see this functional understanding of virtue delineated in a 1759 sermon William Dodd delivered before the Governors of the Magdalen Hospital.[3] In it, Dodd maintains that the prostitutes paradoxically testify to the existence of an inherent female goodness; in them "the nobleness of virtue, and the delicacy of sentiment, have rather been covered over with defilement, than wholly blotted out." If they are provided with temporary shelter from want, and have placed in "their hands the instruments of chearful industry and labour; instruments of industry in hands, which were wantoning in pernicious indolence, and impelled perhaps to the extremity of vice," then they may be "saved to the Community, and made useful to it."[4] Habits of industry, enforced through proximity to other penitents, will finally provide the once fallen woman with an identity whose economic utility testifies to its communal worth.[5]

Dodd's argument for social productivity through the training up of a newly laborious work force typically involves the suppression of desire and difference. "The Rules and Regulations of the Magdalen-Hospital" thus direct the women, referred to throughout as "the objects," to be in "their whole dress . . . plain and neat, and exactly alike" (323). In Dodd's account, the "paternal regard" to which the women are subject while confined in the Hospital will allow them when released to "steal through the world silent and unknown; born again, as it were, to new life, and redeeming the past, by their present good conduct" (34–5). The end to be achieved in their reformation is imagined not as individual cultivation, but as a socially useful self-effacement epitomized in the "humble, meek, and downcast look" (241–2) the women are enjoined to assume.

The characteristic features of the reformed prostitute – self-effacing, silent, acquiescent to paternalistic male definition – are consistent with those prescribed for middle-class women in contemporary conduct literature. Since both charitable foundations and conduct books articulate a moral economy in which female propriety serves bourgeois ideology, this is not surprising.[6] More interesting is the particular verbal form that this proprietorial code assumes. Dodd's *Account of the Rise, Progress, and Present State of the Magdalen Hospital* textualizes the behavioral standards the charity wishes to inculcate through its reformative activities. The rationale behind the initial foundation, the sentimental case histories, the sermons delivered before the assembled governors, the rules directing the behavior of the inmates, the testimonials from grateful relatives: all of these separate strands are drawn into concert by a controlling narratorial presence. It is his function to coordinate the varied meanings that community acquires over the course of the work and to suggest that such plurality justifies active, public support for the charity. The community of penitent prostitutes (once the "instruments of our foulest pollution") thus intersects with the community of the "state" to which the women will be "restor[ed]" when no longer "useless members" (90), and with the community of readers to whom the book is directed. His mediation at once acknowledges the emotional susceptibility variously experienced by the prostitutes, the congregation of the charitable, and the reader, and channels it into the "decent and orderly behaviour" (86–7) that paternalist benevolence sanctions.

Dodd's adherence to the rhetorical strategies of sentimental narrative can be illustrated through one of the exemplary anecdotes, "An Authentic Narrative of a Magdalen." The expectation, created by the title, of a personally "authenticated" voicing of experience is, in fact, frustrated. The "Narrative" disallows the unnamed woman control over a sequentially recounted history. Instead, it embeds an epistolary correspondence with her distraught father within a third-person narrative dedicated to enforcing in the reader's mind the wages of sin and the authority of the narratorial voice who will denominate them for us. Despite the woman's sincere penitence, her reconciliation with her father, and her subsequent exemplary labor in "a family of worth and distinction," she endures a peculiarly horrible death which is clearly designed to be read in symbolically retributive terms. An unattended scratch on her leg "through attention to her duty neglecting, bad consequences ensued; a mortification speedily came on." Like Mrs. Sinclair in *Clarissa*, the woman is advised to have the leg amputated, but, Dodd points out,

> it is easy to conceive from a habit of body so wretched as that which rendered the amputation necessary, what must have been the consequences of such an expedient: a total mortification came on; and in a few days after she expired: expired with blessings on the Charity, as the great means of her salvation; expired with all that serenity of soul, with all that humility, yet confidence of hope, which nothing but true christian principles can inspire; but which those principles will always inspire into the breast of the real Penitent. (42–3)

Her deathbed blessing of the charity as the "means of her salvation," coupled with the ascription of the cause of death to the earlier prostitution, reinforces the fact that in worldly terms, she remains, despite her reformation, defined by the body. As such, she is finally, as a person, incidental to the larger narrative purpose Dodd fulfills in recounting her "appropriate" death. In deducing the moral point of this narrative, he comments at length and with much pathos on the "horrid consequences ... [that] attend a deviation from filial duty," exhorting young women to "settle in their hearts, that no love can be equal to the parental; and that when-ever the syren-voice of seduction wooes them to forsake a tender father's roof, however sweet the sound, however alluring the promises, Destruction waits the fatal step, and Ruin stands ready to close her gloomy doors upon them!" (42–4). As in *The Vicar of Wakefield* or *The Man of Feeling*, the plot of the fallen woman serves as occasion for reinscribing paternal authority.

Such anecdotes can be read as evidence of the reciprocity between novelistic discourse and biographical practice within the period. But they also enable us to understand how, across a wide range of genres, the delivery and reception of stories function to convey obliquely the nature of the power relations to which women are subject. Dodd's drily descriptive title evidences neither the emphatic insertion of his own voice into the characteristically varied accounts of the Magdalen House, nor the monitory ends the text is designed to serve. But as with Sarah Scott's *Millenium Hall*, the conservative import of Dodd's *Account* is formally rendered through the gender and positioning of the witness to the workings of the female community.

In the *Account*, the perspective is that of the male "outsider" whose narratorial priority the texts thematically endorse in their confirmation of hierarchy and in their emphasis on the potential reformation of the large and anonymous community of readers. (A subsequent section will consider *Millenium Hall*'s ironic use of this frame device). Conversely, when the story of the society of women is told by one fully complicit in its realization – by a female "insider" rather than male "outsider" – there are corresponding differences at the level of both form and meaning, differences that substantiate the designation of such narratives as ones asserting principles of confederacy rather than community. As the following section will demonstrate, the *Journey* exemplifies many of the standard features of confederacy narratives. Most obviously, it contests the paradigm of sexual vulnerability that shapes what Nancy Miller calls the "heroine's text": the female-centered plots of the early novel whose alternative, overdetermined endings allow the heroine only social integration or death. In contrast to these, the *Journey* defers closure by employing a Scheherezade-like sequence of stories in which women consistently triumph over their male antagonists. In resisting prescriptive understandings of sexuality as definitive, the female narrator compounds the subversive content of her stories by asserting that in her role as tale-teller she realizes a power that for much of the novel is represented as both self-confirming and as licensing her auditors' assertiveness. But, as the discussion following will suggest, while story-telling may serve as a metaphor for the possibilities of self-making, the reality of women's status as property continues to delimit discursive boundaries.

SARAH SCOTT: "JOURNEY THROUGH EVERY STAGE OF LIFE": "SOONER OR LATER WE BECOME THEIR DEPENDENTS, PERHAPS THEIR SLAVES"

Journey Through Every Stage of Life counterpoints a frame against a core narrative, a structure that allows Scott to make explicit the rhetorical and ideological grounds of her fiction. The frame is occupied by an older woman, Sabrina, who entertains her melancholy mistress, princess Carinthia, with a series of discrete narratives illustrative of women's experience, narratives which the two periodically discuss as story-telling is interrupted by commentary. Scott's formal devices reinforce her feminocentric themes. The privileging of multiplicity over coherence, and of digressiveness over direction, as well as the emphasis on a collaborative, oral narrative have an ideological significance to which

Sabrina directs the reader's attention. She had initially claimed that "all States have equal suffering annexed to them."[7] But she soon revises that judgment and urges that stoical acceptance of female subordination be replaced by an informed awareness of misogyny: "Life at its full Extent, is short, but the Life of Woman is more curtailed by the Fancy and Caprice of Men, than by Age or Distempers...In short, when a Woman is dead in Beauty, she might as well be dead in Law, for she is never after a more agreeable Member of Society than if she was a Ghost ... " (1.6).

Her own spectral position as an older woman and a servant, however, brings with it the compensation of knowledge. This she exercises in the indulgence of a subversive narrative power, fully evident in her first story, "The History of Leonora and Louisa." The former, she tells Carinthia, was "almost the only woman I have ever met with, who endeavoured to conquer the Disadvantages our Sex labour under, and who proved that Custom, not Nature, inflicts that Dependence in which we live, obliged to the Industry of Man for our Support, as well as to his Courage for our Defence" (1.6). Since the impressionable auditor, Carinthia, has been forced into exile by her cousin Frederick's illegal occupation of the throne, the notions of male "support" and "defence" are here invoked ironically. They assume the same function in the history Sabrina offers. Possessed as a result of a liberal education of "female, as well as male, Accomplishments" (1.10), Leonora runs away from home with her cousin Louisa and survives by assuming a series of male disguises. First a clergyman, she serves in a rural parish until "the blooming Divine was changed into a delicate Beau" (1.79). After this, she becomes a painter in London and finally a schoolmaster, with Louisa taking charge of the "Family Oeconomy" (1.115) of the boarders.

The cross-dressing which enables Leonora and Louisa's independence at first provokes discomfort. Leonora "could not reconcile this Metamorphosis of her Sex to the Delicacy of her Modesty, except by assuming the Dress of a Clergyman, which left her Petticoats tho' it took from her her Sex, and obliged People of any Degree of Politeness to behave with much the same Kind of Decorum in her Presence as if she had appeared a Woman" (1.18–19). But she is soon forced to compound the transgression of male dress by enacting codes of masculine behavior, and in doing so discovers first-hand the pleasures of control. The pivotal event in this transition is her leading of a religious service. At first faltering, she becomes "seriously affected with her Subject" (1.26) and ends by deeply moving her audience. Her subsequent careers as painter and schoolmaster, both of which grant to her similar corrective powers, visual and verbal, are entered into without prefatorial comment about their breaches of decorum.

The version of authority played out in the core narrative has both explicit and implicit correlatives in the frame narrative. The conversation between the princess Carinthia and Sabrina provoked by the first cross-dressing anecdote retailed by the latter makes explicit the different notions of power the two women entertain, notions which are, in turn, linked to an opposition between active and passive reading. The princess sees Leonora's male dress as diminishing her authority, since in assuming such garb she loses the opportunity to exercise control over obedient lovers. Given the ability of women to make men "meek humble Creature[s]," Carinthia maintains, "What Lover will venture to say, Woman was made only to be the Property of that nobler Part of the Creation?" Sabrina, typically taking the long view, reminds her charge that "the worshipped Goddess dwindles into the tame useful Drudge, or a disregarded Appurtenance" as soon as courtship ends with marriage. Carinthia "who has known only the idle Lovers in Romance" has been blinded to the conditions of "real Life." These, Sabrina maintains, are determined not by courtly convention but by a sexual economy whose terms are defined by its beneficiaries, men. "Marriage makes the Lover a Convert to the Doctrine" of wife as chattel, Sabrina concludes, a doctrine which ensures that the wife will "pay dearly" (1.34–5) for the seeming authority she enjoyed in courtship.[8]

The interplay here of story and interpretation typifies the twinned narrative impulses that shape the *Journey*. Sabrina mediates between the two in order to wean Carinthia from her consumption of what are seen as misogynistic romances and to suggest alternatives that conform to her own assumption of a fundamental equality: "Learning is of no Sex, tho' it is chiefly arrogated by one, and Virtue should be common to both" (1.119). Yet, as Sabrina herself asserts, in a passage whose paradoxes recurrently inform contemporary treatises on female education, declarations of equality are meaningless if not enacted consensually:

Men hate us if they think us learned, but despise us if we want the Improvements which only Reading can produce . . . They flatter us in our Follies to keep us still Fools, and while our Ignorance, and the Inferiority of our Understandings, are made Arguments for our Subjection, we are persecuted if we aim at Improvement. If we should by Education gain the Learning on which Men value themselves, we must conceal it as if it were a Crime (1.188–9)

For Sabrina, narrative offers the potential both thematically and formally of evading this double bind. "The History of Leonora and Louisa" construes women as members of a confederacy who are able to disprove charges of an innate "Ignorance" and "Inferiority" by appropriating what "Custom, not Nature" sanctions as properly masculine. The conditions of concealment and criminality which men would impose on female learning can be circumvented, she implies, by women's engagement in other narrative modes. Her story-telling is thus made at once to serve as sign of a distinctively female aptitude for language and as agent for the extension of the expressive opportunities fiction offers women.

Sabrina's narrative prowess, in other words, grants her a power that is seemingly distinct from masculine modes and that allows her to confound the notion that "Woman was made only to be the Property" of man. The reader's attention is directed toward a recognition of this intellectual authority by a textual focus on narratorial power. In a manner anticipatory of Sterne's technique in *Tristram Shandy*, for instance, Sabrina playfully enacts the absolute nature of the control she exercises over her creation by commenting on the prolonged suspension of the characters' lives in the intervals during which she moves from telling the history of Leonora and Louisa to discussing its implications with Carinthia. And she suggests by these shifts between frame and core narratives the extension of her authority from the "imagined" to the "actual," as Carinthia is schooled in subversive practices.

But the intellectual property that Sabrina forwards as alternative to existing property relations (defined as male and misogynistic) is ultimately revealed to be unworkable beyond the confines of the story-teller's art. Like Scheherazade's, Sabrina's power is bound up with the act of narration and ends when closure, however indeterminate, is achieved. It does so, because there are no plots, fictional or real, through which women can imagine existences separate from men. After recounting the marriage of Leonora to Calidore, Sabrina thus declares: "And here, with your Highness's Permission, I shall drop her; a Novel would make but a bad Figure carried on beyond Marriage; and as I began *Leonora's* History in order to shew, how capable our Sex might be made of preserving Independence, I could have no Excuse for continuing it after she had done so common a Thing as marrying, and made herself dependent on one of the other Sex; she might rather serve as an Argument, that, let our Talents be equal or superior to them, our Spirits above Meanness, and our Situations above Controul, still sooner or later we become their Dependents, perhaps their Slaves" (1.159–60). "Novel" now joins the earlier discredited "romance" as a form shaped by anti-feminist impulses; the abrupt ending of this particular story (echoed in that of the *Journey* as a whole) suggests that confederacies of women can exist only as long as they remain distinct from the constraints of literary and cultural conformity.

In representing its confederacy of women through discursive practices that are finally revealed to be unsustainable, the *Journey* marks out the practical limits of the adversarial stance that Sabrina assumes. The pleasures of attending to stories in which women triumph over men must pall if their final import is the acknowledgment that "sooner or later we become their Dependents, perhaps their Slaves." In the two novels to which I now turn, Sarah Scott's *Millenium Hall* and Clara Reeve's *The School for Widows*, female authority is rendered more obliquely through reference to an ideal of community rather than confederacy, of a complementary rather than antagonistic relation to men. The indirection characteristic of both works originates in the double strategy each pursues: an overt deference to masculinist, even misogynist, assumptions about women and their capabilities is balanced against a detailed account of communal orders based on what Ruth Perry has called the principles of "utopian maternalism."[9] The reader negotiates these conflicting perspectives by attending to the meanings embodied in the novels' adaptations of structure and genre to questions of gender. Pastoral, associated with the frame narrative's male perspective, and georgic, with the women who describe their work and history in the core narrative, again prove crucial determinants of meaning.

"MILLENIUM HALL" AND "SCHOOL FOR WIDOWS": CONVERSATION AND CONSENSUS

Like Dodd's *Magdalen Hospital*, Scott's *Millenium Hall* is narrated by a male outsider who details the workings of the community to which the title refers.[10] Sir George Ellison's epistolary account of the estate that he and his young charge Lamont happen upon (their carriage has broken down nearby) incorporates the histories of five of the women inhabitants. The narratives are supplied by Mrs. Maynard, a near relation from whom he has been separated by his twenty-year residence in Jamaica.[11] Interspersed with Mrs. Maynard's biographical sketches are tours of the estate, reports on its manufacturing enterprises, conversations between the women, and descriptions of the colonizing activities that have led to the establishment of an adjunct house, with a third about to open. Superficially, then, *Millenium Hall* works like Dodd's *Magdalen House*, as a composite text assembled by a male narrator whose self-proclaimed disinterested stance as "spectator" and "auditor" (54) sanctions his mediation between the real world of the bookseller to whom he directs his letter and the cloistered one he reconstructs for the moral instruction of that reader.[12]

But the complications surrounding the issues of naming and of place that emerge early in Scott's work alert us to ironies that operate at the expense of the narrator, depriving him of the interpretative authority he exercises in Dodd's text. When, on the opening page, he declares that he has elected to "nominate [the place] Millenium Hall, as the best adapted to the lives of the inhabitants, and to avoid giving the real name, fearing to offend that modesty which has induced them to conceal their virtues in retirement" (53), he introduces a trope of false naming – a kind of paralepsis – that comes to distinguish not only the origins of his narrative but also, as we shall see, the generic context through which he defines the community.[13] As his account unfolds, the women's histories that it incorporates textualize this false naming and, by specifying the connections with "modesty" and "concealment," expose Ellison's usage as presumptuous. Repeatedly, these histories draw our attention to the ways in which reputation and fear of defamation control women's lives, at times subjecting them to the designs of the unscrupulous.

In the first of the interpolated narratives, for instance, "The History of Miss Mancel and Mrs. Morgan," a fabricated charge of impropriety forces Miss Melvyn into an unhappy marriage. The false naming through which she is impugned is made possible by the coercive power of reputation – "so delicate a thing, that the least surmize casts a blemish on it" (124). Scott underscores the degree to which reputation operates as a form of social control by distinguishing between its function in the retrospective narratives and in the community as it presently exists. In her earlier life, Miss Melvyn married because she believed that the exemplary authority of rank made appearance definitive. Neither inner consciousness nor outer behavior was allowed to disturb the positive value accorded public estimation. As she comments: "I should never ... esteem myself innocent, however pure my actions, if I incurred the reputation of being otherwise, when it was in my power to avoid it'" (125). This attention to questions of propriety survives in the present Millenium Hall. But within the community of women, the negotiations between the real and apparent that distinguished their former lives are made unnecessary by their shared conviction that here they have instituted an order in perfect conformity to the true meaning of society,

that is: "a state of mutual confidence, reciprocal services, and correspondent affections; where numbers are thus united, there will be a free
communication of sentiments, and we shall then find speech, that
peculiar blessing given to man, a valuable gift indeed . . ." (111).[14]

It might be argued that Ellison's false naming, though a contravention of this discursive transparency, is simply an aspect of his mediatory
role; that is, in his capacity as witness he limits "free communication" in
the interests of "modesty." Paralleling the distortion of false naming,
however, Ellison performs a second misrepresentation in his generic
rendering of the community as pastoral. Together, these narrative
falsifications demarcate his purposive misconstruction of the women's
sphere. In conveying his first impressions of Millenium Hall through a
self-consciously literary vocabulary, he thus disallows the facts of labor
so central to the women's sense of mission: "When we had walked about
a half a mile in a scene truly pastoral [he records], we began to think
ourselves in the days of Theocritus, so sweetly did the sound of a flute
come wafted through the air. Never did pastoral swain make sweeter
melody on his oaten reed" (56). Ellison's former life as a Jamaican
slave-owner has prompted interpretations which read these pastoral
allusions as a figure for the absence of that history which colonialism
enacts in narrowly economic terms. James Cruise thus suggests that
Ellison's attempt to "subtly undermine [Millenium Hall's] intrinsic
value" is in part defeated by the negative fact of his slave-holding past.[15]
More purposively, the representation of women's industry in terms of
georgic could be seen to counter Ellison's perspective by advancing in its
stead a complex understanding of the social and political regeneration
that labor encourages.

Out of the contrast between the observed ideal image of pastoral
leisure and the reality of georgic enterprise emerges the suggestion that
the women's collaborative labor may serve as harbinger of a new social
order. This is one in which "reciprocal communication of benefits" (112)
will be valued over "that state of war, which Hobbes supposes the first
condition of mankind" (111). Thus the generic distinction of pastoral
from georgic parallels a structural distinction of frame from core narratives. Together, these contrasting modes and structures work to enable a
gendered politics in which female industry secures a future of peace and
plenty. This tacit, but ubiquitous, feminist strain within the novel can
also be registered in the discrimination of the men's visual response to
the estate from the women's explication of its meaning. What begins
here as a straightforward opposition of outsider to insider quickly opens

into a series of contrasts – surface and substance, observation and interpretation, cultivated taste and inherent sensibility – each of which functions evaluatively at the expense of the male perspective.[16]

We can see this process at work in the contrast between Ellison's summary account of his approach to Millenium Hall and the first conversation he has the next day with a working woman on the estate. When the men are within a quarter-mile of the house, their attention is caught by "a company of hay-makers in the fields on the other side of the avenue ... .[I]n them we beheld rural simplicity, without any of those marks of poverty and boorish simplicity, which would have spoilt the pastoral air of the scene around us" (57). For Ellison, "poverty and boorish simplicity" are aesthetically offensive and the charms of the scene owe much to their absence.[17] His subsequent introduction into what he calls the "Attick school" conducted by the Millenium Hall ladies builds on his initial impression of this place as an "enchanted ground" (58). But the next morning, he encounters an elderly woman whose conversation returns us to the history and material life of the community. Her narrative disallows Ellison's division of the aesthetic from the political, insisting instead on the complicity of the landowning class in whatever misery and ignorance their tenants experience:

[W]e were half dead for want of victuals, and then people have not courage to set about any thing. Nay all the parish were so when [the Millenium Hall women] came into it, young and old, there was not much to chuse, few of us had rags to cover us, or a morsel of bread to eat, except the two Squires; they indeed grew rich, because they had our work, and paid us not enough to keep life and soul together. (65)

Here the devaluing of labor is seen to undermine selfhood, removing from the starving poor the "courage" of exertion and making "work" signify oppression rather than identity.

As the aged woman elaborates on the distinctions between her former and present life, it becomes clear that this section of the estate reserved for the elderly (it shelters twelve women, each with a small house and garden) serves as a microcosm for the community as a whole. The founders of Millenium Hall, committed to an ethic of service, have made philanthropy a common responsibility and "put us in a way, poor as we are, to do good to many" (66). Industriousness thus at once confirms individual worth, social affections, and the universal duty to "please God" (66). The conservative politics of the novel means that this labor is envisioned in hierarchical terms that naturalize subordination:

"poor folks [Ellison's interlocutor comments] cannot know every thing as these good ladies do," and so both want and need to have someone "to set us to work" (65). But folded within this defense of class difference is, as we have seen, an attack on the gentry who exploit the poor and then refuse to pay "enough to keep life and soul together." The narrative doubly displaces this subversive social commentary, first by having it articulated by a poor and elderly woman, and second, by having her remark that the Millenium Hall ladies "tell me I ought not to speak against [the squires], for every one has faults, only we see other peoples, and are blind to our own; and certainly it is true enough, for they are very wise ladies as well as good, and must know such things" (65). But, of course, the narrative of male oppression and exploitation *is* articulated. And here, as in the biographical accounts offered by the "wise ladies" themselves, there is a pointed contrast established between masculine tyranny and the women's industry, "the basis of almost every virtue" and the foundation of a social order in which "those whose hands and minds were by the favours of fortune exempt from the necessity of labouring for their own support, ought to be employed for such as are destitute of these advantages" (118).

The old woman's conversation with Ellison marks out a local instance of a tactic of equivocation pursued throughout *Millenium Hall* and confirmed in the novel's final uneasy accommodation of critique with affirmation of "things as they are." The ambivalent nature of this ending can best be understood by positioning *Millenium Hall* between two of the works discussed earlier, Dodd's *Magdalen Hospital* and Richardson's *Clarissa*. In the conclusions of all three works, reading emerges as a trope for individual and social reformation. But each negotiates differently the relation between the private sphere of writing and recounting stories and the more public one in which the completed narrative will be circulated among an imagined audience. From these differences can be inferred a politics of reading in which gender is a crucial determinant of meaning.

As we have seen, the narratorial voice in Dodd's *Magdalen Hospital* seeks to regulate the former waywardness of the prostitutes by subjecting them to a paternalism unsympathetic to notions of difference. In *Millenium Hall*, Ellison's narrative is remarkably similar in its rhetorical circumscription of meaning. His pastoralism allows him to construct a closed discursive system in which the order of the community can be made to appear an expression of high feminine art, detached from the concerns of the everyday. Toward the end of his account, he comments:

Till I went to this house, I knew not half the charms of the country. Few people have the art of making the most of nature's bounty; these ladies are epicures in rural pleasures, and enjoy them in the utmost excess to which they can be carried. All that romance ever represented in the plains of Arcadia, are much inferior to the charms of Millenium-Hall, except the want of shepherds be judged a deficiency, that nothing else can compensate; there indeed they fall short of what romantic writers represent, and have formed a female Arcadia. (223)

This celebratory vision of a female Arcadia is as monologic as William Dodd's more punitive one; in both, the frame narrative works to flatten women's experience and to deny the desirability of exchange between inwardness and action. But unlike the *Magdalen Hospital*, *Millenium Hall* has inscribed within it challenges to the totalizing effect of the male narratorial perspective. Formally, the historical specificity denied by Ellison's pastoral is recuperated in the biographies recounted by Mrs. Maynard. And these lives do not simply involve a movement between past and present. Thematically, the identification of the women's activities with georgic enterprise also carries with it a progressive understanding of change: the community itself has expanded from one to three main households, its economy has been diversified with the founding of a carpet manufactory, and, as a result, the women have been able "to enrich all the country round about" (243).

At the end of the novel, however, attention is directed away from the variableness of the women's experience by a summary account of Ellison and Lamont's understanding of what they have seen at Millenium Hall. This final turn toward the male view bears an interesting relation to the conclusion of Richardson's *Clarissa*. There, as here, the reformative impulse, earlier mediated through a woman, comes to be displaced on to a male figure who, in turn, serves as the agent for the conversion of private, female experience into public, circulating text. But in *Millenium Hall*, the two male spectators divide between them what is sequentially represented in the development of Belford's relationship with Clarissa. Belford renounces his libertinism as a result of encounters – personal and written – with Clarissa, and, after her death, dedicates himself to restoring her memory by editing her letters for publication. In the closing scene of *Millenium Hall*, this transition from past to present, reading to acting, private to public is recapitulated in a graduated distinction between the actions of Lamont and Ellison. Lamont's identification with the private emerges in the representation of him as "uncommonly employed" within his room, "reading the New Testament" for "moral evidences" of the "purity of [christian] precepts" of which he now stands "convinced by the conduct of the ladies of this house" (248). Ellison, in turn, the elder of the two, has engagements with the public world beyond Millenium Hall. These public activities are signaled by the posting of his letter – the novel itself – to his bookseller and by his pledge in the final sentence to "imitate ... on a smaller scale" (248) the women's enterprise.

Lamont's turn to serious reading allows him to stand within the text as our surrogate, one whose exposure to the community of the "ladies" has effected a conversion. Ultimately, as the example of the older Ellison suggests, this conversion may ripen into active benevolence, a prospect substantiated by the terms of Lamont's development over the course of the novel. At its beginning, he is disparaged in Ellison's summary account of him as no more than a "coxcomb ... the natural bent of [whose] mind soon led him into all the dissipation which the gay world affords. Useful and improving studies were laid aside for such desultory reading, as he found most proper to furnish him with topics for conversation, in the idle societies he frequented" (55). In the course of his encounter with the women, he has been prompted by their enlightening conversation to renew "useful and improving studies" which may in turn generate a more purposive sense of vocation. Lamont thus begins as a result of their influence the process of fitting himself for a more active life.

In Lamont's transition from self-indulgent coxcomb to responsible gentleman, the contradictory meanings attaching to conversation become clear. Conversation, once coupled with "desultory reading" as a mark of the "idle societies [Lamont] frequented," is transformed at Millenium Hall into the medium of his instruction by the "ladies" and hence the agent of his regeneration. In this latter representation, the women themselves are identified with the socializing functions of conversation in terms that enable the novel's concluding distinction of public from private spheres to be understood as a gendered contrast of masculine (written, active, public) and feminine (oral, circumscribed, private).[18] Comparison with *Journey Through Every Stage of Life* suggests that the constraints on women's potential implicit in these contrastive structures can also be understood more positively as an affirmation of difference. In the earlier *Journey*, the narrative function of story-telling was tied to its release of a fantasy of self-definition, a fantasy that the novel itself disables through the assertion that plots of female authority are entirely factitious: as Sabrina notes, "sooner or later [women] become [men's] Dependents, perhaps their Slaves" (1.160). Because conversation is represented here as an inherently social activity, *Millenium Hall* can, in contrast, allow for a notion of female community pursued in concert with, although formally independent of, a traditional patriarchal order. Lamont and Ellison may return at the end of the novel to the public world, but their departure leaves intact Millenium Hall's reconstruction of that larger world's hierarchies in terms that privilege conversational exchange over Hobbesian competition.[19]

The supposed origins of Millenium Hall confirm that its mandate was from the beginning understood as a reconciliation of traditional hierarchies and communal responsibility. A series of deaths had left the founders free to pool their resources and "[a]s they ordered every thing in their own family with great oeconomy, and thought themselves entitled only to a part of their fortunes, their large incomes allowed them full power to assist many, whose situations differed very essentially from theirs" (159). This interruption of patrilineal inheritance (and the blurring of the nuclear family that it entails) allows the women to recover an older notion of community in which social relations are defined by collective responsibility rather than individual emulativeness or aspiration.

In Clara Reeve's *The School for Widows* (1791), inheritance again proves the spur to a social realization of female identity. But in terms characteristic of the opening stages of the revolutionary decade, the material legacy is tied not to a nostalgic model of politics as in Scott's novel, but to a progressive reading of a specifically middle-class industry.[20] *The School for Widows* presents the self-narrated histories of two widows, conveyed through letters exchanged between long-separated friends. Rachel Strictland has provoked the correspondence by requesting that Frances Darnford "share my heart and fortune, not as a dependant, but as my counsellor and instructress, and my daughter's governess and friend."[21] The desexualized language of courtship here acknowledges both affective and material relationship, but refuses to tie the exercise of authority to exclusionary models of property. In fact, throughout the novel, communal possession serves as a register of the women's reciprocal regard, a regard that places special value on qualities of inwardness. Yet, the women prize financial acumen. Frances Darnford, for instance, arranges a business for Mrs. Martin, who is instructed on how "to realize [the] profits, and to employ the money . . . saved every year," in order that she may become "rich, provident, and easy" (1.36). More importantly, their financial skills distinguish them from their late husbands, who contrastively represent the sins of profligacy and meanness.[22]

The letters of Frances and Rachel pursue their retrospective accounts of the marriage plot through detailed considerations of their husbands' relation to money. In the process, their narratives define a moral economy that is explicitly distinguished as middle class and implicitly gendered as female. Bourgeois women, Reeve suggests, are uniquely able to understand that modesty is the source of civility and not as Mr. Darnford had thought, a "vulgar virtue" (1.64). He had "disdained business of every kind," finding in the *"best company"* men as "idle and dissipated" as himself (1.44, 47). Despite her attempts to "lead him gently into the path of reason and of virtue" by recommending the "study of agriculture," he continued to dismiss her "regularity and oeconomy" as "[p]altry *bourgeois* qualities" (1.48–9) that interfered with his dissipation of her fortune. Mr. Strictland's incorrigibly mean and autocratic behavior, in turn, contrasts with that of his benevolent wife, whose attempts at his reformation are consistently blocked. Yet both women are careful to proclaim the natural, even desirable, ascendency of husbands over wives: Rachel "resolved to do every thing in my power to serve and to save" Mr. Strictland; Frances "detested" women who "had assumed the reins of government, and ruled over their husbands; ... I wished for nothing more than a kind and gentle master, who would indulge my reasonable demands, and check me in what was unusual or improper" (II.282).

These vindications of patriarchal authority within marriage have something of a perfunctory quality, coming as they do from a group of widows who are about to establish a reformed community that very much depends on their freedom from male definition. Moreover, defining the husbands' faults as a function not of gender but of economic and social betrayal – they err not by being men, as in Scott's *Journey*, but by lacking in bourgeois virtues – gives to the projected community a distinctive political meaning. But the disavowal of an aristocratic order for a middle-class one does not entail a parallel endorsement of the competitive behavior often seen as characteristic of the new economic order.[23] In fact, both structurally and thematically, the novel forwards consensus as the surest means to individual and social happiness.

As in both *Journey Through Every Stage of Life* and *Millenium Hall*, narrative form itself rehearses the terms by which the imagined community is constituted. In the *Journey*, as we have seen, the reflexiveness of story-telling serves as metaphor for the restriction of women to fantasies of independence that must, for social reasons, be construed as factitious. In *Millenium Hall*, Mrs. Maynard's interpolated narrative, provoked and developed by the questions of two male interlocutors (and accompanied by a chorus of commentary from the other inhabitants), reproduces the hierarchical conditions that the women enact in the ordering of their estate. In *School for Widows*, questions of form are from the beginning addressed explicitly in terms that imagine gender and genre as collaborating in the construction of meaning.

The novel's prefatorial attack on the "great number of whining, maudlin stories" that feed the current "rage for SENTIMENT" (I.iii) establishes a contested genre as a frame of reference for the reader's interpretation. Sentimental narratives, especially epistolary ones, were increasingly associated during the 1790s with revolutionary excess, an excess that anti-Jacobin commentators located in the novels' sanctioning of female passion.[24] In declaring that her novel will focus not on "false sentiment" but true sensibility, on "those resources which nature intended [the mind] should find within itself," Reeve attempts to recuperate qualities of inwardness in order to argue their social value. Epistolary, as the embodiment of private expression and public communication, represents the formal realization of this double orientation to self and other. The terms of the community anticipated at novel's end afford another variation, one based on the complementarity of bourgeois "regularity and oeconomy" and a sensibility that "ennobles the heart that bears it [because it] is modest and secret" (I.vi). Schooled by their husbands' economic transgressions, the widows represent containment and enclosure as the conditions of the middle-class life they intend to pursue apart from men. Propriety, modesty, decorum, quiet anxiousness about the dangers of upward mobility, an assumed opposition between "real happiness" and "rank, title, or fortune" (I.138): these are the guarantors of identity in both class and gender terms.

CHAPTER 8

Confederacies of women: Phebe Gibbes and John Trusler

In their revaluing of the gendered qualities customarily assigned women, both Scott and Reeve deflect attention from questions of sexual difference. This privileging of attributes currently identified with women, but in fact available to men, marks a key thematic distinction between the narratives of community considered in the previous section and those of confederacy to be discussed below. Before turning to the confederacy narratives of Phebe Gibbes and John Trusler, I would like to map out the larger implications of Reeve's and Scott's choice of a gendered over a sexualized economy of social relations. This should clarify the range and extent of the transgressions enacted in the confederacy narratives and suggest some of reasons for their reconfiguration during the revolutionary decade of the 1790s.

The revaluation of gender that Reeve and Scott attempt balances a commitment to enlarging women's opportunities for social engagement against an acceptance of existing hierarchies. Both authors pursue essentialist interpretations – women are, for instance, assumed to be conversable, innately benevolent, and amenable to change. Since such an essentialist reading refers in the main to terms of inwardness, there exists, potentially, a conflict between its values and those of the economic sphere with which the protagonists are also identified through their businesses and philanthropic projects. The conflict is resolved by the suggestion that women's labor has a regulatory agency that draws private and public into concert. Once again, gendered qualities are central to the underwriting of the universal benefits that follow from women's labor. The collaborative activities that define the novels' distinctive orders – achieved and anticipated – are thus imagined at once as "naturally" feminine and as capable of repairing the existing divisions within the larger society beyond the communities' borders. Women's innate sociability (evidenced in their interest in conversation and story-telling), their sensibility, and their reformist impulses are here invested with an economic purposiveness that rewrites Mandevillean dogma: in these colonies, private virtues become public benefits.

The connection between the work ethic that animates these female communities and the commonly ascribed bourgeois virtues of moderation and industriousness is, then, more than simply rhetorical. In both novels, the repression of sexual difference allows the social order instituted at Millenium Hall and anticipated at the end of *The School for Widows* to be assigned a paradigmatic function. These communities of women represent a compact of interests that men, once alerted to the value of gendered qualities, may adapt and extend to the world beyond their borders. The correspondence between the women's achievement and the men's potential enactment of it is subsequently developed in the sequels, Scott's *History of Sir George Ellison* (both in relation to the eponymous hero and to Lamont in whom "thoughtless vivacity had given place to reflexion" [206]) and Reeve's *Plans of Education* (in which the villainous Lord A of *School for Widows* reveals that after Frances Darnford forced him to "turn my eye inward" he determined to be a "faithful friend and protector" of his family).[1]

In the three works to be considered in this section, Phebe Gibbes's *The Life and Adventures of Mr. Francis Clive* (1764), John Trusler's *Modern Times; Or, The Adventures of Gabriel Outcast* (1785), and the same author's *Life; Or, The Adventures of William Ramble* (1793), the exemplary female community is contraverted in ways that speak to their authors' profound ambivalence about the relation of women to social change. All feature female confederacies bound together by a cunning and opportunism that work to undermine the positive value accorded the gentrification of the hero in the main plot. In Gibbes's novel, the structural rift between the sub-plot (which focuses on rapacious women) and the main plot (which traces the hero's recovery of the material tokens of his good birth) emphasizes the social consequences of the failure to contain or delimit female energy. The confusion of sexual roles is conveyed in Gibbes's novel, as in Scott's *Journey*, by the linking of subversive story-telling with women's successful impersonation both of male behavior and appearance through cross-dressing. In Trusler's works, such confusion is given a more pointedly political meaning, a meaning that in *William Ramble* ties women, and the individual desire for which they stand, to revolutionary excess. While *Millenium Hall* and *School for Widows* represent sensibility and collaboration as gendered qualities possessing a benignly reformist agency, Gibbes's and Trusler's works make sexual difference a cipher of cultural alienation and disorder.

VIRAGO AND HEROINE IN PHEBE GIBBES'S "FRANCIS CLIVE"

Recurrently in the mid-eighteenth-century novel, the desired assimilation of energies associated politically with Whiggish policy, fiscally with new money, socially with the upwardly mobile, and narratively with the momentum of plot development is accomplished through a concluding restoration of property to the reformed hero. *Francis Clive* characteristically makes this pursuit of property central, but does so by nicely inverting the customary genders of the pursuer and pursued. Here it is the errant hero who is the object of conflicting female quests, both of which are driven by ingenious entrepreneurship. The virago Mrs. Smith, in concert with her servant Rachel, devotes herself to the seduction and then fleecing of virtuous men, while Mrs. Clive, animated by different notions of appropriation, strives with the aid of her maid Swinbourn to release her husband from Mrs. Smith's clutches. From the beginning, Mrs. Smith is cast as a female Lovelace, driven by a need for mastery: "love being too soft a passion for her masculine soul, she nevertheless breathed vengeance against the whole sex in general."[2] Like Lovelace, she inveigles her victims by her prowess as a story-teller and then strips them of the male equivalent of female virtue, their fortunes. But, just as Richardson makes his virago figures more sinister than his villains, so too does Gibbes compound the threat of her "female proteus" (1.218) by allowing her to simulate the signs of Clarissa's virtue. After she seduces Francis, for example, "she pretended to weep excessively, and with a most theatrical air and accent, conjured him to kill her, with a penknife she presented him with . . ." (II.24)[3]

Francis Clive's entrapment is initially involuntary, but he finally seeks out her company, hungry for the "succession of diverting tales she found to amuse him" (II.45). The attachment is threatened when Mrs. Smith has him sign, when drunk, a bill for 8000 pounds and a settlement of 4000 pounds a year. The indignant Francis threatens litigation, but Mrs. Smith cows him into submission by recasting the plot of his life's history in a manner familiar to a public attuned to narratives of the good and bad apprentice:

Mr. Frank Clive, clerk in Mr. Benson's compting-house, and Mr. Clive, gentleman, in the possession of a handsome fortune in Ireland, is by no means the same person: narrow circumstances induced him to practice sobriety, chastity, and the utmost parsimony; but no sooner is this check removed, than he discovers himself to be a man of spirit, can take his glass even to intoxication, debauch . . . (II.73–4)

Quelled by this re-telling, Francis would remain the gull of Mrs. Smith were it not for the actions of his long-suffering, but still devoted, wife. In a literalizing of Mrs. Smith's "masculine soul" (i.111), Mrs. Clive disguises herself with "the regimentals of an officer" (ii.107), declares herself Capt. Pain, and determines to inflict some on her rival. After he/she tricks Mrs. Smith into destroying the deeds of settlement and Francis announces his intention to return to his wife, Capt. Pain, "casting off her wig" declares herself. Having secured her husband's reformation, she attempts the amendment of Mrs. Smith's by settling 100 pounds on her for life "to place [her] above necessity or temptation to vice" and "furnish[ing her] with such authors as will both instruct and encourage [her] in reforming of [her] misspent life" (ii.145). But the power of another's plot to shape the future is not spent: the Clives' child dies after being dropped from a window by a drunken maid, an act Francis interprets as a consequence of "my criminal connexion, with an infamous woman, punished, like David's adultery, with the loss of my dear child" (ii.222). After a period of mourning, however, "a second little Spranger [was] bestowed upon them" (ii.230) to inherit the money wrested from Mrs. Smith, and the novel ends with the restoration of the status quo.[4]

The central female characters in *Francis Clive* can be seen at once as entrepreneurial successes and as authors *manqué* who construct elaborate plots based on the premise that female intelligence is sufficient to entrap gullible men and bring them to conform to a standard of behavior that is more or less alien to them.[5] In both fiscal and literary senses, then, they are agents of change within the world of the novel. The cross-dressing motif, however, suggests the limits of female authority. Cross-dressing, here the physical projection of a masculine code of behavior, is confined to the virtuous heroine, and so works to make explicit the distinction between the right and wrong uses of a power that the novel finally suggests is properly vested only in the hero.[6] The heroine assumes male garb in order to pursue the possibility of independent action; once she has achieved the objective made possible by independent action – the reclamation of the hero – she casts off both signs of her deviation from authentic feminine passivity.

In the Trusler novels to be considered in this chapter's final section, the representation of female submissiveness undergoes significant revision. In *Modern Times*, the changes are most evident in the conclusion's refusal to undercut the heroine's plot, which has throughout focused on substantiating female authority. Masculine and feminine plots are here preserved intact, with the latter typically associated with self-fashioning, assertiveness, and the re-writing of individual identity through reference to that peculiar form of gendered property, the female body. By the time of his second novel, *Life, Or, The Adventures of William Ramble*, the negative reaction to the French Revolution is fully in force, and with it, a new set of anxieties centered on the destructive potential of the feminocentric energies that the earlier work had enacted.

JOHN TRUSLER: "PAINTING LIFE AS IT IS"

The Rev. John Trusler was a prolific writer with an acute sense of the varied market for books and the services they could perform. His entrepreneurial instincts provoked a number of schemes related to merchandizing, including one to sell to clergymen (under plain cover) sermons printed in script that they could then pass off as their own compositions, and another to found a Literary Society that would circumvent publishers by printing subscribers' manuscripts and directing the profits back to the author. The subjects on which he himself wrote reveal a comparable talent for locating the opportunities for profit in a range of emergent genres, among them children's literature, novels, conduct books, and garden design. An index to the modish, Trusler provides an invaluable source for modern commentators interested in the formation of a middle-class consciousness. Social historians frequently cite such works as *The Way to be Rich and Respectable* (1775) and *Principles of Politeness and of Knowing the World* (1775), historians of ideas, his *Chronology; or, A Concise View of the Annals of England*, art historians, his *Hogarth Moralized* (1768), *An Essay Upon Harmony* (1789) and *Proverbs Exemplified* (1790). Literary critics have been, by contrast, surprisingly inattentive. But Trusler's two novels, *Modern Times, Or, The Adventures of Gabriel Outcast* (1785) and *Life; Or The Adventures of William Ramble* (1793), have great interest in terms of formal issues relating to plot and gender and of political ones relating to changes in representation prompted by the 1790s revolutionary debate.

One of the few literary contexts in which Trusler's name is now invoked refers to his brief correspondence with William Blake. Blake had rejected a commission by Trusler in response to what seemed to him artistic interference, and then complained to their mutual friend, George Cumberland:

I have made him a Drawing in my best manner; he has sent it back with a Letter full of Criticisms, in which he says It accords not with his Intentions, which are to Reject all Fancy from his Work... Dr. Trusler says: "*Your Fancy*, from what I have seen of it, & I have seen variety at Mr. Cumberland's, seems to be in the other world, or the World of Spirits, which accords not with my Intentions, which, whilst living in This World, Wish to follow *the Nature of it.*"

Trusler's mistaken view of the "*Nature*" of this world, Blake continues, leads him to "be so enamour'd of Rowlandson's caricatures as to call them copies from life & manners, or fit Things for a Clergyman to write upon."[7] Blake's rejection of Rowlandson and Trusler's style is seemingly provoked by their exaggerated focus on minutiae and by the absence of the morally informed point of view that would elevate caricature into satire. Inadvertently, however, he testifies to one of the latter's strengths as a novelist.

Trusler's defence of his manner in the opening chapter of *Life; or, The Adventures of William Ramble* confirms that the kind of reformation satire attempts is no more his object than is the delineation of the World of Spirits. As one "capable of painting life as it is," he declares his mandate to be the education and not the correction of his readers. From this perspective, a novel

fraught with observation, full of incident, and replete with worldly knowledge, is the most instructive book a young mind can read; for thus, learning wisdom from the rashness and folly of others, he will be able to see his way before him, avoid the snares and calamities too often attendant upon life, and, perhaps, make his way to the end of it, with ease and comfort.[8]

This vindication of the novel as form also effectively summarizes the plots of Trusler's two novels, each of which focuses on the hero's search for material success. In the earlier *Modern Times, or The Adventures of Gabriel Outcast*, the first-person narrator's equivocal sense of class conveys the conflicting desire to be considered at once a free agent and one destined by birth for success: "Who my parents were, is, indeed, very immaterial, but it may be necessary to say, that I am the only child of a very respectable, though not very opulent couple."[9] Much of the succeeding three volumes is then spent bemoaning the fact that his lack of money blinds others to his superior status.

The professional equivalent of this disjunction between wealth and worth is realized in Gabriel's choice of occupation. He becomes a ghostwriter for all the corrupt practitioners of the various professions to which he attaches himself: composing sermons for errant clergy, medical texts for incompetent doctors, and parliamentary speeches for "the ignorant and illiterate [who] creep into parliament" (II.52). Quite apart

from the intriguing parallels to Trusler's own career, this plot device is of
interest in its vesting in language the capacity to fabricate identity.
Gabriel's unmasking of systemic corruption consequently works at two
levels: authenticating the personal truth of his own narrative and proving its social value. In a world in which language serves as substitute for
virtuous action, familiarity with its duplicities, he argues, is crucial.

The alternatives to such institutional venality are discovered by
Gabriel in the inverse, but oddly complementary, images of the thieves'
den and of the country estate that occupy key positions in the structure
of the plot. The latter is his reward through inheritance at the end of the
novel. The former becomes his refuge when he faces arrest for what he
believes to be a justifiable homicide. After drinking a toast with the
thieves "as a ratification of their covenant" not to betray their location
in the forest, he accepts their leader's moral justification of their "profession":

"Like the nobles and rulers of the land, we profit, indeed, by plunder; but it is
the plunder of the villain, and such as are the enemies of the community we
belong to . . . Is it not just to take from the oppressor, and make him refund the
wages of peculation? Does not the state benefit by forfeits and escheats, by fines
and confiscations? And if it be lawful to take from a villain his property in *one*
case, it is equally lawful to do it in *another* . . . We live here, secluded from a
wicked world, happy, in a well-regulated society; protectors of the distressed,
and a terror only to the man of rapacity and the smuggler." (II.24–6)

Given Gabriel's conviction of his social superiority, it is typical that
when his turn as leader comes round, he should encourage "salutary
regulations" which "placed the company on a more *respectable* footing"
(II.31). Among these is the exception to the rule of communal property:
of the three women they take on, "one of whom, by the general voice, as
ruler, was to be sacred to me, and the other two were in common with
the rest . . . An event [then] happened that determined me to quit the
connexion; and when it took place, I left my right in her to my
successor" (II.98–9). The alignment of high social status with the ownership of a woman (who will be, like land, inherited by the next to occupy
the position as leader), underscores the entrenchment of this image of
woman as token of male authority. It is an image that denies identity to
the woman in order to grant priority to the fact of ownership and the
power that it confers.

Yet an alternative account in which the woman herself invests in the
body as commodity can be found in the narrative of Miss Biddy

Slash'em, daughter of the vicar of the parish in which Gabriel grew up. To her is given the pleasure in manipulation and self-advancement which Gabriel is disallowed by his genteel status. Hobbled by his sense of elevated birth, he construes the narrative of his life as one shaped by the romance motifs of cruel fortune. His aggrieved recitals of un-rewarded merit are punctuated by chance encounters with Biddy who enthusiastically proclaims the value of assertiveness. If Gabriel is intent on reinvesting authority in patriarchal structures (as the thieves' den suggests), Biddy as strenuously rejects any attempt on their part to restrain her. The plot of her adventures thus serves as foil to the hero's, revealing the possibilities for self-definition and social advance that are opened up by resisting prescriptive roles.

This resistance to patriarchal authority aligns Biddy with a range of marginalized figures. When her father appeals to her to return home after she has been seduced, for instance, she refuses on the grounds that she was "making great proficiency in the profession [she] had taken up, and had the vanity to think, that, in a little time, [she] should be at the top of it" (II.71). She subsequently negotiates a salary, and then a 50 pound annuity to serve as the mistress of the Quaker, Mr. Sly, joins a company of strollers after his death, and then lives with Mr. Dupe who has settled 200 pounds a year on her with a promise to marry, should she "prove with child" (III.171).

Just as Gabriel discovered in his profession as a writer an occupation compatible with his sense of his own gentility, so does Biddy find that words secure her entrance into the world of the distinguished. Mr. Dupe has had her voice trained: "'It has been the means of introducing me into the best company; for so affectedly fond of music are people of fashion, that they will sacrifice every thing to the rage of it. The gentry in this part of the country readily overlook my situation for the sake of my voice, and I visit, and am visited, by every body round me'" (III.171). Biddy cleverly plays on their affectations not only to secure her status, but also to herald her authority over those who would privately deride her. She thus achieves a unique balance between bourgeois self-assertion and social acceptance by a gentry whose style assumes a reciprocity between aesthetic sensibility and wealth.

Biddy's self-awareness recalls the narrator's opening declaration that "he is the richest and happiest of mortals whose resources are within himself, and who depends least upon the assistance of others" (I.i). But this traditional humanist stoic trope clearly loses some of its sententious-ness when acted out by a woman like Biddy Slash'em. The subversive potential of her self-knowledge is heightened by the source of her success: she consolidates her identity by gulling wealthy men who cede authority to her when they invest in her property – her body, and its rarified extension, her voice. Yet the novel makes no attempt to assimilate the heroine's untoward energy by forcing Biddy finally to adhere to the terms of a plot of female contrition such as that enacted for powerful women like Mrs. Smith in Gibbes's *Francis Clive*. Instead, attention is focused on Gabriel, whose actions initially correspond to Biddy's, but who finally substitutes, in ways more typical of masculine characters and conventional endings, real for personal or imaginary property. He makes his fortune by investing the profits of his writing in the funds, a nice instance of the parallel noted by Ronald Paulson between the period's two manipulators of paper currency, writer and broker.[10] The inheritance of his uncle's estate appears at once to reward such self-promotion and to negate the need to continue to engage with a world in which "as Sir Robert Walpole used to say ... every man had his price" (III.185). "Retired from public business, I am set down quietly in my estate in the country," he tells us, where he "enjoy[s] all the blessings of domestic life" (III.214).

Gabriel Outcast, then, finally achieves the material tokens of the respectability he so insistently regarded as his birthright, and he withdraws from a world of contention and anxiety to consolidate his victory over the forces of change. In contrast, Biddy Slash'em's struggle, like Mrs. Smith's in *Francis Clive*, is not to ratify inherited gentility, but to alter her given status. Both of these women represent the possibility of re-writing the future by refusing to adhere to a plot which demands conformity with the past. Both are identified with the power of oral expression – in the form of song or story-telling. And for both, the means to freedom is money and the opportunity it offers to define the female self not as the property of another but through a woman's power to control income in her own right. Such female resourcefulness and capacity for invention could be read as a displacement of bourgeois identity, a reading made credible by the period's recurring link between money and cultural feminization. But whether these representations are interpreted as actual or symbolic, by the 1790s it appears that the parity between female authority and bourgeois activity has acquired more precise political resonances which render it highly problematic.

One of the consequences of this politicization of women's relation to bourgeois culture is that end-of-century novels rarely depict dominant women without censure. The sharp contrast between Trusler's 1785

Modern Times and his 1793 *William Ramble* is most visible in the latter's misogynistic equation of powerful women with lawlessness. *William Ramble* focuses repeatedly on women who by their greater intelligence and deviousness coerce men into actions that are represented as radically compromising a necessary class integrity. Such familiar plot devices as impecunious men marrying for wealth by feigning love or a higher status than they actually possess are present here with a twist; women who are "artful, intriguing, talkative, and obstinate" manipulate young men who are "full of simplicity, and very easily led" into deceptive courses directed toward the particular man's upward mobility.[11] The emphasis in each of these incidents is not on the success of the contrivances, but on the malleability of men and the perfidy of women. Female immorality, as the repeated allusions to France suggest, allows sexual transgression to stand as a figure for political disorder. Female enterprise no longer images the dazzling fiscal possibilities of the unrestrained marketplace, but the spectre of revolutionary upheaval.

Fiscal and sexual systems are drawn into conjunction as Trusler elucidates what he sees as the root causes of the revolution. Adultery, Ramble is told as he searches Paris for his beloved,

"is become the zest of the gay world; the women court it, the men wink at it, and consider it as a relief from a tiresome drudgery. Many a family has pined for an heir; barren soils have been made prolific by new dressing; the state is benefited by an increase of population; of course the man of gallantry becomes a useful member of society, and cuckoldom is growing into credit. It is particularly so here, and I understand they are getting into it in England." (III.54)

The privileging of the state at the expense of the traditional mores of its elite members is tacitly related here to a burgeoning commodity culture. If the profitable state is one whose population grows, then gallantry and cuckoldom are indeed useful and creditable activities.

Yet while he condemns the unrestricted extension of the bourgeois ethic of profit and utility, Trusler remains committed to its limited functioning.[12] The debate on republicanism to which Ramble listens in England – a debate in which the protests of the dispossessed revolve not around principle but their own exclusions from power – suggests that the key objection to such clamorous demands derives from the radical insistence that bourgeois influence circulate freely.[13] Trusler, in contrast, argues that it must be constrained, since the deference of the many, on which the privilege of the few rests, depends on conserving an aura of mystery.[14] Subjugation may not be natural, but it is necessary. His attack on those who act on the knowledge "that a good name is easily acquired by purchase" is a case in point. By doing so, he maintains, they teach the "lower orders" that respect is an "article" to be purchased (II.93–4). Trusler is not disputing the commodification of respect, but rather the universal access to knowledge of how it can be acquired, a knowledge that will ultimately render the commodity worthless. The logic parallels that of Burke in *Reflections on the Revolution in France* with the "super-added ideas" here "furnished" not from the "wardrobe of a moral imagination," but an economic one.[15]

Burke's *Reflections* also shares with *William Ramble* the tendency toward allegorization of the female figure. His depiction of Marie Antoinette situated "just above the horizon, decorating and cheering the celebrated sphere she just began to move in" (169), is famously contrasted with the vision of the "new conquering empire of light and reason" in which "a king is but a man; a queen is but a woman; a woman is but an animal; and an animal not of the highest order" (171). In Trusler's novel, Saunders Macpherson interrupts the debate on republicanism at a London club to declaim that without the monarchy, the English would be " 'aw a parcel of raggamuffins, like the *Sans Culottes* at Paris, running your heeds against each other, in search of a scurvey lassie, ye call leeberty, who has played you monie a shrewd trick. She shewed you a bonny visage, to mack you in loov wi her, and then turned her ragged breech upon you' " (II.8–9). While the depiction of Liberty as a shrewd trickster is an iconographic convention, it also meshes suggestively with the more pervasive vision of female power developed in the novel. Women's calculated use of the body to enthrall men – "she shewed you a bonny visage" – can only end in the flaunting revelation of her sexual corruption – the "ragged breech."

The origins of the Revolution itself are in turn ascribed to the influence exerted by women in France who, "though they are effeminate in their persons ... are masculine in their ideas. This remark, it is said, holds good only with the lower order of women; but we find the same strength of constitution in all orders. A lying-in woman of distinction in France will be up the third day after delivery, and sleep with her husband the ninth day, whereas an Englishwoman requires a month to recover her" (III.79–80). The elision of the biological and the political, the Frenchwoman's bearing of children and "masculine ideas," should be interpreted by the English, Trusler warns, as a sign of things to come. The conflation of female sexuality and aggression (especially fiscal) with revolutionary fervour in the figure of the man/woman makes urgent the need to define more prescriptively masculine and feminine behaviors.

Many novels of the 1790s consequently tend to represent bourgeois activity as exclusively masculine and to render in abstract and social terms the properties of the ideal woman. The transvestitism that accompanied the earlier heroines' rescue of fallen men depended for its efficacy on an essential femaleness that remained undisturbed by the woman's change of garb; her contravention of gender codes was finally a matter of appearances and not reality. In the 1790s, this gives way to the more threatening figure of the man/woman, a figure whose indeterminate sexuality and capacity to cross class boundaries are invested with a power sufficient to topple monarchies. She will recur throughout anti-Jacobin writings in such figures as Rachel Hodges in Maria Edgeworth's *Angelina; Or, L'Amie Inconnue*, and Emmeline in Elizabeth Hamilton's *Memoirs of Modern Philosophers*. Her rise is in turn complemented by the parallel evocation of an ideal of manliness. As Trusler reiterates throughout *William Ramble*, as goes France, so potentially goes England. Anti-Jacobin novelists concur, and female authority is consequently delimited, while bourgeois activity is increasingly defined as exclusively male.

PART IV

The politics of reading

Introduction

In the novels surveyed in the previous section, women possess a remarkably varied agency: they can effect male reformation or corruption, advance or threaten the survival of existing institutions, authenticate or undercut customary representations of selfhood. Contemporary fiction registers these diverse roles through a range of formal constructs: transgressive sub-plots that undermine the more anodyne conventions of the main plot, the relation of gender to genre, the re-alignments of generic categories to signal the novels' concluding restorations of order. Yet whatever the choice of formal strategy, Sarah Scott, Clara Reeve, John Trusler, and Phebe Gibbes make woman's engagement with plot, either through reading or story-telling, a dimension of her authority.

I turn now to the novels of the 1790s, a decade in which the political connotations of plotting gave additional urgency to issues centered on women and reading. Much of what I have considered earlier – questions of community, or property, of the value of women's actual and intellectual labors – comes into sharper focus and acquires additional resonance under the impress of this prevailing concern with the reception and transmission of texts. But, in light of the current scholarly tendency either to isolate the revolutionary decade or to regard it as the harbinger of romanticism, I would stress the reciprocal possibilities of continuity and retrospective clarification afforded by aligning late eighteenth-century novelistic practice with that of earlier writers.

The adaptation of pastoral and georgic in 1790s fiction testifies to the significance of inheritance as a principle governing the evolution of forms and meanings. But, as the following chapters will reveal, the political affiliations of the classical modes undergo a revolution of their own in the period: pastoral loses its aristocratic tenor and becomes identified with utopian radicalism, while georgic's associations with economic expansion and self-making give way to conformity with the conservative view that "[o]ur constitution, for a century ascertained and confirmed, is of all political systems recorded in history, the most perfectly fitted for the attainment and preservation of individual and national happiness."[1]

This political re-orientation of pastoral and georgic is part of a wider pattern of literary adjustment shaped by anxiety about the consequences of blurring the boundaries between genres. Conservative writers assailed radical novelists as demagogues who purvey false doctrine, as "the parrots of metaphysical jargonists."[2] The language of uncomprehending mimicry here refers us to the transliterations of Godwinian doctrine in the novels of writers like Thomas Holcroft. Their assimilation of polemical argument to romance structures made the *"new light"* of radicalism available to all classes, encouraging the disenfranchised to question their condition.[3] Conservative novels of the period most often represent this process though the figure of the innocent but misguided woman, susceptible to the flattering premise of self-definition. As the eponymous heroine of the anti-Jacobin *Dorothea* declares, echoing Mary Wollstonecraft, such novels made her feel "every instant inclined to assert her rights, and rise above her wrongs" (1.14). "to the subtle reasonings in these books," comments the narrator, "what could a young and inexperienced girl oppose?" (1.41). This concluding section will explore the ways in which gender and genre serve as key coordinates in mapping the politics of reading provoked by the "subtle reasonings" of 1790s fiction.

CHAPTER 9

The discourse of manliness: Samuel Jackson Pratt and Robert Bage

In Samuel Jackson Pratt's *Shenstone-Green; Or, The New Paradise Lost* (1779), the antidote to female reading and its political correlative, naive idealism, is masculine *"Common-sense."* The sympathetic identification encouraged by sentimental fictions with their "fancy, and folly, and *fine* sense, which ... is *no* sense at all" is measured by Pratt against the standard of the evaluative detachment exercised by men skeptical of a universal capacity for benevolence. Few, he contends, are now willing to acknowledge the hierarchical values that such a standard ratifies. The ubiquitous non-sense that keeps "the presses in employment" instead exploits the authority of print to nourish the effeminacy on which sentimental reading depends. The habits of private reading in turn infiltrate the political realm by encouraging a belief in social progress and in the efficacy of universal benevolence.[1] In resisting these, *Shenstone-Green* consequently rejects the notion of sensibility, which it construes as a pernicious idealization of human nature. At the same time, the novel condemns the conservative politics of nostalgia, with its tacit assumption that there exists a group of men (*Man of Feeling*) or women (*Millenium Hall*) whose natural disinterestedness would secure social order. But Pratt's intentions are not simply confrontational. While Ruth Perry has suggested that the novel lacks "a serious vision of an alternative way of life,"[2] it does in fact advocate a pragmatic accommodation of "benevolence and business."[3] This middle-class ethos is succinctly expressed in the "GOLDEN RULES OF ŒCONOMY" that concluded his earlier work, *Liberal Opinions* (1775–6): "*Get* honestly, and give cautiously" (VI.221).

Such pragmatism is entirely in keeping with the contemporary reaction against the "culture of sensibility." Its detractors saw sensibility as emasculating, morally suspect, and socially corrosive, and the financial crisis of the late 1770s may well have given an additional edge to prevailing anxieties about the relation between commerce, speculation, and the threat of a more comprehensive class mobility.[4] Pratt's satiric framing of these issues certainly emphasizes their topicality. By drawing on the techniques of his Augustan predecessors, he directs the reader's attention to the invidious social consequences of that naive version of sensibility which sees amelioration as universal. But in establishing the virtues of disciplined labor as the counteractive force to undifferentiated compassion, Pratt also testifies to the influence of increasingly prominent "middle class" attitudes. The brief consideration of *Shenstone-Green* that opens this chapter adapts Pratt's schematic rendering of this middle-class discourse in order to summarize both what it condemns as well as what it values. The more extended treatment of Robert Bage that follows investigates the ways in which that discourse uses women's properties to authenticate the "manly exertions" Bage champions. Bage's novels stand as a demonstration of the ways in which masculine "common sense" is seen to provide the foundation for a "civil society" in which women's labor becomes increasingly specialized.[5]

SAMUEL JACKSON PRATT AND THE DISAVOWAL OF COMMUNITY

An attack on sentimental reading is central to Pratt's satire in *Shenstone-Green*. As the Preface announces, the novel is designed as a warning to those of his own leisured readers "whose weeping eyes and milky tempers render you the slaves rather than the friends of virtue: to you I address the sentiments and adventures of a man who was arrogant enough to suppose he could make human creatures live FOR rather than UPON one another" (1.3). At the opposite extreme from this effeminate sensibility stands Samuel Sarcasm, Sir Benjamin Beauchamp's dedicated steward. His Hobbesian assessment of human nature includes a distrust of literacy as an impediment to the necessary acceptance of life's hardships. To Samuel Sarcasm books "are in general so much *above* or *below* life, that either way one can expect no truth" (1.51). This indictment relies on the conventional contrast of novel to world that contemporary conduct manuals consistently invoke in their denunciations of literature as corrupting and emasculating. Like conduct literature, *Shenstone-Green* proclaims quotidian reality as its standard, defining its truths against the factitiousness of "Romances ... of all atrocious things the *most* atrocious, because they describe matters that never were, and, I hope to heaven, never *will* be" (1.52).

The plot of *Shenstone-Green* provides a metatextual commentary on the seductive powers of such romance texts. Sir Benjamin Beauchamp and his daughter Matilda, impressed by their reading of Shenstone and convinced that imagined social orders can easily be translated into reality, decide to establish a community which will "see a large groupe of ... fellow creatures perfectly independent and uninterruptedly happy." To this end, they consult Sarah Scott's *Millenium Hall* and found their own "commonwealth" on the principle that "every man was to please and enjoy himself *in his own way*" (1.174). The second volume traces the community's rapid erosion as the demotic impulses of Sir Benjamin and his daughter give birth not to another Millenium Hall, with its georgic realization of hierarchical labor, but to a condensed version of London, a place ruled by infatuation with all the invidious forms of luxury contemporary culture can offer. As the traditional contrast of rural innocence to urban corruption dissolves, pastoral itself is unmasked as a damaging literary conceit whose focus on leisure minimizes the actual depravity of the "lower orders." The bored male inhabitants of Shenstone-Green while away time with horse races, cock-fights, and fisticuffs; the women affect aristocratic lassitude which they then dispel by attendance at a "Pantheon, a Play-house, a Concert Room, a Cornely's, ... [and] a Temple for the reception of masques" (III.3). There is also an "*Academy of Dispute* where science and the *belles lettres*, and morality were to be debated, encouraged, and cultivated" (III.47).

Sir Benjamin and Matilda finally realize the fantastical basis of their illusions about human nature and, placing themselves under the direction of the patriarchal Sir Matthew Davies, set out a course of reformation designed to reinforce class distinctions. Central to their plan is the abolition of organized leisure for the poor and of the institutions that sustained it. The concert room will thus be converted to "a Charity-House for poor Welch orphans ... the Pantheon, into a Free-School for boys ... [t]he Theatre into an Alms-House for all good old people past labour" (III.179). The novel ends:

Good order amongst men can only be expected under the check of governments, where wealth and preferment depend on the industry and care of every single individual; where the interest of one is deeply involved in that of another ... where few are *overladen with obligation*, but every man struggles for a little, so that obligations are pretty equally given and bestowed, and where, in fine, there is a regular code of laws which pervades this empire, and provides equally reward and punishment to guard the privileges of one man from the violation of another. (III.190–1)

The communal sharing of property among benevolent women in *Millenium Hall* has given way to an economic individualism which rejects as fanciful a community bound together by anything more than a shared desire for self-advancement. Only through submission to the hierarchy and authority implicit in the patriarchalism of a figure like Sir Matthew Davies can such desire be regulated. Social structures, no longer ratified, as in *The Man of Feeling*, through reference to immemorial principle, derive instead from a "code of laws" presumed to be inherent in political economy. It is clear that Pratt speaks in these final comments beyond the novel and directly to his readers. His terms have little application to the characters themselves whose struggles throughout have been limited to misplaced confidence in human nature. His readers, on the other hand, are assumed to be susceptible to the dual rhetorics of social hierarchy and of possessive individualism, conflated here in order to impress on us the need to retain privilege for the few while ensuring the acceptance on the part of the many that "every man struggles for a little."

Sir Benjamin Beauchamp's "new Arcadia" ultimately founders be-cause his vision of a "golden age ... realized" (I.39) is completely egalitarian. In fact, the novel suggests, left to their own devices the lower orders would not use their leisure to recover a primitive simplicity. Instead, they would mimic the worst excesses of the consumer culture from which their poverty has previously excluded them. Real poverty, Sir Matthew intones after his tour of rural Wales, is most often an inducement to honest virtue, a virtue that money would dissolve into "idleness and dissipation" (III.66). In such concerted attacks on the envisioned pretensions of the poor and on the assumed lack of virtue which disallows their participation in civic life, the novel engages the issue of luxury in ways that we now recognize as typically bourgeois.[6] But as Dror Wahrman has recently argued, "middle-class" attitudes and allegiances during this period can be precisely calibrated to changes in the political scene. For the more liberal Robert Bage, the novelistic implications of this correspondence of class to politics are significant.

ROBERT BAGE: GOOD SENSE AND MANLY EXERTIONS

Writers within the Dissenting tradition were especially prone (at least before the Terror) to affirm the connection between the moral integrity of a middling class consciousness and appeals for social reform. Anna Laetitia Barbauld thus writes in 1790 of that "middle rank of life where industry and virtue most abound ... that class of the community which has ever been the source of manners, of population, and of wealth."[7] In a similar vein, Helen Maria Williams's novel of the same year, *Julia*, lauds the "respectable society of the middle rank, [as] perhaps the society of all others from which the greatest improvement may be derived; for the middle station of life appears to be that temperate region, in which the mind, neither enervated by too full a ray from prosperity, nor chilled and debased by the freezing blast of penury, is in the situation most favourable for every great and generous exertion."[8]

By profession and political inclination, Robert Bage can be placed in this context. A manufacturer with Dissenting sympathies, Bage consistently forwarded liberal views by drawing on the resources of a satire broader and less prickly than the Augustan version favoured by Pratt.[9] The references to Pratt's novel in Bage's first work of fiction, *Mount Henneth* (1781), make explicit the different orientations of the two authors. Disparagement of the poor here gives way to active defence of the middle class. The hero of *Mount Henneth* thus declares that "though I do not intend to follow the example of Sir Benjamin Beauchamp, in the peopling his Shenston Green, I do hope to form a neighbourhood, of the worthy and the good."[10] When this "thriving colony" (II.306) is finally achieved at the novel's end, the worthy and the good are revealed to be those people animated by georgic industriousness. In Pratt's novel, pastoral acquires negative connotations through its associations with the frenzy of female emulation; the more constructive impulses underlying *Mount Henneth* are evident in its use of georgic to authenticate the novel's alignment of manly virtue with middle-class enterprise. Such enterprise, however, is admirable only when expressed in the terms of that disinterested "public virtue" unique to those few in the "middle ranks" who have resisted the "silent operation of finance" (II.120). Gary Kelly has suggested that while the novel "display[s] the confidence of the middle-classes," Bage does not have access to the terms of class consciousness, which remained unavailable to English writers until the translation of *Kapital* in 1887. But as we see in *Mount Henneth*, the discourse of manliness with its prescriptive understanding of gender allows Bage to articulate a vision with social and economic as well as moral implications.[11]

The contrast of substantial bourgeois merit and "paper ... the unsubstantial sign of that evanescent thing, called money" (I.15) is given narrative expression in the history of Camitha Melton. She has been removed from an American ship and claimed as property by an unscrupulous sea captain who subsequently passes her on to a London brothel-owner. The revelation of her history and its significance to the hero, Henry Cheslyn, is structured according to a contrapuntal pattern, in which public and private, circumscribed and sympathetic interpretations are set side by side. Bage alerts us to the varied constructions to which Camitha is liable by presenting her history through a layered series of texts. The first account takes the oral form of gossip: the libertine Sir James Scopton has heard of a recently acquired "nun of Madam P–'s order" (1.74), whom he then sees "sitting at a table, a book in one hand, and resting her cheek upon the other" (1.76). This sentimental and painterly vision of desolation, however, is not encountered directly through Scopton's record, but obliquely, through Cheslyn's account of it. Cheslyn then summarizes for us the woman's history, a history in which Camitha's status as property has repeatedly been negotiated. The captain who had earlier seized her from an American ship "swore she was his property by the laws of war." Drawing upon a more sophisticated understanding of ownership and its privileges, the "well-bred" (1.75) procuress, Mrs. P, to whom she then passes, claims that housing the captive has given her rights to Camitha's labor, a labor from which Mrs. P anticipates great profit: "if I can once bring her to do business . . . I can make two hundred of her the first month, and, before she is blown upon, sell her to some gouty lord for another" (1.82). Miss Melton, however, "asserted her claim to independency and freedom (for she is an American) with great spirit and force of language" (1.75).

The claims of ownership subsequently generate a feverish round of speculative activity. The circle of libertines who have heard Scopton's story bet more than a thousand pounds on the various means by which Miss Melton will finally be raped. Mrs. P, keen to exploit this "very profitable commerce" (1.82), refuses to engage in Henry Cheslyn's haggling over the expenses incurred by Camitha, whom he wishes to save. Cheslyn insists that payment is due only for the expenses actually incurred. But Mrs. P wants recompense for potential losses, losses she estimates as high given the victim's "unwillingness" which "served to enhance the value; the eager volunteers were not the most sought after" (1.99). Mrs. P's terms, of course, are those of the capitalist marketplace, in which the law of supply and demand, rather than any quality inherent in the object itself, defines value. Cheslyn's, in turn, derive from the more traditional moral economy of direct negotiation between individuals who agree that expenditures incurred in the past, and not possible fluctuations of value in the future, determine payment due.

It is in many ways entirely predictable that Bage should use a beautiful and innocent woman to figure opposed responses to property. The sentimental associations of virtue in distress, a stock-in-trade for contemporary novelists, mesh perfectly here with the legal definition of woman as a form of property. But by a series of analogical constructs, Bage adapts this conservative interpretation to more radical ends. He represents property over women as the tyrannical exercise of an illegitimate authority, made parallel here to the American war which has allowed Camitha to be seized as booty. Her history thus acquires the resonances of larger political struggles. Underpinning his critique is a fundamental rejection of claims of ownership over other selves as well as a critique of the definition of female "honor" as vested in the unviolated body which validates such claims. Caralia Duverda, for instance, in one of the novel's many interpolated narratives, believes herself unfit for marriage because she has been raped by marauders, a notion rejected by her lover. But, she points out to him:

"In all those English books your goodness has procured for me, I find it is the leading idea. Women who have suffered it, must die, or be immured for ever. Ever after they are totally useless to all the purposes of society. It is the foundation of an hundred fabulous things called novels, which are said to paint exactly the reigning manners and opinion. All crimes but this may be expiated. No author has yet been so bold as to permit a lady to live and marry, and be a woman after this stain." (1.233)

Bage, of course, does so, twice in this novel alone.[12] His boldness, however, has its limits. At the novel's end, with all of the virtuous characters gathered together at Henneth Castle, Mr. Foston, assenting to the "*postulatum*" that it is "impossible a man should be happy who has nothing to do," proposes that "every man amongst us, should be a man of business, of science, and of pleasure." In pursuit of the first, they agree to undertake trade with America, a "business, in all its branches, [which] may give employment to about one hundred," the practice of physic and of law (without fees), the establishment of a "linen-manufactory" and the "erection of a dome to make glass bottles" (II.304–6). The second will be accomplished by "divid[ing] the country into regions" and exploring "the whole range of natural philosophy" (II.306–7). And the third becomes the province of the women (now all wed to their true loves after quadruple marriages in the closing scenes of the novel): "At the hour of three more properly commences the reign of pleasure, of which the ladies are intire arbiters" (II.309). The reward for the perilous adventures experienced by the novel's male characters is the recuperation of the Horatian ideal, imagined as personally and socially fulfilling; for the female characters are reserved the more circumscribed pleasures of marriage and domestic service.[13]

The resolution of *Mount Henneth*, Bage's first novel, provides a pattern from which he rarely deviates in his subsequent attempts to delineate the bourgeois hero. But as his narrative technique becomes progressively more sophisticated, he discovers further indirect means through which to convey the necessary relation of "good sense and manly exertions," the source of England's laws, "by which personal liberty is as well secured, and private property as well guarded, as is consistent with civil society."[14] The sentiment is Mr. Lindsay's, virtuous tutor to the hero of *Man As He Is* (1792), Sir George Paradyne. Lindsay, James Paradyne, and Mr. Mowbray, all a generation older than the hero, share a scepticism about the present age, a support for the values of "the beginning of the eighteenth century ... when wealth was more moderate and more equal" (1.82), and a conviction that women are to be held responsible for all present ills. As Mowbray claims, "the manly manners of our more immediate ancestors, we have exchanged for the manners of women [and] ... .have lost in firmness of nerve, and strength of constitution" (1.272).

The narrator seemingly concurs with these nostalgic views. Acting on the prefatorial announcement that "[e]xcept the wives and daughters of country labourers, all women read now, or seem to read" (1.iv), the narrator addresses a stream of asides to the "fair reader" (1.220), those "dear inexplicables" (1.215) who are at once solicited as the novel's audience and condescended to as those who "prefer the dulce to the utile" (11.190). No longer the active story-tellers of Scott, Gibbes, or Trusler, women here passively and imperfectly absorb male wisdom. Their status as readers rather than makers of stories textualizes both an inherent submissiveness and a partial intelligence. Inconstant in their attention, women can only attend to "specimens" of what is ironically labelled Lindsay's "antique morality" (1.220).

Lindsay's "antique morality" must be internalized and made current by the hero. But, as in Fielding's *Tom Jones*, and more recently Clara Reeve's *Two Mentors*, the agent of his reformation is, paradoxically, not the unmarried male of the older generation, but a woman of his own. Sir George falls prey to libertine habits despite the best efforts of his coterie of surrogate parents, is restored to virtue and returns to England to die, convinced that through vice he has forfeited the love of Miss Colerain. In his decline, he finds purpose in "the feminine work of framing the drawing [done by Miss Colerain], according to the patterns [she] has left; of choosing for each some tender quotations of four or six lines each; and of arranging them round Miss Colerain's picture, which he had previously caused to be conveyed from his own apartment" (IV.227). As in Fielding's novels, the temporary eclipse of the masculine and its absorption by its opposite serve as prelude to the hero's regaining of both his true love and his virility.

Sir George's engrossment by representations (verbal and visual) and indulgence in lachrymose feeling are parodically feminine. As he sits among his fancy work, he is interrupted by the appearance of Miss Colerain, accompanied by Sir George's sister, Mrs. Birimport. The latter advances both the conversation and the love interest in ways that the principals cannot. Sir George's query, "may I hope," is thus met by his sister's tart rejoinder, "hope, Sir George, if you prefer expectation to possession" (IV.258), followed by the rapid realization of that possession in marriage. The hero's earlier libertinism, like Tom Jones's, had reduced him to a state of passive effeminacy. He now realizes the rewards of a more inclusive possession: the authentic masculine identity known through claiming a female other as his own. But even as Bage conforms to the novelistic conventions he represents as generated by the "fair reader's" expectations, he tilts against them, asserting in the closing pages that "Sir George and Lady Paradyne, may one day be transformed into an Earl and Countess; a most agreeable metamorphosis; and likely to be relished in England, when titles shall be nick names only, in the rest of Europe" (IV.267). Women readers and titled characters, it is implied, may be necessary to the selling of novels, but both run counter to good sense and manly exertions.

In playing out the terms of this double game in which novelistic conventions are at once used and derided, Bage consolidates his own narratorial integrity. The assumption of a female reader is key to the ironic detachment he cultivates in structuring his texts. In his coy and flirtatious relation with her, she comes to stand at once as the other against whom his hero is defined, the audience to which the narrator must appeal, and the source of his inevitable failure. In discursive terms, then, woman represents the unregenerate public: those who read without full comprehension and whose uncritical affective stance precludes serious consideration of the novelist's cultural critique. His self-conscious ironizing of his enthrallment by her in turn reinforces the need to substantiate the conditions of manliness.

Hermsprong; Or Man As He Is Not (1796) opens with an elaborate false start that similarly plays with sentimental conventions in order to authenticate by contrast the more substantial values embodied in the paragon of manliness, Hermsprong. Bage's complex deployment of structure and narrative point of view here comes to serve as metatextual commentary. The first-person narrator, declaring himself "son of nobody,"[15] provides a brief personal history and then launches into an account of Lord Grondale, his daughter Caroline Campinet, and the mysterious stranger, Hermsprong. Only in the tenth chapter, when he first encounters Hermsprong in person, does the writer both name himself as Gregory Glen and abandon first-person for third-person narration. This self-naming seems a consequence of Hermsprong's summary of Glen's character: " 'They say you are an intelligent man; that you are humane; honest in actions, and open in speech. All these are to my taste. I ask your friendship. If you grant it, I hope to convince you that I hold a manly freedom of thinking and speaking, amongst the most estimable qualities of man'" (1.104). Hermsprong's summary omits the one fact of overwhelming import to Gregory Glen, the latter's illegitimate birth. "Was it possible to refuse a friendship so engagingly asked?" writes Glen, "No. From that hour, it has been the greatest source of Mr. Glen's felicity; and you, my dear readers, owe to it this invaluable book" (1.105).

The drawing together here of the originating moment of the narrative and the granting of identity to its writer serves as formal correlative to the values Hermsprong defends. The narrative shift from the intimacy of the first-person ironic voice to the detached and objectively rendered third person allows Gregory Glen to testify to the rational and unbiased turn of Hermsprong's mind, a mind which grants priority to the "manly freedom of thinking and speaking" and ignores the tainted origins through which Gregory has to this point been defined. But while the accident of birth that labels Glen a "bastard" (1.11) is transcended, other forms of illegitimacy which are a function of law and personal tyranny are relentlessly exposed to view. A major theme is Hermsprong's struggle with Lord Grondale's grasping notions of property and his excessive demands for deference. Hermsprong's purchase of an estate contiguous to Grondale's, an estate over which the latter believes he has presumptive rights, represents the younger man's declaration that he will not tolerate feudal notions of an all-encompassing control. Hermsprong extends his challenge from the terms of real property to those of chattels by urging Caroline Campinet to align herself with him against her father. But so enraged is Grondale by his daughter's lack of total compliance that he threatens to call out "the law" in order to crush her revolutionary cant about "the rights of women" (III.170).

Bage renders his programme palatable by making the compliant Caroline Campinet the embodiment of the radical argument concerning individual rights and the limits to tyrannical authority. The political implications would be considerably more daring if the character who plays Anna Howe to her Clarissa, Maria Fluart, were to serve as the revolutionary voice. She is an orphan, a completely free agent, and throughout the novel, she professes her irritation at restraint. Caroline, in contrast, excluded by personality and gender from the realm of purposive action, counsels only limited adjustments to the status quo. Her objections are to the arbitrariness of parental authority, not to authority itself. As she and Hermsprong debate Grondale's control, which fairly rapidly begins to serve analogically as a figure for more complex agents of repression, it becomes clear that women will gain little from revolution.

Hermsprong argues that Caroline's moral justification for filial disobedience lies in her father's having reneged on "obligations" that should be reciprocal. But she is not free to make any choice beyond affiliation with either her father or her husband, he maintains, because women have in marriage a contractual obligation both to their spouses and to society, the latter a function of their "bearing of children" and hence their capacity to confuse the issue of progeny were they not monogamous. The freedom granted to women, in other words, remains subordinated to their function in the transmission of property. The threat to male identity posed by potential female promiscuity in turn underpins a tacit distinction of female mutability from male substance. In a more perfect state, Hermsprong argues, "women would leave the lesser vanities, and learn lessons of wisdom, if men would teach them; . . . more permanent and more cordial happiness might be produced to both the sexes, if the aims of women were rather to obtain the esteem of men, than that passionate, but transient affection, usually called love" (II.171). Women need, then, to control their corrupting narcissism and to direct themselves to securing male "esteem." In this light, Grondale's threat to call the "law" against Caroline because she "knows the rights of women" and "stipulates conditions with her father" (III.170) seems excessive. Bage has throughout the novel carefully circumscribed Caroline's radicalism, tethering it to the love interest rather than developing it in terms of political action. In relation to her, the rhetoric of revolution and understanding of "the rights of women" seem thin indeed.

Caroline thus asserts that her adherence to her father is shaped (as
Anne Elliot will later claim hers was to Lady Russell) by the principle of
respect for parental authority, whatever its reality, an assertion tested by
Hermsprong's revelation that Grondale's claim to his title and estate is
illegitimate. Both belong, in fact, to Hermsprong, who now reveals
himself to be the son of Grondale's older brother and thus the rightful
heir. When Caroline refuses to pledge herself to the man who "reduces
[her] father to adversity" (III.214), Hermsprong advances his plans to
return to America and establish there a utopian community. Fortunate-
ly, Lord Grondale proves penitent and in a lavishly sentimental death-
bed scene, rendered entirely through gesture since he is beyond speech,
joins the hands of his daughter and nephew to signify his approbation of
their marriage. The plot of the novel thus enacts an entirely beneficent
vision of change, no longer revolutionary: the old, illegitimate aristocracy is replaced by a new aristocracy which is both formally indistinguishable from its predecessor and defined in terms that throughout the
Bage canon are identified with bourgeois "manliness" (III.176).

The novel's concluding chapter, in which Gregory Glen emerges to
address the "dear ladies" (III.267) directly, works hard to suggest that this
particular instance of having your cake and eating it too should be seen
as another example of shallow female readers imposing their low tastes
on writers. As Glen explains:

If the careless writer of a novel, closes his book, without marrying or putting to
death, or somehow disposing, not only of his principal personages, but of all
who have acted a part in the drama above the degree of a candle-snuffer, he
creates an unfinished want in the minds of his readers, especially his fair ones,
and they hardly part friends. (III.262–3)

Yet even as he derides the female reader by exaggerating her slavish
adherence to narrative conventions, he himself indulges in a kind of
novelistic excess in the concluding paragraph of the novel:

The union [of Caroline and Hermsprong, now Sir Charles] will prove unfortunate only to the gentlemen of the law; for Sir Charles having no body to go to
law with but himself, is under the necessity of not going to law at all; which will
be so obliging as to give him a full title to his property, by what the gentlemen of
the science call a remitter. (III.268)

The reference is to the principle in common law "by which one having
two titles to an estate, and entering on it by the later or more defective of
these, is adjudged to hold it by the earlier or more valid one."[16]
Hermsprong, that is, acquires his estate through *both* of the means

conventionally invoked by eighteenth-century novels: like Sir Charles Grandison, he inherits property; but like Tom Jones, he also acquires it through marriage. The first means emphasizes the patrilineal transmission of property from father to son; the second, the agency of the woman who, in the absence of an appropriate male heir, becomes the conduit through which the father's wealth flows to the husband. This sly refusal to privilege either is of a piece with the equivocal rendering of gender relations throughout. In the persons of Caroline Campinet and Maria Fluart as well as in the addresses to the reader, femaleness has been tacitly identified both with the incitement of male desire and the potential misdirection of it to unworthy, "unmanly" ends. The slippage between these readings of women's identity follows from Bage's characteristic inability to imagine female agency as operating outside the fixed meanings provided by the clustering of maleness, property, and propriety.

One might assume that Bage's rendering of women and property would be alien to those more fully engaged with the radical program and its vision of redistributed wealth. The eponymous heroine of Holcroft's *Anna St. Ives*, for instance, announces her egalitarian intent "to promote among mankind that spirit of universal benevolence which shall render them all equals ... all participating the labour requisite to produce the necessaries of life, and all combining in one universal effort of mind, for the progress of knowledge, the destruction of error and the spreading of universal truth."[17] Yet, with the exception of Thomas Spence, male English Jacobins most often hedge this supposed equality with various exemptions relating both to class and gender. In their writings, they reveal a persistent reluctance to abandon the notion of a property qualification or a franchise limited by sex. While the utopian agenda advanced by the most radical of the Jacobins envisioned a future in which the entwined terms of class, gender, and property would be nullified, it is, ironically, anti-Jacobins who give substance to theoretical premise in their depictions of the "Amazonian band – the female Quixotes of the new philosophy."[18] Thomas Holcroft's novels, in their fictional adaptations of Godwin's *Enquiry Concerning Political Justice*, suggest some of the reasons for this gap between radical precept and novelistic practice.[19] While he wishes to argue that "mind has no sex" (172), the influence exerted by narrative conventions of representation, as the next chapter will argue, inevitably results in the gendering of political principle.[20]

CHAPTER 10

The gendering of radical representation

Thomas Holcroft's review of *Man As He Is* adapts Bage's stigmatizing of the female reader to the language of criticism, dismissing the "tedious and trifling ... young ladies" who both write novels and, along with "luckless reviewers," consume them.[1] But, he continues, while "the majority of novels merit our contempt," the extent of their influence and potential efficacy in popularizing Jacobin principles argue for a close and prescriptive attention to the form. Ideally, narrative should bring public and private into concert by "playing on the fancy, interesting the affections, and teaching moral and political truth" (297). Or, as he put it more polemically in a review a year earlier:

The labours of the poet, of the historian, and of the sage, ought to have one common end, that of strengthening and improving man, not of continuing him in error, and, which is always the consequence of error, in vice. The most essential feature of every work is its moral tendency. The good writer teaches the child to become a man; the bad and indifferent best understand the reverse art of making a man a child.[2]

Holcroft's identification of "moral tendency" as the criterion of literary value underlines the importance he assigns to educating his audience. In fostering the reader's capacity to reason and to recognize "truth," radical writers believed that they were enabling momentous political transformations. Their conviction was shared by numbers of conservatives, although the anti-Jacobins, of course, had a sharply different response to the prospect of fundamental change. To them, the very existence of an impressionable mass of new readers susceptible to the language of rights and freedoms threatened social and political order.

While I want to reserve until the next chapter a full discussion of the self-declared "anti-Jacobin" novels of such writers as George Walker and Elizabeth Hamilton, the interdependencies of late eighteenth-century conservative and radical fiction suggest that some preliminary comments may be helpful here. Their reciprocal influence has much to do with the inherently partisan interests of conservative and radical novelists; each faction was dedicated not simply to representing its own position, but also to discrediting its opponents'.[3] In narrative terms, this means that novels of the revolutionary decade are often self-consciously intertextual: they deploy the literary conventions that came to be attached to their chosen politics, while alluding to the parallel set of norms that shape their antagonists' work. The objective, as William Hazlitt's summary account of Holcroft's principles makes clear, was to attract a wide circle of readers whose encounters with novels would realize the experience of a political conversion:

He believed that truth had a natural superiority over error, if it could only be heard; that if once discovered, it must, being left to itself, soon spread and triumph; and that the art of printing would not only accelerate this effect, but prevent those accidents, which had rendered the moral and intellectual progress of mankind hitherto so slow, irregular, and uncertain.[4]

A passage from early in Holcroft's *Anna St. Ives* suggests how the novelist embodied the argument for "moral and intellectual progress" in terms that, on the one hand, validate both the radical stance and the language through which it is expressed and, on the other, undermine the rhetoric through which conservative politics was narrativized.

In the passage, the eponymous heroine debates the nature of happiness with the supposedly reformed rake, Coke Clifton. She elucidates for him the distinction between "general and individual happiness," in order to prove the transience and final insignificance of the latter. Clifton's reply is satirical: "Then, madam, we must all turn monks, preach self-denial, fast, pray, scourge away our sins, live groaning, and die grieving." Anna refuses to rise to the bait of his mockery. As she comments to her correspondent, Coke's sister, Louisa Clifton,

I smiled. It is his usual way, when he thinks I am got a little in the clouds, to draw some humorous or satirical picture to bring me down to what he esteems common-sense. But, as I am convinced that truth only needs to be repeated, and insisted on, whenever there is an opportunity, in order finally to be received, the best way is always to join in the laugh, which is inoffensive, unless pettishness give it a sting. (170)

In the course of explicitly avowing a key radical tenet – the irresistible power of truth – this passage comments indirectly on the vocabulary and style of conservative novelists. "Common-sense," for instance, was the rallying cry of the conservatives, the antidote to what they saw as the abstruse theorizing of the "new philosophers." Satire was their preferred means of attack and caricatures of ardent radicals mechanically repeating fragments from William Godwin's *Political Justice* consequently become a standard feature of anti-Jacobin novels.

We can gauge Holcroft's awareness of these hostile parodies from his assured manipulation of them. This scene cleverly epitomizes the narrative strategies of conservative and radical writers in the individual responses of the two characters. Coke Clifton is assigned the role of anti-Jacobin who advocates "common-sense" by the "satirical picture" he draws of the heroine's idealistic theorizing. But Anna maintains the integrity of the radical stance, "convinced that truth only needs to be repeated." In making the mouthpiece of conservative values a very wicked libertine, and in granting the radical heroine both confidence and persistence, Holcroft not only defuses the conservative critique and reiterates radical values. He also establishes that while the conservatives may be able to rouse their audiences through satire, the radicals intend to assert the primacy of the "truth," however plodding and repetitive the exercise may initially appear to the unsympathetic listener.

In making the claim that the moral improvement of his audience vindicates his narrative technique, Holcroft also testifies to another characteristic feature shared by radical and conservative novelists. No matter what their political orientation, both direct their attention to the conversion of the reader. But this focus, however egalitarian in principle, in practice is complicated by inherent assumptions about the nature of that audience. As Holcroft's earlier cited dismissal of "tedious and trifling ... young ladies" implies, the presumed reader was constructed in ways that were potentially compromising to the supposed integrity of radical principles. Contemporary references to "the reader" and to reading practices almost invariably gender as female what is being proscribed – the sensational, the interested, the thoughtless are all labelled "effeminate." The complementary virtues of manliness, improvement, and social responsibility reinforce this gendering of reader and text.

The schematic distinction of female debility from male worth obviously has significant implications for novelists (both conservative and radical) who also wish to assert the role of women's affective gifts in the consolidation of social order. The discussion of *Anna St. Ives* and *Hugh Trevor* that follows will explore how this negative construction of women (and the series of gendered oppositions on which it depends) counteracts

Holcroft's explicit defense of the twinned convictions that "mind has no sex and that woman is not by nature the inferior of man" (172).

MIND WITHOUT SEX

Issues relating to property are central to *Anna St. Ives,* most of them explored through the uneasy relation between the heroine's self-possession and apparent wealthiness. A summary account of the plot reveals how real property serves throughout as an incentive to action, a gauge of character, and a means of advancing Jacobin principles of equality. At the novel's opening, Coke Clifton has been sent by his mother to Paris, ostensibly to settle the "debts of a deceased uncle" (199), but actually to see and fall in love with Anna St. Ives. Their marriage is agreed upon despite her feelings for Frank Henley, whom she disavows out of duty to her family because of his poverty and low birth. (He is the son of her father's corrupt steward, Abimelech Henley.) But a condition is attached to the marriage, namely that she bring to it the 20,000 pounds which is needed to ensure the financial recovery of the Clifton family. They had been left "in absolute distress ... [with] many heavy debts to pay, and mortgages to be cleared" (213) after the death of the father. But Abimelech Henley, who harbors hopes of his own son's marriage to Anna, balks when he discovers that Coke is the intended. Having gained control of the St. Ives money by encouraging Anna's spendthrift father to build elaborate landscapes and by subsidizing her brother Edward's gambling, he refuses to advance the required monies. Coke Clifton, meanwhile, casts off his assumed virtue and swears to ruin Anna (for preferring Frank to him) and Frank (for being his superior in mind if not fortune). The two are kidnapped on Coke's orders, but he finally saves them from imminent death at the hands of their keepers and so begins the process of renewal of virtue with which the novel ends.

Holcroft uses the triangulated relation of Anna and her accepted and denied lovers to develop his critique of aristocratic mores while forwarding radical principles. These opposed political positions have precise narrative correlatives: distinctive plot structures are deployed in order to convey the differences between the moral bankruptcy of the old order and the "energies of mind" released by the new one. In relation to Coke Clifton and Anna, this entails adherence to (or departure from) stereotypical gender and class roles. Coke Clifton's plot is thus the entirely conventional one of sexual and social tyranny made possible by his status as privileged male property owner. Anna's, in turn, is developed by writing against the conventions of standard "feminine" behavior. In developing the relationship between Anna and Frank Henley, Holcroft chooses a more precise analog – the plot of Samuel Richardson's *Pamela* – as the point of contrast against which he can detail the attractions of the new order. The couple's departures from this literary precedent enable us again to register the correspondence Holcroft wishes to affirm between innovation and genuine principle. I want finally to suggest that such a correspondence is compromised by a misogynistic strain in the novel that works to consolidate key social and political hierarchies. This unacknowledged tension that defines central aspects of the radical program occurs despite the novel's dedication to overturning hierarchical principle. Understanding the degree to which this attack on privilege is tied to masculine notions of property and self-definition is crucial to the account of women's exemption from the promise of equality that the revolutionary rhetoric elsewhere endorses.

Coke Clifton exemplifies the compound of sexual and social tyranny that Holcroft represents as the inevitable product of the old order. In Clifton's mind, other men figure as instrumentalities: the virtuous Frank Henley, for instance, will unwittingly be made his "tool" (284), the vicious MacFane, "an implement, with which I will carve the coming banquet" (375). Women, according to his rake's code, must in turn be defined exclusively as physical beings subject to male dominance. Yet while he declares piratically his intention to claim Anna as his property – she is a "prize which I am born to bear away from all competitors" (179) – her intellectual authority at times reduces him to the point of forgetfulness of her beauty. To reassert his primacy, he must affirm his intent to "rob her of all her treasure" (201) and define that treasure in terms exclusively of the body.

Anna patiently opposes Coke's egotistical and appropriative mentality with disinterested "principles of truth" (266), confident of the ultimate victory of reason over passion, candor over sophistry. In doing so, she testifies to the enormous faith the radicals placed in the power of language. Holcroft underlines this power in the novel's distinction of conversation from reading: when Anna offers to transcribe her conversations with Coke in order that he may study her precepts at leisure she subordinates the oral exchange of ideas to their textual form. This local instance of conversation transformed into written record typically points the reader toward the larger, more complicated issue of political conversion. In Anna's reflections on the "laws of necessity," she thus suggests that in the future, men will attain a much higher degree of innocence, length of life, happiness, and wisdom than have ever yet been dreamed of, either by historian, fabulist, or poet: for causes which formerly were equal to the effects then produced are now rendered impotent by the glorious art of printing; which spreads, preserves, and multiplies knowledge, in despite of ignorance, false zeal, and despotism. (294–5)[5]

The alignment of Anna with the authority of print represents a case in point of the enlargement of knowledge made possible by increased literacy. In having Anna proclaim the ultimate defeat of despotism, Holcroft reverses the conventional association of women with oral and interpretive laxness. Voluble female ignorance had long been a novelistic stock-in-trade, especially useful in satirizing an older generation (Di Western, Tabitha Bramble, Mme. Duval) falsely convinced of its mental prowess. The feminist debate throughout the 1790s reinforced the conservative antipathy toward claims of intellectual equality. But Anna's articulateness, like her rejection of Coke's libertinism, challenges this supposed mental and physical authority of men. In proposing to record her comments, she enlists the prestige of political discourse, situating herself beyond the reaches of speculative opinion which customarily marked the limits of women's speech.

This representation of her identity as at once informed and coherent also connects Anna to a sequence of heroines ranging back at least to Richardson's Pamela. In each instance, the protagonist responds to external threat (usually sexual) with a progressively elaborated assertion of selfhood. Holcroft's ironic redaction of *Pamela* in particular, however, underlines the innovative qualities that distinguish his presentation of that self. The substitution of the privileged Anna and her servant lover for Mr. B and his mother's maid typifies the narrative inversions central to his characterization. The socially privileged, intellectually gifted Anna, "distinct and eminent ... above all woman-kind" (363) assumes that reason and cogent argument are sufficient to defeat her would-be seducer. Since "mind is superior to sex" (37), the principles to which she refers are, moreover, universally available. Pamela, by contrast, can only defensively assert her virtue in terms that underline the exceptional nature of her personality and that empty her struggle of political meaning (thus allowing her uniqueness finally to serve as an argument against social aspiration). Identity in Holcroft's novel, in short, is ideally imagined as a capacity of mind rather than body, the expression of a social being rather than of a private consciousness.

The intellectual and moral authority of daughter over father and brother, the political acumen, the capacity to theorize the relation of the private to the public sphere: each of Anna's attributes is remarkable and, in the context of the polarizing of radical and conservative in the 1790s, tendentious. Yet despite this resolute and sincere advocacy of feminist principles, *Anna St. Ives* still relies on gendered oppositions which are entirely conventional in their function and disposition. Cumulatively, they undermine the novel's radical programme in ways that anti-Jacobin parodies were quick to seize on.

These oppositions are generated by a key, but formally unacknowledged, assumption underpinning the novel: everything antipathetic to the Jacobin cause, everything defined as "other," as passional, as subjective, is gendered female. The particular moral and political failings of those male characters in the novel who resist the principles embraced by Frank and Anna are thus consolidated and transvalued under the sign of the feminine. In the process, gender becomes an inclusive category by means of which Holcroft can link such seemingly opposed groups as the aristocracy and the commercial interests as equally odious to the radical program.

The complexity of this process can be seen in the treatment of Frank's father, the St. Ives's steward, Abimelech Henley. Illiterate, with a "language peculiar to himself" (2), he is at once fawning and devious to those whom he deems his social superiors. In this, he clearly resembles those women who, denied status as "rational creatures and free citizens," Mary Wollstonecraft maintains, display a disturbing compound of "[i]gnorance and ... mistaken cunning that nature sharpens in weak heads as a principle of self-preservation." This "little knowledge of human weakness, justly called cunning, softness or temper, *outward* obedience, and a scrupulous attention to a puerile kind of propriety" also ease Abimelech's surreptitious advancement in a culture that insists that only well-born men possess a fully authentic self.[6]

Driven by corrupted private passion and immune to public duties, Abimelech's familial responses predictably assume a highly interested form. His son Frank thus appears to him not as an individual, but as a tool to be used for his own advancement: "a man's son, why a's his son; a's his own; a's his goods and chattels, and law and rite" (214). The legal principle here is most often associated with paternal authority over daughters rather than sons, as dramatized in novels ranging from *Clarissa* (Mr. Harlowe) to *Hermsprong* (Lord Grondale). Abimelech's invocation of it suggests that men who are, as he is, feminized by their exclusion from a full civic existence indiscriminately tyrannize over others. The newly effeminate order thus exceeds the old patriarchal one in its exercise of oppression, extending despotism from the more usual female victims to young, dependent men.

Holcroft associates such feminization, as did many of his contemporaries, radical and conservative, with the narrowing self-centeredness induced by commerce. Burke, perhaps most famously, casts the French revolutionaries as speculators lacking a sense of the past and therefore barred a coherent vision of the future: "All other people," he writes, "have laid the foundations of civil freedom in severer manners, and a system of a more austere and masculine morality. France, when she let loose the reins of regal authority, doubled the licence, of a ferocious dissoluteness in manners ..."[7] In Holcroft's treatment of the same theme, the socially privileged are assimilated to the indictment of the cultural feminization that so consistently features in analysis of commerce. Edward St.Ives thus easily swallows his supposedly intransigent aristocratic principles in exchange for ready cash to pay off his massive gambling debts. Birth and wealth are by such means implicated in the decadence of a social order that violates what Frank Henley deems "one of our first duties": the application of wealth "most to benefit that society from which it first sprang" (381). Frank's disinterestedness appears, in contrast to this feminization, as the radical complement to the "austere and masculine morality" advocated by Burke. When, for instance, he feels himself overcome by the "weakness" (291) of his unrequited love for Anna, he briefly considers escaping to America. The final rejection of this possibility comes by way of an appeal to a masculinized civic identity: "Our duties to society must not cede to any effeminate compassion for ourselves" (316).

The alignments of masculinity and an authentic social identity, on the one hand, and of femininity and culpably interested emotion, on the other, invite us to examine more carefully Anna St. Ives's rhetorical function within the novel. Throughout, this is largely determined by a plot in which the language of sexual contest mediates the opposition between good (principled behaviour) and bad (self-interestedness). As the focus of Coke Clifton and Frank Henley's passion, Anna's person serves as nexus of two forms of possession, sexual and material. According to radical doctrine, both of these should be regulated by reason, which directs that energies of mind prevail over the attractions of person (the property of the individual self) and that private property be allocated according to collective need. But in the working-out of the plot, these two versions of property relations are rendered incompatible because of a gender politics that differentiates Anna's responses from Coke's and Frank's. The result is a conflict between narrative design and political precept, a conflict that compromises Holcroft's intention to represent "mind without sex."

From the novel's beginning, Holcroft details the relation of external and internal notions of property through the figure of Anna. At the level of family politics, Anna is the pawn of her relatives (especially the aristocratic Lord Fitz-Allen) whose conceptions of honour and the integrity of the family estates dictate that she marry within her own class. Coke Clifton is the appointed suitor because his marriage to her will enable him, in turn, to retrieve his own well-born family's wrecked fortunes. Anna embraces the "duty" to marry Coke in the belief that one of the "[f]ew opportunities [that] present themselves to a woman, educated and restrained as women unfortunately are, of performing any thing eminently good" has come to her with the prospect of "restoring a great mind, misled by error, to its proper rank" (37). In this marriage plot, we see two of the novel's representations of property worked out in gender-specific ways: the men affiliated with the transmission of real property, the woman with the improvement of properties of mind (a meaning reinforced by her use of "rank" to designate intellectual ability rather than social place).

This male narrative of real property lost and potentially recovered is supplemented by another that is concerned with more subtle and complex versions of what one may, with propriety, lay claim to. Here, sexual difference becomes crucial in ways that modern feminism – most notably Luce Irigaray's "Women on the Market" – has made central to our understanding of how a commodity culture functions. Holcroft uses the mutual desire of Coke Clifton and Frank Henley to "possess" Anna to distinguish the men's sense of membership within the larger community. Coke, convinced that his innate superiority entitles him to satisfy all of his desires, extends his acquisitiveness to its logical end when he resolves to rape Anna after she denies him preeminence over his rival. Frank, in turn, claims that his right to "meet [her] emanations of mind" (73) is confirmed by Coke's inability to appreciate her fineness. Frank thus asserts that Coke, "[c]onfident in himself, ardent in his desires, unchecked by those fears which are the offspring of true delicacy, his passions violent, and his pride almost insufferable ... thinks he loves. But he is ignorant of the alarms, the tremors, the 'fitful fevers' of love" (123). At the very least, one could say that in these two versions of passion, the language of sexual contest has complementary political significations: Coke believes that the prerogatives of birth entitle him to the possession of Anna's physical beauty (by rape, if necessary); Frank believes that superior "energies of mind" and delicacy sanction his claim to ownership of her. More insidiously, the sexual contest might be seen as a working-out of what Irigaray suggests is the ordering law within modern culture, that is, "exchanges among men."[8] From this perspective, Anna's attractiveness brings into play a sexual economy that requires "that women lend themselves to alienation in consumption, and to exchanges in which they do not participate, and that men be exempt from being used and circulated like commodities" (172).

How appropriate is this model to the late eighteenth-century depiction of social relations on which Holcroft's novel focuses? The account it offers of the male role is clearly inadequate. The commodification of men within an hierarchical class system is not exempted from, but rather central to, Holcroft's critique of things as they are; as Coke's response to Frank reveals, the well-born assume the right of instrumental control over their social inferiors. In relation to Anna, however, Irigaray's comments are more constructive. For the sexual jealousy that serves in the novel as a means of representing conflicting political principles has meaning only in relation to the male characters. Anna is not given even this limited form of agency through which to express her attraction to virtue. Instead, she is made to embody in her person the beauty and grace of the radical cause, appearing as the spectatorial object whom others scrutinize, rather than as an active participant in the creation of the new order.

Hazlitt's judgment of the novel's protagonists – they are less "distinct individuals" than "machines put into action, as an experiment to shew how these general principles would operate in particular situations" – is therefore critical in relation to Anna.[9] The sexual contest that serves as the vehicle for the novel's "general principles" does not simply deny her status as an active agent. It also demarcates a discursive space from which she, by virtue of the novel's complicity with highly conventional notions of female decorum, is excluded.

The most telling instances of such exclusions occur in conversations that turn explicitly on the relation of property to propriety. Anna begins one of these exchanges innocuously enough by summarizing for Coke the radical position on ownership: "You maintain that what you possess is your own: I affirm it is the property of him who wants it most" (264).[10] Seizing on the obvious opening such an assertion offers to one determined to convert political principle into sexual advantage, Coke asks:

"Can appropriation more than for the minute, the hour, or the day exist? Or, among so disinterested a people, can a man say even of the woman he loves – *She is mine?*" (279). Anna is normally in control of the discussions she initiates with Coke, but here she flounders, confessing herself "at a loss" for reply. Frank has to intercede for her, resolving the issue by claiming that in a future, more perfect state, "neither the institution [of marriage] nor the claim [of proprietorship]" (279) will exist.

In an earlier scene, Anna had indulged in a self-deprecatory gesture that similarly marks out the distance from controversy appropriate to women. She ends a spirited account of radical notions of property with the request that her correspondent, "Pardon this prattle!". Her explanation for the effusion – the "heart will sometimes expand" (210) – proffers a sterotypically "feminine" excuse for her lapse into the "manly" discourse of politics. Both here and in the conversation with Coke, the argument for "mind without sex" has been hobbled by a seemingly intractable gendering of language and by the narrative conventions of female representation within sentimental fiction on which political narratives were grafted.[11]

Such conventions are much in evidence in the novel's ending. Intent on achieving an unequivocally political conclusion, Holcroft redirects the balance of power in the triangulated relation between Coke, Anna, and Frank that had to this point shaped the plot. Since Coke's conversion must appear as the embrace of principle and not the repression of sexuality, Anna must effectively be written out of the ending. From the perspective afforded by the terms of her characterization over the course of the novel, this erasure seems predictable. Throughout, ownership of her person has been contested, her possession of real property limited, her affiliation with radical principles constrained by the limiting terms of a specifically female propriety. The imminent marriage to Frank Henley, announced in her final letter, represents the customary reward of that propriety and a formal acknowledgement of the heroine's willingness to surrender title to the property in her body that has to this point nominally been hers (the possibility of rape, of course, suggests the fragility of her tenure). With the resolution of the domestic plot, the two closing letters, from Coke Clifton and then Frank Henley, return the political heart of the novel to the keeping of the male characters. The final paragraph reinforces the gendered division of the plot by celebrating, in terms that explicitly subordinate Anna, the "more glowing" pleasures of male community.

Holcroft's next novel, *Hugh Trevor* (1794–7), as numbers of critics have noted, marks a turn toward the externalized definition of character favoured by Smollett and Bage and away from the "psychological line" followed in *Anna St.Ives*.[12] The dynamics of plot suggest the equally important influence exerted by Fielding. While Holcroft never achieves the final subordination of picaresque contingency to neo-classical coherence that distinguishes Fielding's work, he does borrow from his predecessor the narrative principle of continuity that serves as engine to the plot's action. In terms familiar from *Tom Jones*, schematically rendered versions of woman as debased and ideal serve as externalizations of the hero's conflicting desires for individual and social fulfillment. Like Tom Jones, poised between the eminently available Molly Seagrim and the distant Sophia Western, Hugh Trevor finds himself pursued by Eliza Ellis, whose attempts at seduction prove ineffectual in the face of his "unfaded remembrance of the lovely chaste Olivia."[13] Hugh's resistance to female blandishments, Gary Kelly suggests, owes much to Mary Wollstonecraft's castigation of the sexual double standard; yet Holcroft retains from Fielding the assumed link between class and sexuality that allows Eliza, daughter of a venal clergyman, to be represented as licentious, and Olivia, Squire Mowbray's daughter, as "gentle [and] angelic" (143).

This etherealized representation, and not Olivia's actual presence, dominates Hugh's consciousness. Yet however distanced and idealized she may be, the logic of the plot's unfolding assimilates her to the conventional representation of women as defined by the body. Male characters, contrarily, have access to a community of high-minded peers. The intellectual guidance provided by the novel's succession of mentor figures finds its first exponent in Hugh's boyhood friend Turl, who advises him that his pursuit of "riches and distinctions" (253) must yield to the greater truth that the only advantage of wealth is the means it provides for "a little superiority of knowledge." Hugh, therefore, should be laboring "by giving leisure to the poor or rather to all mankind, to make the acquirement of knowledge the great business of life" (252). Hugh is willing to grant the validity of these Jacobin tenets in the abstract, but not to internalize them: "would you persuade me to renounce those pursuits by which alone I can gain distinction, and respect...Olivia was full in my thoughts, as I spoke" (253). More explicitly than in *Tom Jones*, the pursuit of a woman becomes identified with the winning of wealth and public recognition. The plot of *Tom Jones* ultimately grants material and social status to its hero by means unsought by him and represents their achievement as the positive rewards of heroic civility. Hugh, in contrast, self-consciously dedicates himself for much of the novel to a quest for all three external markers of condition – women, property, and rank – with an acute awareness of their inter-dependence. And he does this in the face of the novel's authority figures' universal condemnation of them as corrupting and inhumane.

The ambivalent relation in which the hero stands to both women and property dramatically informs the novel's crisis. Hugh agrees to resign his rightful claim to the estate originally his grandfather's for motives entirely disinterested and exhaustively explored. He has earlier declared to Wakefield that "If I strictly adhere to the principle of justice, I must not singly consider my own wishes ... I must ask is there no being, within my knowledge, who may be more benefited by the enjoyment of that which I am desirous to appropriate to myself than I can? If so what right have I to prefer self gratification to superior utility?" (434–5). Wakefield now demands that this notion of "superior utility" be acted upon in order to secure his reformation and the happiness of the woman he loves but has wronged, Lydia Wilmot. Property here assumes an integral relation to plot in terms appropriate to its centrality to Jacobin doctrine. Hugh must renounce his inheritance in the name of the public good. In doing so, and in denominating this act of revocation as issuing from "the purest passions of the heart, when they are sanctioned by the best principles of the understanding" (436), he affirms that a standard of equity and disinterested benevolence may be realized through reference to the same structures of inherited property which previously had generated only gross inequality and selfish accumulation. Revolutionary change, in other words, issues most potently from the amendment of individuals; social justice discovers its origins in personality, not law.

Were this the actual ending of the novel, it would mark a radical re-orientation of eighteenth-century notions of plot. The conflation of fiscal and personal appropriation typical of comic endings disallowed, the way would be clear for the kind of possibility William Enfield entertains in his critical comments on *Hugh Trevor* for the *Monthly Review*: "the hero [might] at last [have] fixed on [a profession] which ... might have gratified his moral feelings, and which might have afforded him and his Olivia a liberal competency ... an innocent, liberal, and useful profession."[14] The georgic vision of honest labor forwarded by Enfield, while far from the millenarian pastoralism of the "golden age" antici-pated by Godwin's *Enquiry*, is at least consistent with the emphasis in early radical thought on the necessary relation between individual and social regeneration. But by the mid-1790s confidence had faltered, the victim of government repression (especially following the "Gagging Acts" of 1795), the violent turn of the French Revolution, and the evident failure of the English populace to heed the call to change.

The actual ending of the novel could be seen as a tacit acknowledgment of hopes disappointed. After Hugh's mentor Evelyn dies, his heir Lord Bray calls the notes which the scrupulous Hugh had earlier insisted on signing. Now liable for this "imaginary property" translated into legal tender by Lord Bray's greed, Hugh experiences to the full that sense of himself as "marked in an extraordinary manner as the child of fortune, to whose smiles and frowns I seemed to be capriciously subjected" (467). This recourse to the terms of fortune, with their emphasis on the accidental and contingent so alien to the radical doctrine of necessity, conditions the novel's conclusion. Belmont/Wakefield renounces his claim to the estate, and Hugh himself fortuitously rescues his now immensely rich uncle Elford. Hugh finds himself, as he announces in "The conclusion,"

> the acknowledged heir of a man of great wealth: therefore, I myself am become a great man. Heaven preserve me from becoming indolent, proud, and oppressive! I have not yet forgotten that oppression exists, that pride is its chief counsellor, that activity and usefulness are the sacred duties of both rich and poor, that the wealth entrusted to my distribution is the property of those whom most it can benefit... Neither have I yet shut my doors on one of my former friends. But I am comparatively young in prosperity. How long I shall be able to persevere in this eccentric conduct time must tell. (494)

The note of qualification in the comment that he has "not yet forgotten that oppression exists" ominously tinges this peroration. "At present," Hugh continues, "I must proceed, and mention the few remaining circumstances with which the reader may wish to be acquainted" (494–5). These include an entirely predictable roster of virtuous persons rewarded and vicious ones punished. The injunction to "proceed," in other words, involves at some level the relinquishment of political intent for narrative convention of the most facile kind. After six volumes of intermittent attention to radical principle, the novel lapses into "the usual termination," as Enfield says, the "*quotidien* conclusion" of a "happy marriage" (282).

Anti-Jacobin novels seized with delight on such hesitations. Ever eager to exploit the weaknesses of their political opponents, they interpolated references to both fictional and non-fictional texts into their own, pushing to absurd but entirely logical extremes key radical tenets. What especially attracts their attention are the inconsistencies of novelists like Holcroft who import stereotypical notions of gender and class seemingly without recognizing the damage they do to the integrity of their argument. In adopting this strategy of unmasking, however, conservative satires unintentionally subvert the rationale behind their own virulent attacks on their opponents. While their fictions are filled with alarmist predictions of an English Terror enabled by widespread acceptance of radical doctrine, their practice as novelists reveals the ease with which they dismantled its tenets.

Holcroft's novels in turn point to the limitations imposed on radical fiction by its discursive framework. As we have seen, Holcroft's adaptation of the tropes of female debility undermines his advocacy of a new social order that would release the energies of "mind without sex." Such adaptations also suggest his implication in the structures of thought to which he overtly declares himself hostile. The transvaluing of proscribed qualities in gendered terms ultimately stigmatizes woman as the chief impediment to a masculine capacity for revolutionary change. Such transvaluations prove immensely useful to the anti-Jacobins who argue to the same end, if for entirely different reasons. In the satires of Elizabeth Hamilton and George Walker, essentialist interpretations of women's properties reinforce a prescriptive understanding of women's plots.

History, romance, and the anti-Jacobins'
"common sense"

The mutual dependency that characterizes the relation of conservative to radical 1790s fiction owes much to the shared concern with audience and reading practices that so absorbed writers of the revolutionary decade. In the Dedication to his conservative novel, *The Vagabond* (1799), George Walker touches on one of the consequences of this authorial preoccupation with readers: "I might observe with the late Lord Orford," he writes, "that Romances are only Histories which we do not believe to be true, and Histories are Romances we do believe to be true."[1] The questions of credibility and credulity to which his assertion refers surface repeatedly in the writings of the 1790s. Behind them lie the assumption of a broad and receptive reading public whose varied abilities and loyalties were open to definition by writers bidding for their attention.[2] To the Jacobins, such an audience represented opportunity; as Paine says, "such is the irresistible nature of truth, that all it asks, and all it wants, is the liberty of appearing."[3] In a similar vein, Godwin's powerful metaphorical rendering of the Jacobin doctrine of perfectibility imagines "ten thousand men of sound intellect, shut up in a madhouse, and superintended by a set of three or four keepers," whose "chains fall off of themselves when the magic of opinion is dissolved" under the influence of the communication of ideas.[4]

To the conservatives, however, these newly politicized readers represented danger precisely because of their openness to the communication of ideas, an opennness the anti-Jacobins narrativized as an uncritical susceptibility to story-telling. The public's failure to distinguish romance from history thus rehearses for the conservatives a larger epistemological crisis in which truth is no longer discovered by reference to tradition or precedent but by internalized, subjective criteria. For the radical thinkers the conjunction of "history and romance," as Godwin's essay of that name suggests, is an exciting and fruitful one; for the anti-Jacobins, it is fundamentally problematic.[5] From their perspective, the transvaluing of romance and history points to the confusion of the inward and imagined with the public and actual. For them, it appears an index to the comprehensive political and social crisis which threatened England in the 1790s. When Thomas Mathias writes in 1794 that, "Government and Literature are now more than ever intimately connected," he expresses a widely held belief that Britain's political destiny was inextricably bound to wresting authority over representation – the power of the word or the visual image – from the radical opposition.[6] And when the *British Critic* declares that there exists in England "a state of literary warfare" parallel to the actual revolution in France and trumpets the need for the defenders of order "to wield the pen, and shed the ink," the martial metaphors reinforce the perception of crisis.[7] To the anti-Jacobins, the radicals' success in manipulating the press made urgent the need to find a countervailing discursive strategy that would undercut the appeal of their opponents' story-telling.

An episode from William Beckford's *Azemia* (1797) slyly alludes to this conservative understanding of representation as both form and agent of social control. Wildcodger, a firm proponent of the doctrine that "whatever is, is right," proposes that "various views painted of houses and seats, after the manner of Mr. Repton" be set up in front of the houseless poor:

[I]n contemplating in these representations, the great affluence and flourishing state of their country, the wretched animals whose own folly and indiscretion have not left them forty shillings a year (which is the average price of a cottage), must surely, (at least they ought to do it) forget all *their* trifling inconveniences in the great and patriotic sentiment of rejoicing in the prosperity of their country. I am sure the sans culottes of England, by a little of this management, may become the most *docile* and contented race under the heavens.[8]

Beckford's ironic rendering of Wildcodger's plan mocks the conservative project for containing the poor and disaffected. But the irony, of course, depends on the existence of a widespread conviction that the "wretched animals" were indeed sufficiently credulous that representations of their nation's glory might secure their docility.

Repton's "views painted of houses and seats" provide Beckford with a richly associative complex of ideas for this attack on the sanctimonious. In the *Red Books* which he began to use in 1789, Humphry Repton offered his wealthy clients "charming and highly seductive watercolours, with flaps showing the 'before' and 'after' views" of the changes he proposed for their estates.[9] While his detractors charged that silent amendments rendered the views inconsistent, the scenes answered to

Repton's desire to appeal to the estate owner's appropriative and improving instincts. Beckford's mockery not only spectacularly redefines the relation of book to reality; he also reverses the intent of Repton's texts: according to Wildcodger's scheme the poor will rest content with the status quo, their attention directed to collective abstractions (like the nation and the patriotism it elicits) rather than the individual pleasures of improvement and expenditure.

Wildcodger's faith in the power of visual representation finds its verbal equivalent in the anti-Jacobin commitment to satiric fiction. But conservative writers understood that the "wretched animals" were unlikely to "become the most *docile* and contented race under the heavens" unless rigorously counteractive measures were taken against radical writers, the "metaphysical jargonists" who made novels key to their revolutionary strategy.[10] Reading audiences would not be prompted to "forget all *their* trifling inconveniences" through the kinds of "contemplation" that Wildcodger commends, in other words, as long as radical fiction made the prospects of change and progress so attractive. The result of this recognition on the part of the conservatives was a prolonged discursive battle with the radicals, a battle distinguished by the political authority both vested in fiction and by the insularity fostered by their appeal to a shared audience. As the decade unfolded, increased taxation and the threat of invasion from France made the task of securing allegiance from the newly politically aware more urgent, especially given the powerful claims for individual rights mounted by radical writers.[11] These the conservatives resisted, H. T. Dickinson suggests, in profoundly reactive ways, constructing their ideological position as rejoinder to the English radical interpretations "of the natural state of man, of the origins and foundations of civil government, and of the aims and purposes of political society."[12] Edmund Burke's version typically engages the reader in a rhetorical conflict:

The body of the people must not find the principles of natural subordination by art rooted out of their minds. They must respect that property of which they cannot partake. They must labour to obtain what by labour can be obtained; and when they find, as they commonly do, the success disproportioned to the endeavour, they must be taught their consolation in the final proportion of eternal justice. Of this consolation whoever deprives them, deadens their industry, and strikes at the root of all conservation.[13]

Competing voices are here imagined as struggling for control of the body of the people: the artful radicals who root out that which consoles the individual and sustains the state set against the conservatives whose commitment to natural subordination comes complete with divine approval.

In the culture of the 1790s, both visual and verbal structures participate in this enclosed and self-defining rhetorical world. David Bindman's summary judgment that "the story of the British response to the French Revolution is about British rather than French politics" holds as true for the visual tradition he explores as for the dramatic one considered by Jeffrey Cox.[14] But insularity and reflexiveness seem more often to produce anxiety, than confidence. Even the most ringing pronouncements are, like Burke's, shadowed by the awareness that positions must be contested not only with one's peers, but also and more alarmingly with a public that seemed increasingly to be both unknowable and capricious. The categorical instability to which this chapter's opening quote from George Walker's *The Vagabond* refers when it makes belief the determinant of genre – history or romance – emerges with the parallel suspicion that judgments now issue from subjective rather than objectively determined criteria. It is at this point that conversion becomes a central aim in the politics of narrative. In defense of "genuine Religion, Morality, and Liberty," Walker declares, the author must seize whatever means come to hand, even if these involve engagement with the frivolous: "a *Novel* may gain attention, when arguments of the soundest sense and most perfect eloquence, shall fail to arrest the feet of the *Trifler*, from the specious paths of the new Philosophy" (i.vi). To this end, he traces in his novel the disasters that ensue when the radical sympathizers Dr. Alogos, Frederick Fenton, and his tutor Stupeo decide to live out in practice the radical precepts they have uncritically absorbed in their reading of Godwin, Paine, Wollstonecraft, and Rousseau.

"THE VAGABOND" AND MASCULINE COMMON SENSE

In the Preface that follows the Dedication to *The Vagabond*, Walker prepares us to interpret these activities in more inclusive terms by developing the political concomitants of good and bad reading. "[M]en of real genius and erudition," he suggests, understand that the proper relation of the individual to the social can be grasped only by those whose disinterested commitment to the public sphere originates in their knowing and sanctifying the past. Reformers, on the other hand, indulge the personal vice of imaginative self-projection both in what they write – the "*political romances*, which never were, and never will be, practical": – and in their construction of audience – those persons whom the delusive powers of imagination "hurry away" from a proper concern with "common life." In the end, Walker charges, the public sphere envisioned by the radicals can only resemble the confusion of their private lives; the looseness and immorality of those whose "dreams of ideal felicity" make them inattentive to "precedent and continuity" disallow a genuinely productive social order (1.[ix]–x).

The argument for the priority of public definition over private interest inverts the model of one of Walker's favorite targets, Mary Wollstonecraft. Her assertion in the *Vindication* that "public virtue is only an aggregate of private" (281) tacitly allows women as guardians of the domestic sphere a key role in defining its terms. And, since "the private duty of any member of society must be very imperfectly performed when not connected with the general good," the logic of her position leads inevitably to the advocacy of "political privileges" and a full "civil existence" (271–2) for women. To Walker, such arguments are anathema. They not only "root up and overthrow every thing which has received the sanction of ages" (1.x), they also do so in the name of an entirely misplaced faith in universal virtue. As the honorable Vernon in *The Vagabond* argues to his boyhood friend and Jacobin sympathizer, Frederick Fenton, "'look at the private life of any one of them [the "new philosophers"] and you will find the liberty they seek to be no other than the right to practise every licentiousness, unchecked by the *law*, and unstigmatised by sober and religious men'" (1.59).

The Vagabond combines this attack on private licentiousness and inattention to public decorum with a more specifically verbal critique. Typically of anti-Jacobin fiction, *The Vagabond*'s focus on textuality censures radical fiction and politics by representing both as equally formulaic in their use of literary conventions. Radical narrative is made to appear a closed discursive system in which consummate story-tellers and faulty interpreters collaboratively evade the test of history, a test described by Bisset as "induction," by Elizabeth Hamilton as "common sense," and by Walker as "common life."[15] Viewed in isolation, this critique is persuasive. But when set in the context of either conservative or radical practices, its weaknesses become clear. On the one hand, the conservatives' own intertextual relation with radical writers makes them adhere to a parallel set of discursive boundaries. As a result, they attack revolutionary politics not primarily by direct reference to public events, but through a process of refraction that works through the medium of radical narrative. And, on the other, the terms of the critique are finally

extraneous to the radical understanding of the ends of narrative. Not
only is the test of history irrelevant to their vision of future perfectibility
(history is what they want to resist, not endorse), they also *intentionally* use
those narrative conventions for which the conservatives mock them in
their anti-Jacobin satires.

Radical fiction works self-consciously with the customary meanings
attaching to genre and place, developing them in distinctive ways that
answer to the political principles they wish to impress upon their
readers. Pastoral allusion, for example, points in radical fiction to the
golden future that will be recovered once government has been rejected.
That future is, in turn, often realized in an idyllic utopian community
discovered in America. America's freedom from the strictures of the
past allows it to appear in novels like the anonymous *Henry Willoughby*
(1798) as source of millenarian hopes for a republican Europe and as
reward to those characters who begin as acquisitive picaros in the old
world and end as converts to the egalitarianism implicit in the new one.
The precedents for such novelistic uses of pastoral and America appear
throughout radical literature. Paine, for example, writes that America
appears "the beginning of time . . . The real volume, not of history, but
of facts, is directly before us [there], unmutilated by contrivance, or the
errors of tradition."[16] And Priestley comments, in a refinement of this
orientation toward the future: "whatever was the beginning of this
world, the end will be glorious and paradisaical, beyond what our
imagination can now conceive."[17] The terms of pastoral shape Godwin's vision of this blissful state which would follow were man able "with
perfect facility [to] obtain the necessaries of life." Free of grinding labor,
at one extreme, and palling indolence, at the other, men would discover
that "[p]rivate interest would visibly accord with public good; and civil
society become what poetry has feigned of the golden age."[18]

The conservatives' willful misconstruction of radical representations
– especially of romance and pastoral – acquires a logic of its own,
however, when set in the context of the anti-Jacobin endorsement of
satire and georgic. This conservative reliance on a satiric vision that
relates intertextually to radical romance can be seen as a response to
what many in the 1790s considered the unprecedented nature of the
crisis faced by the nation.[19] As Jeffrey Cox suggests, the widespread
"turn to parody" evident in the artistic dominance of caricature in the
1790s typifies antirevolutionary attempts to "undo or revise the forms
adapted by one's opponents."[20] *The Vagabond* is entirely typical in its
programmatic "undoing" of the tropes of radical romance. In Walker's

novel, perfectibility gives way to the assumption of a universally debased human nature and to the austerely unsentimental "common sense" which serves as its standard of judgment. Idealized notions of community are unmasked as self-serving and interested. Faith in the recreation of a pastoral "golden age" (1.1) is exposed as a specious excuse for indolence; the advocacy of independent thought is shown to lead to the universal breaking of all "natural" ties to the point of matricide; universal "genuine liberty" (1.40) and female emancipation work to the benefit of heartless cads who seduce and then abandon women; America, that supposed "second Arcadia," is at once an urban nightmare infested with yellow fever and a rural wilderness of "impassable native grasses, and swarms of insects, snakes and toads" (II.146).[21]

Convinced that legislative sovereignty offers the surest defence against human weakness, Walker maintains "that coercion and laws are necessary to restrain the arm of destruction and violence" (II.255). In rendering Jacobin philosophy as story through his own satiric narrative, he emphasizes the seemingly innocuous guises that the "arm of destruction and violence" can take. From the petty hypocrisy, selfishness, and egotism of the "new philosophers" issue a damaging range of offenses against social and individual integrity. The threat to order posed by their theories of the origin of society, by the civic ideal they project, and by the gender biases they question: all of these are touched on in the peripatetic adventures of the Jacobinical Dr. Alogos, Frederick Fenton, and the tutor Stupeo. In their different ways, each of the men conforms to the opprobrious tag of "vagabond": "inclined to stray or gad about, without proper occupation," "not subject to control or restraint," a "disreputable or worthless person."[22] That they do so despite their material, intellectual, and social advantages is presented by Walker as further evidence that external agents of "control and restraint" are necessary to counteract irresponsible self-delusion.

The climactic representation of Jacobin iniquities occurs appropriately enough in the ideal republic that Alogos, Frederick, and Stupeo accidentally discover in the American interior. Intent on "promoting their pastoral scheme" (II.126) the three emigrate to America, expecting to discover there the golden age realized. Their first chastening occurs in Philadelphia where they discover not a "second Arcadia" (II.133) but a relentless dedication to grinding work: "we have no honest gentlemen here – no idle hands," they are told, "if a man will not work, he may starve" (II.129). After a complicated series of adventures that take them deep into the American interior, they happen upon a distant prospect that seems to offer the pastoral marvel they have been seeking: "A fine, level country interspersed with gentle swellings, and intersected with limpid streams, watering extensive groves" (II.179–80). Closer scrutiny reveals a state of total disrepair, the consequence of the inhabitants' philosophical bent. The parodic account of their preference for theory over actuality reveals the absurd extremes to which Berkeley's immaterialism has been taken here:

A man striking a tree sometimes with his fist, and then with his head, induced the Doctor to inquire the meaning of so singular an action. – "What are you doing?" said the Doctor. – "I am endeavouring to drive this *idea* out of my path" – "That is not an idea," said the Doctor, "that's a reality." "All things are ideas," replied the man: "every thing which appears to exist is merely an idea." (II.182).[23]

As in the third voyage of *Gulliver's Travels*, one sane voice among the multitude of misguided projectors emerges to provide the history of the madness. What follows is a skeptical synopsis of the state of England should Jacobin theories be enacted. Parescho recounts that the once orderly society founded on inequality gave way to an electoral system which was, in turn, undermined by the "middle class," who were unfortunately "universally influenced by the powers of oratory. Any man who could rant and declaim was certain of their support" (II.190). A civil war annihilated the monarchy and aristocracy with the intent that "[e]quality in every sense of the word was to be established, and all laws, sacred and civil, were abrogated" (II.191). When it becomes apparent that a laboring class is still necessary, it is decided that, since the women have "declared themselves no longer dependents on the men, but equal in every point," they should be subjected "by force to the labour necessary for providing food, raiment, and shelter for the community, while the men should be employed studying the public good" (II.192). When the women "[droop] under this usage," a "prodigious great philosopher" proposes an ingenious solution: "were all men necessitated to work, the labour would scarcely be felt by any" (II.193). The result is not Godwinian pastoral, but the present utter breakdown of society.

The reader has been prepared for this sequence in which the middle class unwittingly contrives its own destruction (in part through disturbing gender relations) by an earlier encounter with an "ideal" community. Before Alogos had emigrated, he attempted to create in England "a little republic" (II.10) of his own. As in Pratt's *Shenstone-Green*, a disregard of function signals the spuriousness of the enterprise. Alogos directs the conversion of "a large barn into a Hall of Reason, where they undertook. . . to read moral lectures" (II.15) proving the falseness of religion. But when the parish becomes fully conversant with the "Principles of Universal Equality" and the *"Rights of Man,"* it falls into ruin, the men refusing to labor and their wives becoming "what is vulgarly called lazy and slovenly, but which, in the language of refined philosophy, is independent, and superior to prejudice" (II.19).

If working women are seen here as the regulators of their husbands' labor, upper-class women exercise a parallel function in the sphere of desire. In Walker's sexual economy, the danger of feminism lies not in its release of Amazonian energy, but in the sanction it seems to provide to the open expression of *male* passion. That passion is represented as indiscriminately appropriative and levelling: "'If genuine liberty were established,'" Stupeo declares,

"all the female sex would be within our choice... What business has one man to monopolise a woman to himself? Affection and love is as various as any other passion. What are the names of mother, and wife, and daughter, and sister? In a state of nature men will pursue their own inclinations, and not each grasp a female being to himself, the slave of his caprice, and the object of his disgust." (1.40–1).

The imperfectly veiled misogyny here reinforces Walker's argument that the sexual freedom enjoyed by men could only be experienced as enthrallment by women. Without their social functions as mother, wife, daughter, and sister, women would be entirely subject to the wandering "inclinations" and capacity for "disgust" of feckless men.

The sophisticated double tack effected here – sexual equality as destructive both of social order and of the female identity it supposedly liberates – is evident as well in the working out of plot and character. Frederick, determined to "gratify the pure and natural desire" of seducing his best friend Vernon's betrothed, easily converts Amelia to the "new doctrines. . . for they carried self-evident proofs in the latitude they allowed for the passions and weakness of human nature" (1.51). Jacobin rhetoric also provides a convenient rationalization for his betrayal of Vernon whose outré attempt to "[exclude] all others from their natural right" in the "fancied property" of Amelia apparently sanctions her seduction. Amelia's end – she dies, pregnant, in a fire from which Frederick, lost in metaphysical speculation, fails to rescue her – enforces the impossibility of women's eluding definition as property. As Vernon's property, Amelia was cherished and protected; as Frederick's, she is abandoned and consumed by a fire that literalizes passion's destructiveness.

The crude sexual politics invoked in this episode depends on the sentimental pathos to be wrung from the woman-as-victim topos. In Laura, Alogos's niece, Walker offers a comic alternative: a female character who possesses all the expected attributes of Jacobin heroines – beauty, intelligence, articulacy – but who uses them not to confirm but to counter radical doctrine. She asserts the nature and value of the essential differences that divide the sexes, arguing that these "should teach us that [men and women] are designed for different pursuits" (I.10). Walker underscores the validity of this assertion by aligning the radical attachment to theory with misogyny and narcissism. Alogos, bombastically spouting snippets from *Political Justice*, attacks Laura's "perverse disposition," complaining that "she will not exert the divine privilege of resistance, and throw off the shackles of domination." Moments later, however, his abstract commitment to her independence yields to cries of "idle slut" (I.10) when he discovers that she has visited an old woman in the village and neglected to set his room in order. His selfish rant, all bluster and no substance, throws into relief her active benevolence and its meliorative social consequences.

While Alogos in his role as surrogate father pays lip service to equality while demanding subservience, Frederick as potential suitor enacts a complementary hypocrisy in matters sexual. Mouthing Godwinian arguments linking marriage to monopolistic tyranny, Frederick develops a variation on Locke's epistemology: Laura appears to him "a blank, a mere white sheet of paper; and it remains for me to stamp upon her any character I please" (II.33). In fact, Laura finds Frederick supremely resistible and, like Alogos, easily outmaneuvered in argument. While the men uncritically absorb suspiciously expedient notions from their reading of radical texts, Laura actively counters what she considers their baleful influence. In her view, arguments for sexual equality only pretend to disinterested attention to women: "those men who preach up promiscuous intercourse of sex do it merely to cover up their own depraved desires and avoid the stigma of the world by rendering it common" (II.24).

While Laura serves throughout as authorial mouthpiece, the politics of the novel demand that the conclusion of *The Vagabond* produce a realignment of gender relations. As a result, she is assigned a severely diminished role that is consistent with the moral recovery of Frederick and Alogos and with the novel's final celebration of the hierarchies enforced by "coercion and laws" (II.255). The conversion of Frederick and Alogos to the principles of British liberty (following fast on the heels of their rejection of the "horrid and impracticable system of equality" [II.233]) thus coincides with the silencing of Laura. Excluded from direct speech, she is transformed into an emblem of transcendent femininity. As with so many eighteenth-century heroines, she achieves this apotheosis when she becomes the object of others' interpretations, rather than the originator of her own. This moment, appropriately enough, occurs at her wedding to the stalwart Vernon. Witnessing it, Frederick acknowledges "that the endearing and tender smile of a modest woman, has more real pleasure than the most wanton blandishments of promiscuous intercourse" (II.263), while her uncle, in a parallel vein, lauds "that modesty and [those] maternal feelings [which] are the chief ornaments of a celestial mind [in the] fair daughters" (II.265) of England.[24]

"MEMOIRS OF MODERN PHILOSOPHERS" AND FEMALE VIRTUE

Elizabeth Hamilton's *Memoirs of Modern Philosophers* (1800) also debunks Jacobin doctrine, but does so in terms that reveal how authorial gender often operates as a powerful determinant of meaning. *The Vagabond* casts its misguided radicals as privileged men whose politics seek to mask their exploitation of women by labeling it feminism. True masculinity, Walker implies, demands acceptance of the full range of proprietorial relations, be they social, economic, or sexual. For Hamilton, the political and sexual are similarly entwined, but attention is focused more directly on the beguiled and exploited women. Ultimately, the texts concur in affirming the civilizing capacities of women and in insisting that these can be realized only within the confines of masculine convention and law. But the use of the socially distanced paired heroines – the vulgar Bridgetina Botherim and the gentle Julia Delmond – also allows Hamilton to consider the dangerous release of female sexuality (apparently hastened by Jacobinism) as symptom of a wider cultural decay.

The *Monthly Review* identifies this crucial link between radical politics and sexual impropriety as the novel's key weakness: "In the volumes before us, the pretended philosophers are a set of miscreants, who would equally disgrace any opinions to which they might pretend an attachment; and they are only represented as seducing two females, whose characters are marked with the strongest traits of folly."[25] The *Monthly*'s scoffing at the banality of seduction and its tilt against the depiction of the "modern philosophers" as "heroes of Grub-street" (413) point to a conjunction fundamental to the novel's attack on radicalism. Its dangers, Hamilton insists, lie in the insidious power it exercises over the culturally marginalized, both socially and expressively: women and the "novels and metaphysical essays" (II.42) that they read. England may have avoided the flamboyant excesses of revolutionary France, Hamilton implies, only to be destroyed from within.

Typically of the anti-Jacobins, she adopts for monitory purposes the very form against which she inveighs, using the novel to represent the machinations of its evil genius, Vallaton. The meanly born son of an executed mother (an allusion to the mother of the heroine of Mary Hays's recent feminist novel, *The Victim of Prejudice*), he advances from hair-dresser to "philosopher," a transition from literal to figurative tending of the female head made possible by women's gullibility. As is appropriate for a "hero of Grub-street," Vallaton uses the seductive powers of fiction to exploit the debilities of gender. In George Walker's *The Vagabond*, distinctions between history and romance are confused when readers (and not externally defined criteria) determine authenticity. Hamilton is also interested in the negative social consequences that follow from such transvaluings.

Julia Delmond's father, in slighting religion and allowing unrestricted reading, has compromised his daughter's ability to discriminate truth from falsehood. As a result, she credulously accepts the fantastic account of himself offered by the interloper, Vallaton. The story which he tells in order to gain entrance to a world from which ordinarily he would be excluded draws on egregiously romantic and aristocratic conventions: abandoned as a baby, he maintains, the "richly embroidered" cloth in which he was wrapped identified him as well-born to the "lady of great family and fortune" (I.93), who supposedly found and raised him.

This local instance of the defeat of truth by romance intersects in the novel with a number of variants that open on to a larger social sphere and a different set of generic assumptions. In the seduction of the well-born Julia Delmond by Vallaton, romance remains the dominant mode. He manipulates its conventions in order to satisfy her naive desire for heroic status. The more public world in which the déclassé Bridgetina Botherim moves allows broader satiric strokes. When the radical circle to which Bridgetina belongs, for instance, resolves to enact Godwin's theories of social perfection by joining the "Gonoquais Hottentots," Hamilton indulges her talent for rhetorical parody in listing the charms of the Hottentots to the radicals: they "had no trade, no commerce, no distinctions of rank, no laws, no coercion, no government; [they were a group] who had among them no physicians, no lawyers, no priests, and who, to crown all, *believed in NO GOD!*" (I.331). In order to raise funds for their emigration, they accept Citizen Glib's circulating library as a donation and then sell off its "superfluous books, such as history, travels, natural philosophy, and divinity" while retaining the "novels and metaphysical essays ... for the instruction of the philosophers" (II.42).

Hamilton deftly marshals the conservatives' favorite cluster of targets: the "state of the most rigid simplicity" advocated by Godwin devolves here into a string of negations – "no trade, no commerce, no distinctions of rank" – signifying absence of meaning and purpose; the association of women with city speculators (alternatively expressed as an association of imagination with money) and the connection of both with circulating libraries is entirely typical. And once again, the relation of text to audience serves as a trope for the depredations radicalism encourages: under the cover of supposed political principles, the substantial accomplishments of the past will be jettisoned in favour of the airy delusions of the present. Any sense of an authority beyond the individual, whether social or religious, will be deemed as "superfluous" as those disciplines that offer a vision sanctioned by tradition: history, natural philosophy, divinity.

The two heroines' plots will represent all of these negative consequences as the outgrowth of bad reading habits exacerbated by a spurious freedom of thought allowed women. Mrs. Fielding, the novel's exemplar of "social sensibility" and agent of the heroines' final conversions, pronounces on Bridgetina's slide from novels to metaphysics in terms that parallel the more rarified encounters of Julia Delmond: "To an imagination enflamed by an incessant perusal of the improbable fictions of romance, a flight into the regions of metaphysicks must rather be a dangerous excursion. I am afraid Miss Botherim has gone too far astray in the fields of imagination to be easily brought back to the plain path of common sense" (III.164).

In the event, Bridgetina is cured of the delusions bred by indiscriminate reading not by the invocation of a corrective text, but by the spectacle of Julia Delmond's protracted dying in Mrs. Fielding's "Asylum of the Destitute." In this substitution of visual for verbal instruction, class and gender assumptions converge. Reading, the source of the low-born Bridgetina's seduction by Jacobin delusions, gives way to the immediacy of an encounter that is experiential rather than speculative. Julia's sleeping form is thus initially presented to Bridgetina as an emblematic realization of "the fruits of your boasted system of happiness and virtue" (III.282). When Julia wakes, she glosses this connection between female aspiration and death by declaring that she sought in radical doctrine "a new and nobler path to glory than the quiet duties of domestic life" (III.311). Visual and oral witnessing here displace the textual enthrallment that the logic of the novel wishes to establish as the necessary prelude to sexual violation. The *Monthly Review* reserved its most stinging criticism for this scene. While the whole of Julia Delmond's "history approaches too closely to that of the penitent prostitute in Mackenzie's Man of Feeling," her death in particular "reads as if it were copied from the earlier work" (413). In fact, although Emily Atkins's father declaims to Harley, "Her death I could have born! but the death of her honour has added obloquy and shame to the sorrow which bends my gray hairs to the dust," *The Man of Feeling* does not move beyond this figurative extinction of honor to an actual death-bed scene.

The reviewer's mis-remembering testifies at once to the period's sense of the negligible distinction between figurative and literal loss of female identity after seduction and to the two novels' powerfully visual representations of penitence. For both Mackenzie and Hamilton, the freezing of the action at moments of intense pathos and the organization of scenes in accordance with spectacle or tableau constructions register discomfort with the fluidity and pleasure in change that novels were seen to foster. Such pleasure appeared to conservatives a covert invitation to more active participation in the public sphere that novels of all political stripes depicted as enticingly variable and demanding. The relation of text to female reader thus comes finally to be seen by both Mackenzie and Hamilton as profoundly reflexive, since each contains latent energies whose release intitiates the erosion of things as they should be or, rather, things as they were. Mackenzie clusters women, verbal prowess, and financial speculation as inimical to Harley's archaic pastoralism. For Hamilton, writing at the end of the century, the susceptible female reader figures not only the threat of the nouveau riche (as it did for Mackenzie), but also that of the masses below.

Hamilton's attack on the iniquitous consequences of undisciplined reading by women who are "naturally" disposed to credulity finds its complement in her censure of those who fail to police their female relations. We are invited to applaud Mr. Delmond's "attachment" to his unfeeling wife, which while neither "sentimental or sublime ... was, nevertheless, cordial and sincere. As an helpless object depending on his protection, he had been accustomed to cherish her. As *his own*, he had considered her with that regard which self-love attaches to property; and even the very sufferings she had occasioned to him, were, perhaps an additional motive of his affection" (1.42). His failure to construct his relationship with his daughter along similarly protective and proprietorial lines leaves her open to the textual seductions of Jacobinism and the sexual ones of Vallaton. Hamilton's logic at this point depends on two key assumptions about female identity: first, women are molded by forces external to them; and second, in a world defined by rampant acquisitiveness to which women are entirely subject, it is in any case absurd to consider them as anything other than the ciphers of male desire.

But male desire itself operates in accordance with rhythms of possession determined by social status. While the "self-love [that] attaches to property" encourages compassion and solicitude in the well-born Delmond, the restive urge to possess that drives the vulgar Vallaton produces exactly contrary emotions. The threat he represents to established order at the individual level finds its social correlative in the mass organizations of industrial workers. Discontent, we are told, is endemic near the "stupendous cotton-mill, or other great work where [men and women] ... were earning, it may be, three times the wages of the laborious cottager" (1.221). The erosion of the georgic ideal of honorable labor translates the individual "cottager" into the faceless mass of what appears a standing mob: "the men, riotous, profane, and brutal; the women, bold, squalid, and shameless" (1.243). That same attraction to change which loosened the ties of Delmond's paternal authority, Hamilton suggests, has altered the social and physical landscape of Britain in profoundly destructive ways. "[I]nnocence and simplicity of manners," the distinctions of class and sex, have yielded to a peculiar confusion in which the women – "bold, squalid and shameless" – are figured as at once masculine and, in the weighted vocabulary of eighteenth-century sexuality, shamelessly promiscuous (1.243).

The Conclusion returns the attack on the Jacobins' impossibly idealized vision of human nature to formal grounds. A group of "pretty critics[s]" (III.353) meets to demand that after the necessary reformations of the wicked have been effected, and splendid fortunes acquired by recently discovered rich relations or prize lottery tickets, all should be happily married. The allusion here to *Hugh Trevor* identifies its hackneyed resolution with the fantastical basis of radical doctrine and the romance conventions through which it is promulgated. But Hamilton elects instead to reward the surviving, steadily virtuous characters only with "a competence in middle life," a stroke she declares to be "quite a bore, and shews the author to be a mere quiz" (III.355).

"Middle life," the source of "regulated desires, social affections, active benevolence, humility, sincerity, and a lively dependence on the Divine favour and protection" (III.365–6), has, of course, served as implicit ideal throughout Hamilton's novel. In the works of Jane West, as we will see in the concluding chapter, the defense of the middle class provides an opportunity to define more explicitly the proper relation of reader to text and world.

CHAPTER 12

Jane West and the politics of reading

In the concluding pages of *A Tale of the Times* (1799) Jane West disparages the literary form she herself has adapted to her defense of domestic virtue: "the novel, calculated, by its insinuating narrative and interesting description to fascinate the imagination without rousing the stronger energies of the mind, is [by the radicals] converted into an offensive weapon, directed against our religion, our morals, or our government, as the humour of the writer may determine his particular warfare."[1] As we have seen, the dedication of fiction to political purposes in fact defines the literary production of both radicals and conservatives in the 1790s as they competed for the allegiance of an audience envisioned as peculiarly susceptible to calls for institutional change. West's determination to contrive fictions capable of "rousing the stronger energies of the mind" in order to defeat Jacobin principles, however, stands in potential conflict with the idealization of private life and female inwardness her works enforce, an ideal centered on the notion that "virtues shunned observation, and only courted the silent plaudit of conscience" (*Tale* III.333). In each of the novels written in the 1790s, *The Advantages of Education: or, the History of Maria Williams* (1793), *A Gossip's Story* (1796) and *A Tale of the Times* (1799) the conflict is resolved by invoking the "muse of history" in aid of "the muse of fiction" (*Tale* II.5).[2] Constructing the discourse of private life in accordance with the model afforded by linear history allows her obliquely to confirm its consonance with the forces of tradition and continuity. But investing the quotidian with exemplary status also, and more problematically, grants to culturally marginalized women political significance. The desire to harmonize these competing impulses shapes West's commitment to the education of her female readers. This chapter will consider how attention to genre and history finally enables West to address the intersections of private and public in terms consistent with her advocacy of "things as they are."

TEXTUAL AUTHORITY AND THE "NARRATIVE WAY"

The voice of the narrator in each of these three novels, Prudentia Homespun, gives coherence to the various levels on which the texts operate, its idiosyncracies allowing her at once to court and to deflect the charge of "egotism" (*Tale* III.388) she levels against her radical opponents. She represents herself both in personality and literary interests as existing at the edges of official culture: living in a small village in the north of England sufficiently insular to have generated its own "vocabulary," she possesses an annuity of a hundred pounds a year, is unmarried, and delights in that quintessential form of female converse, gossip, for which she claims to be suited by virtue of "a retentive memory, a quick imagination, strong curiosity, and keen perception."[3] The insistent ordinariness of her life in turn infiltrates her writing, which she declares has "no splendour of language, no local description, nothing of the marvellous, or the enigmatical" (*Gossip* I.xi–xii). In avoiding the "high heroick" mode of "memoirs and adventures" (*Gossip* 1.39), however, she claims to achieve not inconsequentiality but a moral purposiveness keyed to the needs of her female readers. More specifically, her "narrative way" – the linear organization of events, their causes and consequences – counters the pernicious influence (both literary and ideological) of "those refined principles and delicate distinctions, invented by several French writers" (*Gossip* 1.25).

Prudentia's attempted reformation of the public through redefinition of the private sphere attaches to the notion of scrutiny a powerful corrective influence. The "actual observation of life" (*Gossip* 1.39) to which she dedicates her fiction draws on terms familiar from Adam Smith's *Theory of Moral Sentiments*, where personality is stabilized by reference to two spectatorial presences, one located in the social world that surrounds the self, the other in the man "within the breast."[4] In West's formulation, women should act in accordance with the terms by which "[m]en [currently] educate their youth" and "look to the general esteem of worthy people, and the approbation of their own hearts, for the recompense of their merit." But in the process, they must guard against imbibing "those notions which novel reading in general produces," especially that most invidious expectation that "matrimony [is] the great desideratum of our sex."[5] Despite her declaration to the contrary, the novels do reward good characters with happy marriages and assign to the misguided miserable ones. This seems to confirm Janet Todd's identification of West with the "reactionary moral novel" whose characterized narrator allows her to avoid the "self-centredness of sensibility."[6] But Prudentia Homespun as she is developed over the course of West's novels is not simply a narrative expedient. She exists in a relationship to both reader and text whose multiple ironies allow her creator to mark out a stance more complex and purposive than the oppositional role of "reactionary" suggests.

One of the earliest of these ironies turns on Prudentia's lineage. While she claims in *Advantages of Education* relationship to the Vicar of Wakefield, contemporary readers might well recognize her affiliation with the unfortunate Harriet Homespun of Samuel Jackson Pratt's *Pupil of Pleasure* (1776).[7] Harriet's fall originates in affective and uncritical reading; she rejects "such *low* stuff" as *Joseph Andrews* and "such old things" as the *Spectator* in favor of the highly wrought sentimental novels that her clergyman husband disparages as the "trash that circulates at a watering place amongst the women," trash that the villain of Pratt's novel, Sir Philip Sedley, will use in conjunction with Chesterfield's *Letters* to effect her seduction.[8] As the reference to circulation suggests, Harriet's credulous acceptance of sentimental fiction as authoritative has its roots in a commodity culture that Pratt represents as inciting women to emulation and egotism.[9] The implicit parallel here between social and readerly relations, by means of which textual infatuation figures class confusion, also attracts Prudentia Homespun's attention. But she, unlike her namesake in Pratt's novel, is the controller rather than the victim of the text. She advocates at every level the maintenance of evaluative distance by aligning herself with those "sensible people" who deplore "this inundation of affected fashion, which sweeps away before it distinction and oeconomy" (*Advantages* 1.35).

Her attack on categorical confusion and advocacy of social difference extend beyond declarative statement to inform virtually all aspects of the novels' structure and meaning. Verbal irony affords one of the more obvious instances of this commitment to detachment, and Prudentia attends carefully to the compact between reader and narrator on which the success of such irony depends.[10] Addresses to the reader, whom she assumes to be drawn from "the younger part of the female world" (*Gossip* 1.4), are another, and occasionally take the form of unmediated admonitions, as in her commendation of "[t]hat philosophy which I wish my readers to possess, [which] is constantly occupied in assimulating our desires with our situations" (*Advantages* 1.109). More frequently, however, the disciplining of the implied reader proceeds indirectly

through critical representations within the text of the characters' sentimental indulgence in romance.

As we have seen, anti-Jacobin narratives frequently render the radical
agenda in terms of pastoral romance. Such recourse to genre allows the
conservative author to conflate the aristocratic origins of pastoral and
the idealist constructs of the radicals in order to suggest the commitment
of both political extremes to the factitious and improbable. But while
Hamilton's and Walker's satires associate romance with misguided
radicals, West attends to the dangers it presents to ordinary readers
attracted by the seductive promise of heightened sentiment. Romances,
Prudentia implies, despite their vaunted emotional intensity, actually
inhibit genuine compassion by encouraging stock responses. The dull-
ing effects of formulaic writing on characters within the text serve as
covert warning to actual readers that fiction acquires value only to the
degree that it intersects with the concerns of "common life" (*Gossip* 1.33).
For the more sympathetic characters, such as Marianne in *A Gossip's
Story*, the consequences of responding to events only through the medium of the novels she has read are disastrous: "the *spring* of [her] mind
was entirely broken" (II.210), we are told, by the failure of actual
experience to meet the expectations roused by pastoral romance. In less
attractive characters, romance provides a vocabulary which excuses
brutality by re-naming it fine feeling. To Geraldine's assertion in *A Tale
of the Times* that familiarity with the industrious poor makes apparent the
empty satisfactions of luxury, Arabella responds that her "sensibility"
could not bear such proximity: "You certainly must have very strong
nerves, sister. I protest, when I have seen several little dirty, starved,
naked children, peeping out of those smoky hovels which stand by the
road side, I have often thought that it would be a great mercy to shoot
them, as one does worn-out horses" (II.126).[11]

The construction of reading as the quintessential female activity thus
allows the narrator not only to consider such attendant issues as interpretation, authority and judgment, but also to absorb actual readers
within the discourse that governs the characters' existences. The sophistication with which Prudentia marshals good and bad readers (both
actual and fictional) in order to reinforce the need for critical engagement with the text is most evident in the interpolated "Rudolpho, Earl
of Norfolk; A Legendary Tale" in *A Gossip's Story*. Her introductory
comments expose the tenuousness of the compact between the writer
and those readers "who choose to skip over adventitous matter," while
they cement the alliance with "the few, who still love to see nobility clad

in the respectable robe of virtue; and eminent rank described in unison with dignified sentiments and generous actions" (1.116). These "few," of course, must read ironically, understanding that the inflated style of "Rudolpho" marks the tale, in one sense, as escapist romance. The circle of characters who listen to the story and serve as the actual readers' surrogates represents the potential range of responses: Captain Target tries to keep himself awake, while Marianne's "eyes swam with tears"; only her sister, the heroine Louisa, deduces the moral import of the tale. The characters' responses, in turn, play out at the level of the audience the ethical core of "Rudolpho," which has argued that man "must from labour's strenuous grasp / The palm of triumph gain" (1.128). In stark contrast to the effortless gratifications of pastoral, "Rudolpho" argues that without industry there can be neither knowledge nor pleasure. For West, then, the conditions of reading particularize a more inclusive faith in the civilizing value of labor.

The multiple viewpoints of good and bad readers both inside and outside the text are further complicated in *Advantages of Education* and *A Gossip's Story* by Prudentia's location of her narratorial function within a version of the conversational circle used by Richardson in *Sir Charles Grandison*.[12] Interpolated exchanges between Prudentia and her more severe friend Mentoria in West's first novel provide the narrator with an internal audience for her ruminations on the morality of fiction. With *A Gossip's Story* that audience has expanded to a group of "single ladies" who gather in a "very agreeable society, which meets three times a week, to communicate the observations which the levity of youth, the vanity of ostentation, or the meanness of avarice have suggested" (1.2). Their field of inquiry is much expanded by the arrival of Richard Dudley, his elder daughter Louisa, and his younger one Marianne, the latter of whom, raised by her grandmother after her mother's death, has recently inherited 50,000 pounds on condition that she be "uncontrolled mistress" (1.19) of the sum. The narrator comments on the flurry of speculation that greets each new piece of information about the Dudleys: "[t]he incertitude of public opinion has been exemplified by histories of degraded heroes and persecuted patriots. I choose to illustrate it by an instance from common life" (1.33). In giving to the intimate details of "common life" dignity and substance, Prudentia at once marks out the explanatory limits of "public opinion" (of degraded heroes, persecuted patriots, or new neighbors) and privileges her own private insights. In the process, she obliquely confirms the novel's centrality to the representation of inwardness and her own role as mediator between this subjectivity and the public world on which its consequences are visited.

Forsaking history for private life, Prudentia nevertheless assumes an intrinsic connection between the two, a connection formalized through her narratorial role. The seeming contraries of public and private, objective and subjective, real and fictional, are consistently broken down by her double alliance with each of the opposed terms. She is thus at once a member of the gossips' circle and an ironic observer of the shifting grounds from which its judgments issue. She is, as well, both the authoritative medium through which the implied reader encounters the characters within the text and, as she ruefully admits in the novel's conclusion, the dependent creature of that same reader: ". . . I am afraid readers care little about an author's private history, and after all the civil things we *can* say, only appreciate our merit by our ability to entertain and instruct *them*" (II.216). Patricia Meyer Spacks's comment that gossip "epitomizes a way of knowing as well as of telling" is apposite here, for Prudentia's recognition of her instrumental function closes the gap between narrator and character.[13] Throughout *A Gossip's Story* the female characters have been urged to accept self-denial as normative and to avoid the specious illusion of power that romance grants its heroines. Prudentia's authority, having been exercised through acts of narration, now yields to the recognitions that identity is contingent on performance and that the efficacy of her performance is finally unknowable. Those readers who "care little about, an author's private history," in other words, also remain private to the author who has attempted to reform their reading habits.

The anxieties of authorship implicit in the ending of a *A Gossip's Story* acquire additional urgency in *A Tale of the Times*, where social collapse is depicted as frighteningly imminent. The undermining of authority to which the text obsessively refers touches even Prudentia who shares her authorial gifts of acuteness and ability to intuit weakness and repressed emotion with the novel's Jacobin villain, Fitzosborne. This confusion of powers for good and evil disturbs the wry superiority of tone characteristic of the earlier work and makes more pressing the need, at the level of overt commentary, to align narrative with a clearly articulated vision of social order. Like Thomas MacDonald who argues in *Thoughts on the Public Duties of Private Life with Reference to Present Circumstances and Opinions* (1795) that "the utter destruction of political balance in Europe compels us at last to turn our eyes inward," Prudentia works on the assumption that coherence in the public realm can only be re-affirmed through an intimate knowledge of private life.[14] In re-orientating her fiction toward representations of "the times" – the realm of memorialist or historian – she thus abandons ironic distance to pursue the private not in its mediated form of gossip, but directly through the "power of Gyges' magic ring, invariably possessed by all novel writers, [which] has enabled me to peep behind the curtain" (II.24).

In keeping with this transformation from gossip to novelistic spy upon human hearts, Prudentia alters the tone of her address to the reader. She poses less often as the chiding observer of venial sins and more as the righteously angry prophet brooding over a world in which the "torrent of enthusiastic sentiment" (II.7) threatens all that she values. The warm complicity provided by the gossip's circle also gives way to a world imaged as bristling with the offensive textual products of the "new code" (III.70) of Jacobinism against which she situates her own writing. Her narratorial stance, then, draws together the perspectives of novelist and historian in order to revile the "New Philosophy," which, in an elaborate paralepsis at the beginning of the novel, she stigmatizes for its rejection of "filial and conjugal ties," of religion, of inherent female virtue, and of appropriately constraining clothes, the latter superseded by the "loose drapery of Grecian Bacchanals" (I.4–5).

In its confirmation of the reciprocal verities of private and public, novelist and historian, the narratorial voice acquires powerful ideological resonances that allow it to serve as a model of response to the complexities of "the times" themselves. At the heart of the novel, Prudentia's scrupulously contextual judgment thus offers a focused instance of the link between individual action and social integrity which the plot more expansively represents. These formal and structural paradigms of mediation open into engagement with questions of historical representation. History itself is now understood as a process in which momentous political change originates in the seemingly inconsequential details of private life. This conviction that altered relations in the sphere of private life are causally prior to changes in the public realm, or, as Edmund Burke suggests in *Letters on a Regicide Peace*, that a "silent revolution preceded the political, and prepared it,"[15] in turn gives both urgency and moral sanction to West's efforts to forestall an English revolution by rendering in fiction a single instance of its anticipated dire effects:

When posterity shall know that these principles characterize the close of the eighteenth century, it will cease to wonder at the calamities which history will then have recorded. Such engines are sufficiently powerful to overturn governments, and to shake the deep-founded base of the firmest empires. Should it therefore be told to future ages, that the capricious dissolubility (if not the absolute nullity) of the nuptial tie and the annihilation of parental authority are among the blasphemies uttered by the *moral* instructors of these times: should they hear, that law was branded as a vain and even unjust attempt to bring individual actions under the restrictions of general rule; that chastity was defined to mean only individuality of affection; that religion was degraded into a sentimental effusion; and that these doctrines do not proceed from the pen of *avowed* profligates, but from persons *apparently* actuated by the desire of improving the happiness of the world: should, I say, generations yet unborn hear this, they will not ascribe the annihilation of thrones and altars to the successful arms of France, but to those principles which, by dissolving domestic confidence and undermining private worth, paved the way for universal confusion. (II.274–5).[16]

Prudentia's appeal here not only to the monumental achievements of the past, but also, and more unusually, to the future assumes that history and fiction draw on parallel notions of plot. The sequential logic underlying this shared narrative allows her novelistic version of "the times" to serve both as cautionary tale and prescriptive antidote to the threat of "universal confusion."

The counter-attack she mounts against the "illustrious sophists" (1.163) adapts the terms of Burke's "commercial humanism." As J. G. A. Pocock writes, Burke stigmatizes speculation in order to advocate an "aristocratic and commercial order which could be represented as at once natural and progressive and defended by reference to a system of civilized manners."[17] But despite the clear rhetorical need for characters capable of resisting speculation in the economic sphere and licentious Jacobinism in the sexual–political one, the exemplary commercial humanists of West's novels appear rear-guard apologists, retired from public life and defending their integrity by reference to past accomplishments. Richard Dudley in *A Gossip's Story*, who "united the character of the true Gentleman to the no less respectable name of the generous conscientious merchant" (1.14) "glor[ies] in having stimulated the industry of thousands; increased the natural strength of [his] country; and enlarged her revenue and reputation, as far as a private individual could" (1.182). But Dudley has been undone by others' speculative activity and finally proves an inept defender of his "remaining treasure" (1.181), his daughter Louisa.

If men possess an identity conferred by commercial enterprise, women by the same logic are denied coherence and forced, by their legal status as property, to resign their disposition to male authority figures. When Louisa Dudley begs her father not to marry her off to the odious Sir William Milton, he responds: "Am I too sanguine in supposing that a man, who can make the liberal offers he has done, will be influenced by the sweet and candid partner he has purchased with his liberty and his fortune?" (1.65). In the event, Milton is unmasked by the fortuitous revelation of a cast-off mistress and his "purchase" is refused. While the contingencies of plot thus allow the terms of fiscal exchange to remain unchallenged, the confirmation of Louisa's initial response offers a covert rebuke to the emotionally uninflected masculine world of commercial enterprise. Yet another of the signs of its potential to pervert and diminish can be found in the increasingly active female participation in the commerce of the sexes that *A Tale of the Times* sees as evidence of contemporay decadence. "[A] wife's affections, in this age," we are told, "are but a transferable commodity of little permanent value" (II.200–1).

THE WORK OF WOMEN: GEORGIC, FICTION, AND HISTORY

What then is the appropriate form of the female enterprise which, at least potentially, serves as corrective to its male equivalent? How can it be represented in narrative in terms that respect West's desire at once to sanction female inwardness and to argue for its centrality in the resistance to revolutionary change and in the construction of history as the product of individual effort? Genre provides the solution. By discrediting the responses variously elicited by Gothic, Jacobin, and pastoral and by espousing in their stead the redemptive power of labor central to georgic, West is able to formulate a coherent politics of reading. Such a politics at once confirms the central role women play in the constitution of private life and excuses their incursion into the domain of public speech by reference to the threat posed by French revolutionaries. As her *An Elegy on the Death of the Right Honourable Edmund Burke* (1797) suggests, Burke himself apparently recognized and encouraged the key role of women in the censuring of the French:

> Daughters of Britain! let the grateful Tear
>   Of kindred Worth your Champion's Ashes dew;
> His Breast, like your's, impassion'd and sincere,
>   Glow'd with the Virtues he rever'd in you.

> Like you, he sorrow'd for a noble Train,
>   Once the bright Gems that grac'd the Gallic Throne,
> Now scorn'd and slander'd by the Base and Vain,
>   Chas'd from all Countries, and proscrib'd their own.[18]

Gothic, Jacobin, and pastoral attract West's censure because each engages with the reader in terms that are represented as insufficiently rigorous given the acuteness of the danger now menacing Britain. William Beckford's *Azemia* (1797) mocks even as it exploits this studied inconsequentiality; Gothic, he maintains, allows him "to fill up my little book without a word of politics, revolutions or counter-revolutions, and prattle through my volumes as prettily, and beat up my literary *pap* with as innoxious ingredients as the most strait-laced matrons or rigid elders, can recommend for their babes and sucklings."[19] West's objections are less playfully expressed, but grow out of a parallel recognition of the genre's preciocity: Gothic, with its "ghosts and dungeons, incident without character, or character without effect" (*Tale* 1.164) is culpably escapist in its focus on the "terrific and romantic [rather than] the moral and the probable" (1.11). Jacobin writings offer an even greater threat to the susceptible reader:

Combining Pagan superstitions with the exploded reveries of irrational theorists, they place at the head of their world of chance a supine material God, whom they recognize by the name of Nature, and pretend that its worship supersedes all other laws human and divine. By the side of this circumscribed Deity they erect the idol shrine of its viceregent, Interest; by the monstrous doctrines, that "whatever is profitable is right," that "the end sanctifies the means," and that "human actions ought to be free," they dissolve the bonds of society. (11.273)

Jacobin doctrine, in its promise of unstrenuous gratification and of individual interest banishing the rigors of law and society, offers a corrupted reconstruction of pastoral in the realm of politics.

Each of her novels witnesses a progressive elaboration on this negative reading of pastoral. *Advantages of Education* suggests that excessive tenderness leagued with a credulous faith in "arcadian scenes of felicity" (11.235) destroys domestic peace. More problematically, since pastoralism speaks to the prevalence of fashion and the class emulation on which it depends, there exists the dangers of the latter's extension beyond the middle class:

Suppose for one instant [Prudentia comments] that the rage for idleness (I beg pardon, I mean refinement; I always mistake those words) should spread to the next order in society, and our housemaids and cooks, weary of their dirty occupations, should grow as refined as their young ladies. The industrious mother cannot perform all the domestic affairs herself; and as we do not live in Utopia, but in a country, where exertion must precede enjoyment, our elegant girls must be either useful or starve. (1.34)

As this passage suggests, the attack on pastoral is predicated on its openness to the claims of universal leisure advanced by radical thinkers. In the world of "common sense," "exertion must precede enjoyment," and enjoyment must be keyed to social status.

By a series of deft moves, West manages to implicate aristocratic codes in this Jacobin valorization of leisure. In this way, she undercuts the opposition between the two political extremes and advances her claim for the special moral status of the enterprising middle class. In *Advantages of Education*, the villain Stanley, actually Sir Henry Neville in disguise, exploits pastoral rhetoric in his efforts to seduce Maria, whom he dubs the "village nymph" (1.130): "The lover, who had a few *aristocratic* notions, (I use that word to prove my knowledge of modern politics) seemed to think it impossible that [Maria's mother] should object [to the seduction], when acquainted with his rank and character" (1.158). Prudentia's ironic evocation of the radical vocabulary in this context develops from her conviction that men are limited in their relations with women either to protection or predation. Jacobins and aristocrats, in the political sphere, achieve coherence with pastoral in the literary, and with romantic rhetoric in the discursive spheres, by virtue of their shared willingness to negate distinction in the pursuit of self-interest. Reader and writer are, in turn, drawn into this complex by the suggestion that formulaic sentimentalism encourages rote responses; the value of interpretation, conversely, hinges on the difficulties involved in exercising meticulous judgment. Marianne, in *A Gossip's Story*, thus stands at once as a figure for the pastoral character, writer, and reader:

Marianne had now an additional employment, besides playing upon her harp, reading pastoral poetry, walking in the woods by moonlight, and listening to distant waterfalls. She kept a journal of the events of the day, and every morning dispatched two sheets of paper, closely written, to her beloved Eliza. If any sceptical critic should censure this as a violation of probability... I shall pity his ignorance, and refer him to the productions of many of my contemporaries; where he may be convinced, that sentiment is to the full as ductile as gold, and when beaten thin will cover as incalculable an extent of surface. (1.225-6)

Self-referential writing, in its eliciting of shallow emotion from the reader, participates in the debilitating effects of leisure, formally represented in these novels under the sign of pastoral.

West's reading of pastoral thus allows the conflation of gender, genre, and the politically specious. Countermanding its exclusion from the grace of labor are the georgic values she ascribes to the heroines of her first two novels. West's particular interest in the problematic status of women's enterprise results in a construction of georgic that aligns it with a female rhetoric expressive of middle-class ideals. *The Advantages of Education* and *A Gossip's Story* retain the conventional emphasis on the civilizing and reconstructive powers of georgic. But in both novels, mundane financial failures necessitate industriousness and so situate georgic within the domestic sphere. While war is not then causally prior to the re-forging of order, as it is in the classical *Georgics*, the resonances of that tradition encourage the reader to understand domestic reconstruction as related to the threat of revolutionary France and of civil war.

The imminence of this danger and the vigilance it demands typically emerge through contrast with pastoral's irresponsible idealizations. When Louisa's father loses his money the pair are forced to retire to the Lancashire estate left to her by her grandfather "as a supply for pin-money" (II.48). Characteristically, Marianne congratulates her sister on the prospect of living in a cottage, since "that name suggested every thing that was pastoral and charming" (II.40). In fact, the "most enthusiastick imagination could hardly associate pastoral ideas with the neglected wilderness of Seatondell, could suppose it peopled by Naids [sic] and Dryads, or fancy that Pan ever awoke its echoes with his tabor and pipe, while Cynthia and her maids of honour danced cotillions" (II.48). West's deflation of pastoral rhetoric, with its unseemly and factitious conjunction of nymphs and cotillions, sharply contrasts with the substantial virtues ascribed to Louisa's program of georgic enterprise: "We shall find [she informs her father] both health and amusement in improving our farm in summer, and in winter books and musick will afford a never-failing resource from chagrin" (II.52–3). The significant and adult world of georgic here displaces the illusory and childish realm of pastoral. In their complementary alignments with conservatism and radicalism, West's generic adaptations shape the progressive social model which her fiction advances.

The actual tilling of the soil at Seatondell, of course, is effected by a "party of labourers" (II.55).[20] Louisa's georgic exercises exchange literal for supervisory labor in order to confirm the distinction of tenants from property owners: "Accustomed to oeconomick attentions, she knew how to husband her bounty, and by adding to it her personal services, to render a trifle valuable. She visited the sick, consoled the afflicted, instructed the ignorant, and reproved the idle" (II.62). This feminized and class-specific interpretation of georgic may seem at first to assign to Louisa a merely local function. But her investment of the labor of "personal services" gives a value to her husbandry that is associated throughout West's works with effective social control. Active intercession in the lives of the poor through charity allows the rod of correction to be applied to the "ignorant" and the "idle." If her father "stimulated the industry of thousands" through his "mercantile pursuits," Louisa's more intimate connection with labor achieves complementary results. Georgic's meliorating capacity thus affects the social registers above and below the middle class with which West primarily associates it, becoming the conduit through which the reform of both the licentious rich and the idle poor is attempted.

A Tale of the Times more rigorously defends georgic industry by elaborating on the supervisory relation of women to the rural poor, their correlatives in class terms. Yet it finally disallows the redemptive power of labor to its heroine, Geraldine, Lady Monteith, condemning her instead to a flattened and reductive variation on Clarissa's death following rape. The failure of georgic here reflects a fundamental division within the novel itself, a division that follows from West's attention in the second volume to the destructive machinations of the archrevolutionary (and highly derivative) villain, Fitzosborne. The first volume focuses on the conventionally paired West heroines, rendered less schematically than in earlier works since both are actively virtuous – though Lucy, who is the less wealthy of the two, has the edge of "superior energy" (I.105) of mind.[21] The more privileged Geraldine, "like Pygmalion, became deeply enamoured with the creature of her own imagination" (I.115), Monteith, whom she marries despite his intellectual and moral inferiority to her. In the first four happy years of their marriage she dedicates herself to improving her husband's Scottish estate on which she intends to build a "neat little village" inhabited by those tenants who "seem to fulfil their duties with marked propriety." Her role she imagines in terms conventionally deemed paternalistic, but which West's novels re-write as the province of women: "I will frequently visit them; I will be their legislator, their instructor, their physician, and their friend. They shall look up to me with gratitude, and my own heart shall enjoy the pure recompense of conscious beneficence" (II.10). Such appropriation of male virtue is made necessary by Monteith's feckless inattention to dissent and by his dangerously feudal notions of the necessary distance between master and laborer. He regards Geraldine's project as a leisurely diversion, a way to "amuse" herself when she has "no other employment," and stipulates only that she install "no manufactories in my neighbourhood. – All our family hate the very name of them. – They only encourage a horde of idle insolent vagrants, who fly in your face upon every occasion" (II.18).

Geraldine's grasp of political relations is, in this instance at least, considerably more complex than her husband's. While he insists that women and children be "fed at the castle gate," she understands the social dynamics of obligation: "No, let them eat the bread of industry, and enjoy those delights which the active exertion of our native energies always inspires." Such "provident benevolence" will ensure that they "will long need the protecting care of their benefactor, and consequently cannot affect an insolent independence on his bounty" (II.19–20). The social utility of labor expressed generically here through georgic once again acquires additional force through the contrasting associations of pastoral. Geraldine's nemesis, Fitzosborne, embodies the seemingly opposed but equally pernicious attributes of Jacobin and aristocrat, united (as in *The Advantages of Education* and *A Gossip's Story*) under the sign of pastoral. While Monteith's failures are those of a man profoundly bored by "every scheme not immediately connected with his own pleasures" (II.22), Fitzosborne is positively evil in the "covert war which he waged, not merely against the chastity, but also against the principles of his victims" (II.153). As with Lovelace, Fitzosborne's intelligence and lack of a coherent identity (in both figured as protean changeableness) fuel his capacity to exploit weakness. Countering Arabella's comment (quoted earlier) that the poor should be shot like worn-out horses in order that she not be offended by the sight of them, Fitzosborne, alert to Geraldine's presence, but at this point misreading the latter's charity as the product of copy-book idealization, declaims on the beauties of "those obscure cots, the chosen abodes of innocence and virtue." To this, she responds in turn: "My long residence in retirement allows me positively to contradict the popular notion, that the country is the seat of Arcadian happiness and purity, though much may be done to ameliorate the condition of the lower classes of society; and I am convinced, that residing among them is one of the more probable means of effecting that important design" (II.128–9).[22]

But even as West accords Geraldine's sentiments all the positive resonances of georgic industry and suggests that women are peculiarly fitted to the supervisory control of the extended household, she is bound for reasons of both politics and gender to punish Geraldine and her husband. In West's earlier novels, the combination of wealth and unhappiness characteristic of the less successful of the paired heroines is made to correspond to private failures of generosity or inner strength. Here the pathos of the heroine's fate depends on the virtual absence of such personal weakness. Geraldine is "[a]dorned with every natural and acquired accomplishment; 'chaste as the icicle on Dian's temple'; attached to her husband; the fondest of mothers; domestic, prudent, and religious." Yet with all of these attributes, she, nevertheless, must fall. Active virtue alone is insufficient to withstand the "covert assault" (II.149) prepared by the devious Fitzosborne. And her intemperate husband, prey to aristocratic vices and so lacking the attentiveness characteristic of genuine "manliness," fails to repulse the danger.

While *A Tale of the Times* is not an allegory, its tethering of politics to sexuality invites us to consider character as an index to larger cultural preoccupations. The conservative programme of the 1790s held to two imperfectly meshed paradigms of femaleness generated by the "culture of sensibility": woman is both a physical being susceptible to masculine appropriation and an agent of the civilizing values of domesticity that are a product of her moral acuteness. Geraldine's integrity and, more especially, her identification with the distinctive national virtues exemplified by georgic encourage a reading of her, in the light of the second of these paradigms, as a figure for Britain itself. But her openness to the blandishments of the insinuating radical Fitzosborne points to the shadowy presence of the first paradigm and implicitly argues the need for Britons' continued vigilance, for resistance to any influence imported from France, for strong government. The merging of sexual and political discourses here under the sign of woman and the implication that such merging figures Britain's vulnerability to French radicalism also makes compelling the need to gender politics in definitively masculine terms. Patriotic "manliness" thus marks out the preserve of politics as masculine and sanctions the representative function of the chaste woman as symbol of the integrity and security of the state.

The conclusion to *A Tale of the Times* draws generously on these conservative standards. In the narrator's retrospective survey of Geraldine's rape and death, only a "latent spark of vanity" can be isolated as their possible cause. But even this is sufficient, we are told, in the absence of a husband's "firm judgment, the manly tenderness, which should guide and direct this attracting woman through the thorny maze of public life" (III.278–9), to guarantee her destruction. The lack of protective manliness allows the "pestilent notions" (III.372) inherent in revolutionary rhetoric to mimic the course of infectious disease; the "attracting" host, the undefiled body of the woman, tempts the Jacobin villain to sully and pollute. "Manliness" alone stands as a barrier between the achievement of domestic felicity, with its public expression as "*amor patriae*," and the forces destructive of "our religion, our morals, or our government" (III.388). If women represent what is best in any culture, they also, and more importantly, may become the vessel through which that culture is corrupted.

West's commitment to the commonplace stands, in her own view, as the source of the insight that enables both narratorial omniscience and political acuteness – the complementary spheres of the textual and actual worlds. Attention to "real life" and not to the "Utopian geography of many modern novelists" (*Gossip* II.96) allows the confirmation and hence preservation of this densely textured quotidian vision with its powerful impulse toward conformity. Through the resolute ordinariness of her narratorial voice, of her sense of the reader, and of her didacticism, West draws into conjunction public and private. By a parallel logic, the extraordinary or exceptional is vilified, both in its philosophical form of the "scepticism [which] owes most of its adherents ... to the pride of human reason, and the love of singularity" and its authorial one of the "singularity" courted by successful writers, "these huge Leviathans [who] toss and sport as they please in the great deeps of literature" (*Tale* III.62, I.99). She, in contrast, identifies her efforts as writer and polemicist not with the insouciant freedom assumed by "modern novelists," but with the obligation of the "lesser fry [to] submit to some precautions, or endure the harder alternative of annihilation. Our morose taskmasters ... impose upon us the hard laws of having a beginning, a middle, and an end" (*Tale* I.99) – the same "hard laws" of the "narrative way" which links "the muse of history and the muse of fiction." Such emphasis on discipline and commitment in relation to her own authorial efforts locates them within the moral imperatives that govern georgic. The framing of writer and audience within this context alerts us to the wider implications of the politics of reading that West painstakingly constructs in all three novels. The decade in which they appeared was marked by a succession of near famine years that provoked, from one side of the political spectrum, calls for revolutionary change and, from the other, the anti-utopian prescriptions of such authors as Thomas Malthus. For West, the georgic mode, with its urging of unremitting labor, its acceptance of necessary pain, and its promise of political stability after great upheaval, served at once as a literary and political paradigm for the relation of "common life" to history that her novels represent.

Epilogue

In the eighteenth century, emergent genres took as their province the problematic relation of the inward and private to the social and public. As this book has argued, among the novel's strategies for the mediating of these spheres was a plotting of women's relation to property through reference to two classically sanctioned and masculine modes, pastoral and georgic. Through this conjunction of the marginal and interiorized with the elite and hegemonic, the novel is able to render self-making an issue of cultural moment. A fuller understanding of the conditions informing early fiction's representations of identity can be realized through comparison with an established genre, such as historiography.[1] Historiography, while clearly enjoying an authority and prestige denied the novel, nevertheless reveals in its accommodation of sentimental impulse to political narrative a susceptibility to comparable pressures.[2] These discrete, internal adjustments also have an external dimension, apparent in the responsiveness of each genre to the narrative challenges posed by the other: novel and historiography reciprocally incorporate many of the distinctive features of the competing form, even as both lay title to bordering genres such as memoir and biography.[3] Questions of audience are, of course, central to this process of mutual re-definition throughout the period. But, as Part IV has argued, in the closing decade of the century, the need to secure readers is both intensified and complicated by the pervasive tendency to formulate generic issues through reference to gender. The perception that women not only formed a significant constituency within an enlarged reading public, but that they also had the potential to exercise both literary and political influence made gender a key element in the revolutionary debates. These two strands – the novel's generic competition with historiography and the implicit recognition of a potential female authority that the focus on gender in 1790s literature confirms – are at once modified and regulated in the new form of historical fiction.

In the 1790s, the proximity of novel and history had generated a discursive conflict in which the political implications of story-telling or plotting were understood to have material (and not simply speculative) correspondences. For many radical and conservative writers, as we have seen in both Godwin and Walker, history and romance now appeared on formal and epistemological grounds virtually indistinguishable.[4] In their shared conviction that interpretation is subjectively grounded, such writers allowed the possibility that the power of fiction might well reside in its ability not simply to record but actually to make history. Both imagined that readers of novels might translate the imperatives of self-making into actions that would reconfigure the public sphere, making it increasingly susceptible to demands generated by private desires.

The politics of reading that so agitated the last decade of the century invested the conventions of pastoral and georgic with new partisan meanings. Jane West's drawing together of the "muse of fiction and the muse of history" situates the plain-spoken narrator and her surrogate, the female reader, within the context of a georgic enterprise imagined as capable of renovating a nation imperiled by radicalism. In her account, the defeat of pastoralism (identified with a radical self-interestedness whose politics disavow the achievements of the past) would enable a purposive female georgic to collaborate with male commerce in the construction of a progressive history.

The investment of pastoral and georgic with political significations did not, however, survive the diminishing revolutionary threat. Paradoxically, the separate attempts of radical and conservative writers to realize in their fictions the consequences of the collaboration between private and public virtue (with the meaning of that virtue construed differently by each) had as one of their effects the reinforcement of division. The social consequences have been thoroughly documented by Davidoff and Hall in relation to the construction of gendered, separate spheres.[5] The later literary history of the problem of genres I have been tracing here would require another book, but the outlines of at least one part of a subsequent genealogy can be suggested by a final glance at one of the characteristic new forms of the nineteenth century, the historical novel: fictions in which the narratorial voice, at once intimate and skeptical, has as its correlative the evocation of the protagonist's emotions filtered through the distance of passed time. Romance and history, denied the political immediacy they possessed at century's end, register in the historical novel a collaborative appeal to the present-day reader's judicious detachment from the factionalism seen to

distinguish the past. In the exemplar of the new form, Walter Scott's
Waverley, the perspective of "sixty years since" also imposes changed
meanings on the relation of gender to genre. Under the impress of
historical fiction, pastoral and georgic are profoundly altered, serving as
markers of temporal and gender difference rather than as contrastive
tropes for political positions whose respective verities radical and conservative novels had contested. Within Scott's *Waverley*, pastoral is thus
associated with the vanished romance of the Jacobite cause, while a
commitment to georgic reconstruction initiates Edward Waverley's final
entry into the realm of "real history."[6]

The novelistic representation of that "real history" is crucially dependent on a series of removes: the temporal one of "sixty years since"
and the literary and aesthetic ones through which Scott distinguishes his
fictions from those of his peers. We can see how this distancing effect
works by contrasting Jane West's sense of the novel's relation to its
cultural context with Scott's. In the "Introductory" first chapter of
Waverley, Scott provides a tongue-in-cheek list of the alternative running
titles he considered to accompany the "uncontaminated name" of his
main title. Among them is "A Tale of the Times":

Or again, if my Waverley had been entitled "A Tale of the Times," wouldst
thou not, gentle reader, have demanded from me a dashing sketch of the
fashionable world, a few anecdotes of scandal thinly veiled, and if lusciously
painted so much the better; a heroine from Grosvenor Square, and a hero from
the Barouche Club or the Four-in-Hand, with a set of subordinate characters
from the elegantes of Queen Anne Street East, or dashing heroes of the
Bow-Street Office? I could proceed in proving the importance of a title-page,
and displaying at the same time my own intimate knowledge of the ingredients
necessary to the composition of romances and novels of various descriptions.
But it is enough, and I scorn to tyrannize longer over the impatience of my
reader, who is doubtless already anxious to know the choice made by an author
so profoundly versed in the different branches of his art. (4)

Scott's construction of a "tale of the times" as merely a "dashing sketch
of the fashionable world" contradicts the meanings carried by the actual
title of West's 1799 novel. In contrast to the dismissiveness implicit in
Scott's phrasing, West foregrounds, by way of searching inquiry, the
forms of betrayal that constitute "the times." In adopting the "narrative
way," *A Tale of the Times* integrates the political and personal in order to
engage the reader's judgment of prevailing mores. Prudentia and her
readers, acting on the assumption that only a critical scrutiny of present

error will secure future order, collaboratively undertake the analysis of widespread corruption.

Scott's relation to the reader whom he variously characterizes in the quoted passage as gentle, impatient, anxious and subject to authorial tyranny is developed in quite different ways. His mocking account of the eager consumers of romances and "private scandal" distances him from the existing reading public he here derides and from the literary culture that encourages its debased taste.[7] The irony that signals his literary and aesthetic detachment from his surrounding context relates suggestively to the historical distance he exercises in relation to the events of "sixty years since" and to the ideal reader constructed through his mediation of that distance. In *Waverley*, the present exists not directly through focused inquiry, but inferentially as product of the distinction between the sentimentally rendered political history of the Jacobite rebellion and the "real history" of private life that Waverley's disenchantment authorizes. The substitution of "sixty years since" for the rejected "tale of the times" as running title allows that "real history" to be plotted individually as the maturing of Edward Waverley and culturally as the change in manners effected by the "gradual influx of wealth, and extension of commerce" that followed the defeat of the "Jacobite party" (340). The feminized "muse of fiction and the muse of history" who enable Prudentia Homespun to explore with a female readership the corruptions of present times give way in Scott's work to the Author of the Waverley Novels whose specialized knowledge of the past is imparted to a gentlemanly reader attentive to the origins and progress of an accomplished civil society.

Notes

INTRODUCTION

1 Alexander Pope, *Imitations of Horace* Sat.II.ii.167–80, vol. IV ed. John Butt, *Twickenham Edition of the Poems of Alexander Pope* (London: Methuen, New Haven: Yale University Press, 2nd edn. rpt. 1961).

2 For a succinct account of one of the most influential theorists of property, C. B. Macpherson, including the notion of possessive individualism, first outlined in his *Political Theory of Possessive Individualism* (Oxford: Clarendon Press, 1962), see Andrew Reeve, *Property* (London: Macmillan, 1986), 45–51. J. G. A. Pocock offers a critique of Macpherson's thought as insufficiently dialectical in "Authority and Property: the Question of Liberal Origins." See J. G. A. Pocock, *Virtue, Commerce, and History: Essays on Political Thought and History, Chiefly in the Eighteenth Century* (Cambridge University Press, 1985), 51–71. On the relation of property rights to political argument within the period, see Thomas A. Horne, *Property Rights and Poverty: Political Argument in Britain, 1605–1834* (Chapel Hill and London: The University of North Carolina P, 1990).

3 Renée Hirschon has noted the lack of critical attention paid to the issue of property, despite Engels's early recognition that female subordination follows from the conjunction of the institutions of private property and monogamous marriage. But, while advocating an "historical perspective," she overlooks the eighteenth-century contribution to this complex of ideas and details instead the ways in which the Victorians' "intellectual preoccupation" with the relation between property, marriage and women's position survives in the work of modern anthropologists. See Renée Hirschon, "Introduction: Property, Power and Gender Relations" in *Women and Property: Women as Property* ed. Renée Hirschon (New York: St. Martin's Press; London and Canberra: Croom Helm, 1984) 6, 1. Susan Staves's *Married Women's Separate Property in England, 1660–1833* (Cambridge, Mass.: Harvard University Press, 1990) redresses this imbalance.

4 See, Joyce Oldham Appleby, *Economic Thought and Ideology in Seventeenth-Century England* (Princeton University Press, 1978) and *Liberalism and Republicanism in the Historical Imagination* (Cambridge, Mass.: Harvard University Press, 1992); Isaac Kramnick, *Republicanism and Bourgeois Radicalism: Political*

Ideology in Late Eighteenth-Century England and America (Ithaca: Cornell University Press, 1990). In the opening summary chapter of *Republicanism and Bourgeois Radicalism*, Kramnick usefully distinguishes his argument for the centrality of a fully formed bourgeois ideology from the positions of Harold Perkin, Albert Hirschman, and R. S. Neale.

5 See J. G. A. Pocock, *The Ancient Constitution and the Feudal Law: A Study of English Historical Thought in the Seventeenth Century* (Cambridge University Press, 1957), *The Machiavellian Moment: Florentine Political Thought and the Atlantic Republican Tradition* (Princeton University Press, 1975), and *Virtue, Commerce, and History* (Cambridge University Press, 1985). See also Quentin Skinner, *The Foundations of Modern Political Thought* (Cambridge University Press, 1978). Appleby's *Liberalism and Republicanism* offers an interesting interpretation of Pocock's model.

6 See John Barrell, "'The Dangerous Goddess': Masculinity, Prestige, and the Aesthetic in Early Eighteenth-Century Britain," in *Cultural Critique* 12 (1989), 101–31.

7 As Claudio Guillén argues in "On the Uses of Literary Genre," genre is "a problem-solving model on the level of form." Guillén, *Literature as System: Essays Toward the Theory of Literary History* (Princeton University Press, 1971), 120. Michael McKeon develops Guillén's insight in terms that allow for a more dynamic model of historical specificity: genres, he writes, "provide a conceptual framework for the mediation (if not the 'solution') of intractable problems, a method for rendering such problems intelligible." *The Origins of the English Novel, 1600–1740* (Baltimore and London: Johns Hopkins University Press, 1987), 20.

8 On the repositioning of georgic and pastoral over the course of the eighteenth century, see Ralph Cohen, *Innovation and Variation: Literary Change and Georgic Poetry* in *Literature and History. Papers Read at a Clark Library Seminar. March 3, 1973* (Los Angeles: William Andrews Clark Memorial Library, 1974); Richard Feingold, *Nature and Society: Later Eighteenth-Century Uses of the Pastoral and Georgic* (New Brunswick, N.J.: Rutgers University Press, 1978); and Alastair Fowler, *Kinds of Literature: An Introduction to the Theory of Genres and Modes* (Cambridge, Mass.: Harvard University Press, 1982). Fowler analyzes the contiguous ascendency of georgic and of related didactic forms such as the essay, biography, and novel.

9 James Thomson, *The Castle of Indolence* Canto II, stanzas xxix, lxi, lxv in *James Thomson: Poetical Works* ed. J. Logie Robertson (London: Oxford University Press, rpt. 1971). On the ambiguities attaching to the contrast of indolence and industry in Thomson's work, see John Barrell, *English Literature in History, 1730–80: An Equal, Wide Survey* (London: Hutchinson, 1983).

10 John Chalker, *The English Georgic: A Study in the Development of a Form* (Baltimore: Johns Hopkins University Press, 1969), 15.

11 The "great cultural insecurity" of the mid-eighteenth century, J. Paul Hunter writes, derives "from a pervasive male sense that men were holding their place only nominally and that women were beginning to control

energy, vitality, and ultimately identity." See Hunter, "Clocks, Calendars, and Names: the Troubles of Tristram and the Aesthetics of Uncertainty" in *Rhetorics of Order / Ordering Rhetorics in English Neoclassical Literature* ed. J. Douglas Canfield and J. Paul Hunter (Newark: University of Delaware Press and London and Toronto: Associated University Presses, 1989), 194. G. J. Barker-Benfield has detailed the gendering of consciousness that ratified this new understanding of identity in *The Culture of Sensibility: Sex and Society in Eighteenth-Century Britain* (Chicago and London: University of Chicago Press, 1992). The initial focus among feminist critics such as Dale Spender, Mary Anne Schofield, and Jane Spencer on the recovery of female-authored works has recently been supplemented by a number of studies that point to the conjunction of the emergence of the novel and of the professional woman writer, to whose concerns the novel was seen to give authoritative expression. See Janet Todd, *The Sign Of Angellica: Women, Writing and Fiction, 1660–1800* (New York: Columbia University Press, 1989); Cheryl Turner, *Living by the Pen: Women Writers in the Eighteenth Century* (London and New York: Routledge, 1992); Catherine Gallagher, *Nobody's Story: The Vanishing Acts of Women Writers in the Marketplace, 1670–1820* (Berkeley and Los Angeles: University of California Press, 1994). A fuller comprehension of women's signifying functions within the novel, this book argues, is made possible when female-authored works are supplemented by consideration of male-authored ones (canonic and less familiar).

12 Nancy Armstrong, *Desire and Domestic Fiction: A Political History of the Novel* (London: Oxford University Press, 1987).

13 See David Vincent, *Literacy and Popular Culture: England 1750–1914* (Cambridge University Press, 1989); Alvin Kernan, *Printing Technology, Letters, and Samuel Johnson* (Princeton University Press, 1987); Cheryl Turner, *Living by the Pen: Women Writers in the Eighteenth Century*; and J. Paul Hunter's " 'The Young, the Ignorant, and the Idle': Some Notes on Readers and the Beginnings of the English Novel" in *Anticipations of the Enlightenment in England, France, and Germany* ed. A. C. Kors and P. J. Korshin (Philadelphia: University of Pennsylvania Press, 1987) for a representative range of interpretations of literacy and its consequences in the period. James Raven, *Judging New Wealth: Popular Publishing and Responses to Commerce in England, 1750–1800* (New York: Oxford University Press, 1992) argues that while individuals read more in the eighteenth century, literacy rates in fact remained fairly constant over the period.

14 See Appleby, *Liberalism and Republicanism*, especially chapter four, pp. 124–39, "Ideology and the History of Political Thought."

15 Michael McKeon, "Historicizing Patriarchy: the Emergence of Gender Difference in England, 1660–1760," *Eighteenth-Century Studies* 28 (1995), 295–322.

16 John Dryden, *The Works of Virgil: Containing his Pastorals, Georgics and Aeneis. Translated into English Verse* (London: 1697), quoted from *The Poems of John*

Dryden volume II ed. James Kinsley (Oxford: Clarendon Press, 1958), *Georgics* I.217–18.

PART I

INTRODUCTION

1 Pocock, *The Machiavellian Moment*, 466.

1 "CLARISSA" AND THE GEORGIC MODE

1 Samuel Richardson, *Clarissa, or, The History of a Young Lady* ed. Angus Ross (Harmondsworth: Penguin Books, 1985), 1191.
2 Thomas McLaughlin, "Figurative Language" in *Critical Terms for Literary Study* ed. Frank Lentricchia and Thomas McLaughlin (Chicago and London: University of Chicago Press 1990), 84.
3 Margaret Anne Doody, "The Man-made World of Clarissa Harlowe and Robert Lovelace" in *Samuel Richardson: Passion and Prudence* ed. Valerie Grosvenor Myer (London: Vision Press; Totowa, N.J.: Barnes and Noble Books, 1986), 55.
4 John Locke, *The Second Treatise of Government* in *Two Treatises of Government* ed. with intro. and notes Peter Laslett (Cambridge University Press, 1988), 288, 289. For Margaret Anne Doody's perceptive reading of Locke, see "The Man-made World of Clarissa Harlowe and Robert Lovelace," 54–5. For a discussion of the *Second Treatise* within the context of the mid-century debate over the legal status of intellectual property, see Irene Tucker, "Writing Home: *Evelina*, the Epistolary Novel, and the Paradox of Property," *ELH* 60 (1993), 419–39.
5 Appleby, *Liberalism and Republicanism*, 81.
6 Locke, *Second Treatise of Government*, 289–90.
7 For a reading of Lockean notions of contract as profoundly anti-feminist, see Carol Pateman, *The Sexual Contract* (Stanford University Press, 1988).
8 *Critical Remarks on "Sir Charles Grandison," "Clarissa," and "Pamela"* (1754), Augustan Reprint Society, no. 21 (Los Angeles: William Andrews Clark Memorial Library, University of California, 1950), 29–30.
9 Thomas O. Beebee, *"Clarissa" on the Continent: Translation and Seduction* (University Park and London: Pennsylvania University Press, 1990), 102, 104–5.
10 Terry Eagleton, *The Rape of Clarissa: Writing, Sexuality and Class Struggle in Samuel Richardson* (Oxford: Basil Blackwell, 1982), 56.
11 See Christopher Hill, "Clarissa Harlowe and her Times," *Essays in Criticism* 5 (1955), 315–40; Ian Watt, *The Rise of the Novel: Studies in Defoe, Richardson, and Fielding* (Berkeley and Los Angeles: University of California Press 1957); Eagleton, *Rape of Clarissa*; Pocock, *Virtue, Commerce, and History*; John Barrell, *The Political Theory of Painting from Reynolds to Hazlitt:. "The Body of the Public"* (New Haven and London: Yale University Press, 1986); John Zomchick, *Family and the Law in Eighteenth-Century Fiction: The Public Conscience in the Private Sphere* (Cambridge University Press, 1993).

12 Pocock, *Virtue, Commerce, and History*, 112.
13 Charles Taylor, *The Sources of the Self: The Making of the Modern Identity* (Cambridge, Mass.: Harvard University Press, 1989), 211.
14 Appleby, *Liberalism and Republicanism*, 138–9.
15 Paul Langford, *Public Life and the Propertied Englishman, 1689–1798* (Oxford: Clarendon Press 1991), 1, 305–6.
16 Adam Ferguson, *An Essay on the History of Civil Society* intro. Louis Schneider (New Brunswick, N.J. and London: Transaction Publishers, 1980), 82. For a wide-ranging consideration of the concept see David Spadafora, *The Idea of Progress in Eighteenth-Century Britain* (New Haven and London: Yale University Press, 1990).
17 Anthony Low, *The Georgic Revolution* (Princeton University Press, 1985), 221.
18 See Chalker, *English Georgic*, Richard Feingold, *Nature and Society*, Low, *Georgic Revolution*, Ronald Paulson, *Breaking and Remaking: Aesthetic Practice in England, 1700–1820* (New Brunswick and London: Rutgers University Press, 1989), Raymond Williams, *The Country and the City* (New York: Oxford University Press, 1973). For the Romantic period, see John Murdoch, "The Landscape of Labor: Transformations of the Georgic" in *Romantic Revolutions: Criticism and Theory* ed. Kenneth R. Johnston, Gilbert Chaitin, Karen Hanson, and Herbert Marks (Bloomington and Indianapolis: Indiana University Press, 1990), 176–93.
19 Low, *Georgic Revolution*, 7.
20 Dryden's prefatorial claim to his 1697 edition that *Georgics* is "the best Poem of the best Poet" is elaborated in mid-century by Joseph Trapp and John Newbery, both of whom emphasize the poem's fusion of beauty and didacticism. "*Virgil* has omitted nothing that would contribute to make his precepts pleasing;" Newbery writes in the *Art of Poetry*, "and his fables, allegories, descriptions, similies, reflections, remarks, digressions, &c. seem all to spring spontaneously out of his subject." In a similar vein, Trapp's *Lectures on Poetry* commends the "Pleasure that naturally results from reading them [as] chiefly owing to the Pleasure and Advantage which attends a Country Life." The "Pleasure and Advantage" Clarissa herself garners from the "Country Life" at both Harlowe Place and her grandfather's estate signal her complementary dedication to purposive action. See Dryden, *Poems*, "The Dedication of *The Georgics*," p. 913; John Newbery, *The Art of Poetry on a New Plan* (1762) (New York and London: Garland Publishing, 1970), 1.185; Joseph Trapp, *Lectures on Poetry, Read in the Schools of Natural Philosophy at Oxford* (1742) (New York: Garland Publishing, 1970), 194.
21 For the relation between the discourses of sensibility and politeness, see G. J. Barker-Benfield, *The Culture of Sensibility: Sex and Society in Eighteenth-Century Britain*.
22 John Allen Stevenson, "The Courtship of the Family: Clarissa and the Family Once More," *ELH* 48 (1981), 757–77, suggests that the question of familial opposition to Lovelace has traditionally been construed through reference to property relations as in the marriage and courtship patterns

outlined by Christopher Hill. But the "emotional struggle" (758) in the triangle of suitor, father, and child, a struggle best understood in light of Levi-Strauss's discussion of the incest-taboo, is also crucial. The Harlowes attempt to circumvent the normative "reciprocal exchange" of women in marriage with a "particularly literal form of endogamy" (760) in which Clarissa weds Solmes, who "clearly represents a more endogamous match than Lovelace in terms of class, background, and outlook" (760). See Raymond F. Hilliard, "*Clarissa* and Ritual Cannibalism," *PMLA* 105 (1990), 1083–97, for another anthropologically inflected reading of the novel.

23 See Nancy K. Miller, *The Heroine's Text: Readings in the French and English Novel, 1722–1782* (New York: Columbia University Press, 1980).

24 William Blackstone, *Commentaries on the Laws of England* (1765) (New York and London: Oceana Press 1966), 1.430. William Alexander will later argue that this extinction of personal identity has corollary advantages in terms of women's relation to real property: "By the laws of this country, the moment a woman enters into a state of matrimony, her political existence is annihilated, or incorporated into that of her husband; but by this little mortification she is no loser, and her apparent loss of consequence is abundantly compensated by a long list of extensive privileges and immunities which, for the encouragement of matrimony, were, perhaps, contrived to give married women the advantage over those who are single." *The History of Women* (London: 1779), II.323.

25 Low, *Georgic Revolution*, 6.

2 MAKING MEANING AS CONSTRUCTIVE LABOR

1 Robert Bage's *Mount Henneth* (1782) literalizes Lovelace's implicitly piratical imagery in the plot of Camitha Melton, a woman who, being seized on the high seas, provides the occasion for arguments concerning legal title to a woman's person. See below, chapter nine.

2 See Blackstone, *Commentaries*, 1.298.

3 For a detailed account of the juridical interpretation of personality within eighteenth-century fiction, including *Clarissa*, see, Zomchick, *Family and the Law*.

4 Relations among the Harlowes are established by reference to a careful network of allusions to real and portable property, the narrative assumption being that such allusions establish the salient characteristics of individuals and the structures by which they order their responses to others. Clarissa, for instance, tends to use property metaphorically in order to describe her difference from her family. She thus envisions herself as enacting "agreeable schemes of making others as happy as myself by the proper discharge of the stewardship entrusted to me (are not all estates stewardships, my dear?)" (104). Uncle Anthony's relentlessly mercenary understanding of stewardship clarifies the larger meanings intended by Clarissa: "But now I think of it, [he writes to her after she has complained of Solmes's illiteracy] suppose you *are* readier at your pen than he – you will make the more useful wife to

him; won't you? For who so good an economist as you? – And you may keep all his accounts and save yourselves a steward. And, let me tell you, this is a fine advantage in a family: for those stewards are often sad dogs, and creep into a man's estate, before he knows where he is; and not seldom is he forced to pay them interest for his own money. I know not why a good wife should be above these things. 'Tis better than lying abed half the day, and junketing and card-playing all the night, and making yourselves wholly useless to every good purpose in your own families, as is now the fashion among ye" (155). Her brother, in turn, is characterized as grasping, self-aggrandizing and insatiably acquisitive: "(for when was ever [Clarissa writes to Anna Howe] an ambitious mind, as you observe in the case of avarice, satisfied by acquisition?)" (105). And Bella, who attacks Clarissa for squandering her money, is answered by Clarissa's withering allusion to the parable of the talents: "Better than to lie rusting in my cabinet, as yours does … " (195).

5 The phrase is from the heading to chapter seven, "The Humanist Sublime: *Clarissa* as the Agent of a Humanist Ideology," in William Warner's *Reading "Clarissa": The Struggles of Interpretation* (New Haven and London: Yale University Press, 1979). For useful summaries of the flurry of critical responses to *Clarissa* that appeared in the 1970s, see the "Bibliographic Postcript" in Terry Castle's *Clarissa's Ciphers: Meaning and Disruption in Richardson's "Clarissa"* (Ithaca and London: Cornell University Press, 1982), 189–96, and Sue Warrick Doederlein, "Clarissa in the Hands of the Critics," *Eighteenth-Century Studies* 16 (1983), 401–14.

6 Samuel Richardson, *The History of Sir Charles Grandison* ed. with intro. Jocelyn Harris (London: Oxford University Press, 1972), III.235.

7 Richardson to Aaron Hill, November 7, 1748. In *Selected Letters of Samuel Richardson* ed. John Carroll (Oxford: Clarendon Press 1964), 99. For an account of the novel's relation to Restoration tragedy, see chapter five, "Tyrannic Love and Virgin Martyr: Tragic Theme and Dramatic Reference in *Clarissa*" in Margaret Anne Doody, *A Natural Passion: A Study of the Novels of Samuel Richardson* (Oxford: Clarendon Press 1974), 99–127.

8 *Oxford English Dictionary*.

9 Francis Bacon, *The Advancement of Learning and New Atalantis* intro. Thomas Case (London: Oxford University Press, 1957, rpt. 1974), 177–8. The editor of the 1733 *Philosophical Works of Francis Bacon*, Peter Shaw, includes in the "Small Glossary or Explanations of certain Philosophical Terms, either Invented, or Used in a New Sense, by the Author" a listing for "Georgicks": "This expression of *Georgicks* is transferr'd from Agriculture into Ethicks; so as to denote the Art of cultivating, or improving the Mind in Moral Virtue." *The Philosophical Works of Sir Francis Bacon, … Methodized, and made English, from the Originals with Occasional Notes, to explain what is obscure …* (London: 1733), I.i, I.v.

10 The language of reciprocal labor which comes increasingly to define Belford's moral stature in the novel is anticipated in his conversation with Mrs. Smith. The conversation, Belford writes to Lovelace, "gave me high credit with the good woman: so that we are perfectly well-acquainted already: by

which means I shall be enabled to give you accounts, from time to time, of all that passes: and which I will be very industrious to do, provided I may depend upon the solemn promises I have given the lady, in your name as well as my own, that she shall be free from all personal molestation from you. And thus shall I have it in my power to return *in kind* your writing favours; and preserve my shorthand besides: which, till this correspondence was opened, I had pretty much neglected" (1073).

11 Ann Louise Kibbie, "Sentimental Properties: *Pamela* and *Memoirs of a Woman of Pleasure,*" *ELH* 58 (1991), 561–77.

12 Samuel Richardson, *Pamela; Or, Virtue Rewarded* (London and Melbourne: Dent, 1914, rpt. 1983), 1, 3.

13 See April London, "Placing the Female: the Metonymic Garden in Amatory and Pious Narrative, 1700–1740" in *Fetter'd or Free: British Women Novelists, 1670–1815* ed. Mary Anne Schofield and Cecilia Macheski (Athens, Ohio and London: Ohio University Press, 1986), 101–23.

14 See Ros Ballaster, *Seductive Forms: Women's Amatory Fiction from 1684 to 1740* (Oxford: Clarendon Press 1992), 126–8.

15 That contract, of course, also retrospectively sanctions an interpretation of Pamela as ironic in her invocation of place.

16 McKeon, *Origins*, 366. For a complementary account of Pamela as at once an incarnation of bourgeois industry and of aristocratic achievements, see Christopher Flint, "The Anxiety of Affluence: Family and Class (Dis)order in *Pamela: or, Virtue Rewarded,*" *Studies in English Literature* 29 (1989), 489–514.

17 See Peter Linebaugh, *The London Hanged: Crime and Civil Society in the Eighteenth Century* (Cambridge University Press, 1992) for an account of the mid-century transition from a system of vails and perquisites to regular wages. See also J. Jean Hecht, *The Domestic Servant Class in Eighteenth-Century England* (London: Routledge and Kegan Paul, 1956), and Bruce Robbins, *The Servant's Hand: English Fiction from Below* (New York: Columbia University Press, 1986).

18 Henry Fielding, *"Joseph Andrews" and "Shamela"* ed. with intro. Martin Battestin (Boston: Houghton Mifflin Company, 1961), 313.

19 Samuel Richardson, *Pamela. Volume II* intro. Mark Kinkead-Weekes (London: Dent, New York: Dutton, rpt. 1976), 314–15.

3 WICKED CONFEDERACIES

1 Judith Wilt, "He Could Go No Farther: a Modest Proposal about Lovelace and Clarissa," *PMLA* 92 (1977), 19–32. Wilt argues "that the rape either was not fully carried out or was carried out by the man's female 'accomplices'" (19).

2 The betrayal of virtue by middle-class women driven by emulation is a recurring feature of eighteenth-century fiction. Sarah Fielding's *The History of the Countess of Dellwyn* (1759) is a particularly striking instance, but Frances Burney, Charlotte Smith, Ann Radcliffe, and a range of less well-known authors also include variations on the theme.

4 "THE WORK OF BODIES": READING, WRITING, AND DOCUMENTS

1   The relation of sentiment to sensibility has been variously represented by
     modern critics. While acknowledging that the two are often used synony-
     mously, Janet Todd argues that "there is, none the less, a useful distinction
     to be made in historical usage and reference": sentiment refers to literature
     in which the expression of opinion or principle depends on the collabor-
     ation of thought and emotion; sensibility is an "innate sensitiveness or
     susceptibility revealing itself in a variety of spontaneous activities such as
     crying, swooning and kneeling." See *Sensibility: An Introduction* (London and
     New York: Methuen, 1986), 7. Chris Jones's "Introduction" to his study of
     the social constructions that inform radical sensibility surveys the secondary
     literature, notes the various "damagingly simplifying" attempts to delimit
     the meaning of sensibility by considering it as a later manifestation of
     sentiment, as a conservative, patriarchal movement, or as a form of "body-
     language," and resolves to use sentiment and sensibility interchangeably. In
     addition to the persuasive methodological reasons provided, he makes the
     practical point that there is no adjectival form of "sensibility." See Chris
     Jones, *Radical Sensibility: Literature and Ideas in the 1790s* (London and New
     York: Routledge, 1993), 5–6.
2   *The Vicar of Wakefield* provides a particularly striking instance of the tonal
     ambiguities created by authors who wish at once to retain the patriarchal
     authority afforded by the didactic mode and to exploit sentimental pathos.
     Primrose's hortatory speech to the assembled prisoners effects their instan-
     taneous and universal conversion, but the reader is left unsure of the Vicar's
     status as surrogate author: does the speech represent Goldsmith's advocacy
     of paternalistic authority or a satire of it?
3   Leo Braudy, "Penetration and Impenetrability in *Clarissa*" in *Modern Essays
     on Eighteenth-Century Literature* ed. Leopold Damrosch, Jr. (New York and
     Oxford: Oxford University Press, 1988), 274, 276.
4   William Enfield, *Observations on Literary Property* (London: 1774), rptd. in *The
     Literary Property Debate: Eight Tracts, 1774–5* ed. Stephen Parks (New York:
     Garland, 1974), 11. Quoted in Trevor Ross, "Copyright and the Invention
     of Tradition," *Eighteenth-Century Studies* 26 (1992), 6. Justice Joseph Yates, in
     Millar v. *Taylor*, April 20 1769, in *English Reports* 98:242. Quoted in Ross,
     "Copyright," 7. See also, Mark Rose, *Authors and Owners: The Invention of
     Copyright* (Cambridge, Mass.: Harvard University Press, 1993).
5   Warner, *Reading "Clarissa,"* 57. Warner's influential account envisions the
     text as a "vast plain where Clarissa and Lovelace, and their respective allies,
     and the two ways of interpreting the world they embody, collide and
     contend" (viii). While the misogynist edge to this study has been anathema-
     tized by such subsequent deconstructionist analyses as Terry Castle's
     Clarissa's Ciphers, the oppositional paradigm tends to be retained.
6   Terry Eagleton, drawing on the possibilities of *l'écriture féminine* enunciated
     by Luce Irigaray and Michele Montrelay, suggests that "men and women

under patriarchy relate differently to the act of writing. Men, more deeply marked by the 'transcendent signifier' of the phallus, will tend to view signs as stable and whole, ideal entities external to the body; women will tend to live a more inward, bodily relationship to script. Whatever the dangers of such stereotyping notions, nothing could be more appropriate to *Clarissa*. Clarissa herself exerts the fullest possible control over her meanings, sustaining an enviable coherence of sense even through her worst trials ... Lovelace's writing is mercurial, diffuse, exuberant." See *Rape of Clarissa*, 52–3. See also Beebee, *"Clarissa" on the Continent*, 128ff.

7 Zomchick, *Family and the Law*, 26.
8 Ibid., 27.
9 Ferguson, *Essay on the History of Civil Society*, 12.
10 Kibbie, "Sentimental Properties," 562. In Kibbie's reading, Pamela colludes with the process by which she becomes B's property through marriage, "a transformation that his assaults on her person could not accomplish" (562). See also John Allan Stevenson, "'A Geometry of his Own': Richardson and the Marriage Ending," *Studies in English Literature*, 26 (1986) 469–83, in which the argument about Richardson's novels as anti-courtship narratives parallels Kibbie's. I am interested in the way in which reading and writing work to legitimate this process by translating an understanding of the female self as property into the property of a text which in turn renders private experience publicly accessible and morally functional.
11 The experience of Harriet Byron in *Sir Charles Grandison* underscores this point by revealing how inflected by the terms of gender the process of reading is. In *Grandison*, it is Harriet who reads, and is profoundly impressed by, the epistolary correspondence of the virtuous hero. In *Pamela* and *Clarissa*, male reading and reformation go hand in hand; in neither of these novels does the female reader undergo internal change. The often remarked flatness of *Sir Charles Grandison* can also be related to a further distinction from his earlier novels: *Grandison* lacks the female confederacies against which the virtues of Pamela and Clarissa are defined.
12 For an account of the changes in contemporary domestic architecture that led to the distinction of private from public space, see Mark Girouard, *Life in the English Country House: A Social and Architectural History* (New Haven and London: Yale University Press, 1978) and Cynthia Wall, "Gendering Rooms: Domestic Architecture and Literary Acts," *Eighteenth-Century Fiction* 5 (1993), 349–72.
13 The collaboratively written letter describing the wedding of Sir Charles and Harriet anticipates this privileging of the general over the specific both in the terms of its production (Charlotte and Lucy take turns recording the events) and in its attempt to balance "sentiment" – in the sense of maxims – and action: "But here comes Lucy. – 'My dear girl, take the pen – I am too *sentimental*. The French only are proud of sentiments at this day; the English cannot bear them: Story, story, story, is what they hunt after, whether sense

or nonsense, probable or improbable'" (III.228).

14 Eagleton, *Rape of Clarissa*, 4. Christopher Flint pursues a complementary argument in "The Anxiety of Affluence."

15 The first phrase serves as heading to the opening chapter of John Millar's *The Origin of the Distinction of Ranks* (1806 edn.) intro. John Valdimir Price (Bristol: Thoemmes Antiquarian Books, 1990), the second to Sketch VI of Henry Homes, Lord Kames's *Sketches of the History of Man. A Second Edition* (1778) (Hildesheim: Georg Olms Verlagsbuchhandlung, 1968). William Alexander offers a succinct account of the representative function of women in his *History of Women* (1779): "[T]he rank, therefore, and condition in which we find women in any country, mark out to us with the greatest precision, the exact point in the scale of civil society, to which people ... have arrived" (1.103).

16 Kames asserts that "[w]omen have more imagination and more sensibility than men; and yet none of them have made an eminent figure in any of the fine arts ... Nature has avoided rivalship between the sexes, by giving them different talents. Add another capital difference of disposition: the gentle and insinuating manners of the female sex, tend to soften the roughness of the other sex; and where-ever women are indulged with any freedom, they polish sooner than men" (*Sketches* II.3–4). Sylvana Tomaselli notes that the "idea that women were the barometers on which every aspect of society, its morals, its laws, its customs, its government was registered had gained much ground since the publication of Montesquieu's *De L'Esprit des Lois* in the middle of the century." This implication of women in the making of culture that is so consistently a feature of eighteenth-century stadial theory, Tomaselli argues, provides a powerful corrective to the modern feminist tendency to align woman with nature and to make both victims of patriarchal constructs. Sylvana Tomaselli, "The Enlightenment Debate on Women," *History Workshop Journal* 20 (1985), 114.

17 Millar, *Origin*, 57.

18 G. J. Barker-Benfield argues for the counterpointing of the powers of conversion granted women in narrative against their inscription as susceptible creatures who are physiologically subordinate in *Culture of Sensibility*, 250–8.

19 As Ruth Salvaggio argues in her assertion that the "exclusion and displacement of what the age regarded as feminine was *necessary* in order for these [classical and enlightened] systems to exist and thrive" in *Enlightened Absence: Neoclassical Configurations of the Feminine* (Urbana and Chicago: University of Illinois Press 1988), ix.

20 Ferguson, *Civil Society*, 255–6, 79, 260.

PART II
INTRODUCTION

1 This generic ambivalence helps to account for the diversity of readings *The Man of Feeling* has provoked. The absence or presence of satire has proven a

particular source of debate. While for Brian Vickers, the novel evidences a "non-ambiguous mood of pathos and sympathy" (See the "Introduction" to his edition of *The Man of Feeling* [London: Oxford University Press, 1967], xiv), for John Sheriff, *The Good-Natured Man: The Evolution of a Moral Ideal, 1660–1800* (University: University of Alabama Press 1982), the "several layers of fiction and several narrators" (83) point to an unrelenting satire of Harley. Barbara Benedict develops the metaphor of framing invoked by Sheriff to argue that Mackenzie uses linguistic and structural irony to critique sentimentalism in her *Framing Feeling: Sentiment and Style in English Prose Fiction 1745–1800* (New York: AMS Press 1994).

2 Henry Mackenzie, *The Lounger* (20), June 18, 1785. In *Novel and Romance 1700–1800: A Documentary Record* ed. Ioan Williams (London: Routledge & Kegan Paul, 1970), 331, 328.

"THE MAN OF FEELING"

1 G. A. Starr, "Sentimental De-education" in *Augustan Studies: Essays in Honour of Irvin Ehrenpreis* ed. Douglas Lane Patey and Timothy Keegan (Newark: University of Delaware P; London and Toronto: Associated University Presses, 1985), 253. See also, G. A. Starr, "'Only a Boy': Notes on Sentimental Novels," *Genre* 10 (1977), 501–27.

2 McKeon, "Historicizing Patriarchy," 314.

3 For differing interpretations of the politics of sentimental narrative, see Robert Markley, "Sentimentality as Performance: Shaftesbury, Sterne and the Theatrics of Virtue" in *The New Eighteenth Century: Theory, Politics, English Literature* ed. Felicity Nussbaum and Laura Brown (New York and London: Methuen, 1987), 210–30, and Patricia Meyer Spacks, *Desire and Truth: Functions of Plot in Eighteenth-Century English Novels* (London and Chicago: University of Chicago Press 1990), 6.

4 Oliver Goldsmith, *The Deserted Village* in *The Poems of Thomas Gray, William Collins, and Oliver Goldsmith* ed. Roger Lonsdale (London: Longmans, Green, 1969), lines 1, 285, 58.

5 Andrew Ettin, *Literature and the Pastoral* (New Haven and London: Yale University Press, 1984), 149. Betsy Thoughtless's acid response to Trueworth's encomiastic account of the joys of rural life in Eliza Haywood's *Betsy Thoughtless* (London: 1751) substitutes the realities of the female condition for his ritualized invocation of place. While he lauds "shady bowers" and "purling streams," her version of pastoral centers on the role it will impose on her: "What! to be cooped up like a tame dove, only to coo, – and bill, – and breed?" (II.89). Betsy, in other words, clearly grasps the relation of gender to genre, and recognizes the deceptions of a received vocabulary which purports to be neutral.

6 On the repositioning of georgic and pastoral over the course of the eighteenth century, see Cohen, *Innovation and Variation*, Feingold, *Nature and Society*, and Fowler, *Kinds of Literature*.

7 George Crabbe, "The Village" 1.18 in *Tales, 1812 and Other Selected Poems* ed.

with intro. Howard Mills (Cambridge University Press, 1967).

8 Henry Mackenzie, *Julia de Roubigné. A Tale. In a Series of Letters. Published by the Author of The Man of Feeling, and The Man of the World. In Two Volumes* (1777) (New York and London: Garland Publishing, 1979) i.viii.

9 Mackenzie, *Julia de Roubigné*, i.x. In *Desire and Truth*, Spacks groups *The Man of Feeling* with such novels of the 1760s and 1770s as *Tristram Shandy*, *Sentimental Journey*, and *Humphry Clinker* and reads their "near rejection of plot" as an "ideological challenge" (6) to contemporary understandings of sexuality and power.

10 Mackenzie will invoke the same pattern in his introductory explanation of the origins of *Julia de Roubigné*. There, the manuscript is rescued from "the ordinary uses of his [the grocer's] trade" for which a young boy, accidentally encountered, has offered to sell the "bundle of papers" (i.viii).

11 Henry Mackenzie, *The Lounger* (20), June 18, 1785. In Williams, *Novel and Romance*, 328–9.

12 Frances Burney, *Evelina or The History of a Young Lady's Entrance into the World* ed. with intro. Edward A. Bloom and Lillian D. Bloom (Oxford University Press, 1968, rpt. 1991), 7.

13 James Fordyce, *The Character and Conduct of the Female Sex* (London: 1776), 48. Barker-Benfield comments that Emily Atkins "had been warmed up, in accordance with the traditional belief in the physiology of female arousal, by a combination of oral and literate culture" (*Culture of Sensibility*, 334). Paul Kaufman's analysis of the account books of the Bath Municipal Library, "the first solid evidence of the sex of patrons," reveals, however, in terms contrary to those of most commentators in the eighteenth century, that women "constituted less than thirty per cent" of the patrons. See "In Defence of Fair Readers" in *Libraries and their Users: Collected Papers in Library History* (London: The Library Association, 1969), 223, 224.

14 Susan Staves, "British Seduced Maidens," *Eighteenth-Century Studies* 14 (1980), 109–34, comments on the notable "prominence of the girl's father, who both in law and in fiction is frequently seen to be the chief victim" (110).

15 The contemporary privileging of wealth over birth is censured early in the novel in the course of the narrator's description of Harley: "Some part of his external appearance was modelled from the company of those gentlemen, whom the antiquity of a family, now possessed of bare 250l. a year, entitled its representative to approach; these indeed were not many; great part of the property in his neighbourhood being in the hands of merchants, who had got rich by the lawful calling abroad, and the sons of stewards, who had got rich by their lawful calling at home: persons so perfectly versed in the ceremonial of thousands, tens of thousands, and hundreds of thousands (whose degrees of precedency are plainly demonstrable from the first page of the Compleat Accomptant, or Young Man's best Pocket Companion) that a bow at church from them to such a man as Harley, – would have made the parson look back into his sermon for some precept of Christian humility" (9–10).

16 Henry Mackenzie, *The Man of the World. In Two Parts. The Second Edition Corrected.* (London: 1773), II.54.

17 Spacks, *Desire and Truth*, 129.

18 John Brown, *An Estimate of the Manners and Principles of the Times* (London: 1757), a2, 29, 42–3, 155. See also, *An Estimate of the Manners and Principles of the Times, Volume II* (London: 1758) and Brown's *An Explanatory Defence of the Estimate of the Manners and Principles of the Times. Being an Appendix to that Work, occasioned by the Clamours lately raised against it among certain Ranks of Men. Written by the Author of the Estimate, In a Series of Letters to a Noble Friend* (London: 1758). For the publication history of the *Estimate*, see Donald D. Eddy, *A Bibliography of John Brown* (New York: The Bibliographical Society of America, 1971). J. C. D. Clark's reading of the *Estimate* as a millenarian response to a short-lived series of military crises in the prosecution of the Seven Years War does not speak to the ways in which the cluster of ideas invoked by Brown continues to provide the organizing terms for much contemporary fiction. See *English Society 1688–1832: Ideology, Social Structure and Political Practice during the Ancien Regime* (Cambridge University Press, 1985), 307–8.

19 James Fordyce, *Sermons to Young Women, In Two Volumes. The Third Edition, Corrected* (London: 1766), 148, 273. The anonymous *Fordyce Delineated. A Satire* (London: 1767) attacks those "*Scottish–English* apes" (9) like "*Miss James*" (23) who come to London "to seek their fortunes" and stay to "laugh and sneer at their countrymen" (14). Fordyce's appeal to the "young of the fair female kind" (24) meets here with a skeptical response:

> These female sermons are so famous grown,
> That they've the fourth edition undergone;
> Their sale to fair *Londina*'s not confin'd,
> Abroad they go to form the female mind;
> To teach the fair their duty to their spouse,
> As soon as fetter'd in the marriage noose,
> Seldom to gossip, but at home abide,
> And lie, all night, pleas'd by their husband's side. (20)

The complement to Fordyce's advocacy of women's attentiveness to men appears in Thomas Gisborne's injunctions against unregulated female novel reading: "The appetite [for novels] becomes too keen to be denied; and in proportion as it is more urgent, grows less nice and select in its fare. What would formerly have given offence, now gives none. The palate is vitiated or made dull." *An Inquiry Into the Duties of the Female Sex* (London: 1797), 216–17.

20 Miss Walton might thus be seen as a vestigial narrative embodiment of *Fortuna*, a late manifestation of what J. G. A. Pocock identifies as a recurring feature in Augustan journalism: "She stands for that future which can only be sought passionately and inconstantly, and for the hysterical fluctuations of the urge towards it ... [for a] renewed feminization of time and of the process of actualization of fantasies on which – though never quite com-

pleted – the speculative society depends." See Pocock, "Modes of Political and Historical Time in Early Eighteenth-Century England" in *Virtue, Commerce, and History*, 99. John Mullan's argument, that the "domain of sensibility and sentiment in novels is constituted, in various ways, out of an opposition to a 'world' of masculine desire, commercial endeavour, and material ambition" (*Sentiment and Sociability*, 150) seems, in the context of a novel like *The Man of Feeling*, to misconstrue the contemporary understanding of masculinity. "Commercial endeavour and material ambition," as the example of the nouveau riche squire suggests, are associated with inattentiveness to tradition (especially in relation to property, as when the squire pulls down the buildings that interfere with his "prospects") and orientation to the future. Harley's imprecation, "And from his [the squire's] derogate body never spring / A babe to honour him" (96), hints moreover, in its adjustment of Goneril's gender, not only at the femininity of the squire, but also at his potential eclipsing of the values of continuity and stability. Such feminization accords with Adam Smith's account of the effects of commerce in his *Lectures*: "Another bad effect of commerce is that it sinks the courage of mankind, and tends to extinguish martial spirit . . . By having their minds constantly employed on the arts of luxury, they grow effeminate and dastardly." Quoted in Albert O. Hirschman, *The Passions and the Interests: Political Arguments for Capitalism before Its Triumph* (Princeton University Press, 1977), 106.

21 The cultural shift is nicely epitomized in Smeaton's 1764 comment, "I have heard a mighty bustle of late about securitys of our libertys and *properties*; pray sir is not the *time* and *skill* of any artist employed in design, his property, his estate . . . ?" Quoted in Margaret C. Jacob, "Scientific Culture in the Early English Enlightenment: Mechanisms, Industry, and Gentlemanly Facts" in *Anticipations of the Enlightenment in England, France, and Germany* ed. A. C. Kors and P. J. Korshin (Philadelphia: University of Pennsylvania Press 1987), 153.

22 Mackenzie, *Lounger*, 328.

23 Mackenzie himself aspired to the writing of history. As his correspondence reveals, he planned to complete Hume's *History*, projected a biography of Pitt, and read to the Royal Society in 1812 a paper on the "Life and Writings of Mr. John Home," a much longer version of which was published in 1822. See *Literature and Literati: The Literary Correspondence and Notebooks of Henry Mackenzie. Volume I. Letters 1766–1827* ed. Horst W. Drescher (Frankfurt am Main: Verlag Peter Lang, 1989), 141, 210–11, 242–4. For a discussion of *The Man of Feeling* and Scottish Enlightenment historiography, see April London, "Historiography, Pastoral, Novel: Genre in *The Man of Feeling*," *Eighteenth-Century Fiction* 10 (1997), 43–62.

24 Thomas Cogan, *John Buncle, Junior, Gentleman* (London: 1776–8), 1.145.

25 Laurence Sterne, *The Life and Opinions of Tristram Shandy* ed. Ian Campbell Ross (Oxford University Press, 1983), 71.

26 John Mullan analyses *Tristram Shandy*'s representation of the "currency of

sentimentalism" in terms of a "fellow-feeling" that transcends language and is "largely a male prerogative" (170) in *Sentiment and Sociability*.

27 John Gregory, *A Father's Legacy to his Daughters* (Edinburgh: 1821), 161.

28 Susannah Gunning's *Coombe Wood* (1783) offers a particularly explicit example of the connection between property and female identity invoked in novels from *Tom Jones* through to *Mysteries of Udolpho*. At the end of Gunning's novel, the self-sacrificing heroine, Miss Altam, is rewarded with marriage and the deed to the estate, Coombe Wood. For a brief moment, before marriage secures Lord Edwin's title to both wife and property, Miss Altam possesses Coombe Wood in her own right. That moment represents her inherent and independent virtue as most perfectly realized at the point of its eclipse; recurringly in sentimental and gothic novels women secure their titles to property only when the redefinition of the heroine through marriage is imminent. What Miss Altam experiences only briefly, of course, uncle Toby has continuously.

29 William Ray, *Story and History: Narrative Authority and Social Identity in the Eighteenth-Century French and English Novel* (Oxford: Basil Blackwell, 1990), 277.

30 While Mackenzie and Sterne define current inadequacies through emblematic representations of women who are contrasted with the masculine virtues of the past, Cogan focuses on woman as a figure of corruption without the opposing vision of a retrospective pastoralism. As quintessentially middle-class in its sentiments, Cogan's work perhaps must dispense (for ideological reasons) with the elite framework of pastoral, but the persistent gendering of decadence as female points to the ubiquity of misogynist constructs.

31 Markley's "Sentimentality as Performance" argues that paratactic structure is ideologically significant in its capacity to "undermine the fictions of socioeconomic and technological progress promoted by the Whiggish ideology of Addison, Steele, and Locke" (229). Cogan's novel also conforms to Spacks's perception in *Desire and Truth* that the novels of "Sterne, Brooke, and Mackenzie deny the effective presence of a separate shaping intelligence sufficiently single and powerful to ordain coherence. Such denial of power amounts to a denial of self understood as unified and unifying consciousness, of self as constituted by what Freud would call *ego*" (127–8). On the sentimental novel's resistance to closure, see Leo Braudy's classic "The Form of the Sentimental Novel," *Novel* 7 (1973), 5–13.

32 Clara Reeve, *The Progress of Romance Through Times, Countries, and Manners; with Remarks on the Good and Bad Effects of it, in Them Respectively; In a Course of English Conversations* (1785) (New York: Garland Publishing, 1970), II.39. Amory's novel had a long history of provoking partisan commentary. Hazlitt saw it as a Rabelaisian curiosity reminiscent of Walton's *Compleat Angler*. See "On John Buncle," *The Complete Works of William Hazlitt* ed. P. P. Howe (London and Toronto: J. M. Dent, 1932) IV.51–7. But *The Saturday Review*'s 1877 dismissal of "that queer style of stilted sentimentalism characteristic of his time, and heightened in his case by the absurdity which suggests the

disturbing influences of a disordered brain" is a more typical judgment. See *The Saturday Review of Politics, Literature, Science, and Art* (43), May 12, 1877, 585–6. The contemporary sense of the novel's generic ambivalence and its popularity are attested to by the Bristol Library Records of 1773–84. *The Life of John Buncle* is categorized under the rubric "History, Antiquities, and Geography" and was withdrawn 29 times (20 times in the period 1779–82 and 9 times between 1782 and 1784). See Paul Kaufman, *Borrowing from the Bristol Library, 1773–1784: A Unique Record of Reading Vogues* (Charlottesville: Bibliographical Society of the University of Virginia, 1960), 25.

The eccentricity of the novel depends on the numbing reiteration of the eponymous hero's encounters, in which he stumbles upon a house in the middle of a wilderness, is warmly greeted by the owner, invited to share a sumptuous meal, and asked to recount his adventures. Remarkably, his hosts are always of his rather peculiar religious persuasion (modified deism marked by violent attacks on the doctrine of the Trinity), or quickly become converts.

33 See the Earl of G–'s comment regarding his London house in Richard Cumberland's *Arundel* (London: 1789) for an interesting variation on this conventional association of the feminized city and prostitution: "compared to my hereditary residence it is but as a mistress to a lawful wife, and I shall throw it off without a sigh" (II.283). The sophistication of the connections between *John Buncle, Junior, Gentleman*, its cultural context, and its readers is especially marked when compared to more typical reworkings of an earlier influential text, such as Sophia Briscoe's crudely opportunistic *Miss Melmoth; Or, The New Clarissa* (1771).

6 COLONIAL NARRATIVES: "CHARLES WENTWORTH" AND "THE FEMALE AMERICAN"

1 Langford, *Public Life*, 530.
2 This felicitous phrase heads chapter three, "The Flight from History in Mid-Century Poetry," of John Sitter's *Literary Loneliness in Mid-Eighteenth-Century England* (Ithaca and London: Cornell University Press, 1982).
3 Locke, *Second Treatise*, 301.
4 Edward Bancroft, *An Essay on the Natural History of Guiana, in South America* (London: 1769), 326.
5 For details of his double career as spy, see Samuel Flagg Bemis, "British Secret Service and the French–American Alliance," *American Historical Review*, 29 (1924), 474–95.
6 Mary Louise Pratt, *Imperial Eyes: Travel Writing and Transculturation* (London and New York: Routledge, 1992), 4.
7 John Nicholl, "The Voyage of the *Olive Branch* (1606–7)" in *Wild Majesty: Encounters with Caribs from Columbus to the Present Day. An Anthology* ed. Peter Hulme and Neil L. Whitehead (Oxford: Clarendon Press 1992), 67.
8 D. A. G. Waddell, *The West Indies and the Guianas* (Englewood Cliffs, N.J.: Prentice-Hall, 1967), 42.
9 Raymond T. Smith, *British Guiana* (London and New York: Oxford Univer-

sity Press, 1962), 14.

10 Smith, *British Guiana*, 14 and Waddell, *The West Indies and the Guianas*, 60.

11 Edward Long, *History of Jamaica* (London: 1774), II.327. Robert C. Young, *Colonial Desire: Hybridity in Theory, Culture and Race* (London and New York: Routledge, 1995) argues that hybridity was the nineteenth century's word for "the crossing of people of different races" (6). A "key issue for cultural debate," hybridity emerges as a question in the eighteenth century and is subsequently pursued in terms that reveal how theories of race were also "covert theories of desire" (6, 9). The quotation from Long's *History* is from Young, 175.

12 Bancroft, *Natural History*, 116.

13 Ibid.

14 Virgil, *Georgics*, II.458. Bancroft amends the original of the opening line of this most famous section of the *Georgics* – '*O fortunatos nimium, sua si bona norint*' – in order, presumably, to remove the specific occupational reference ("Oh happy husbandmen! too happy, should they come to know their blessings!" Virgil, *Eclogues, Georgics, Aeneid 1–6* trans. H. R. Fairclough in Loeb Classical Library edition [Cambridge, Mass. and London: Harvard University Press, rpt. 1994]).

15 David Spurr, *The Rhetoric of Empire: Colonial Discourse in Journalism, Travel Writing, and Imperial Administration* (Durham, N.C. and London: Duke University Press, 1993), 92–3.

16 Edward Bancroft, *The History of Charles Wentworth* (1770) (New York: Garland Publishing, 1975), I.255. The theft that launches the hero into his colonial adventure thus recapitulates the terms of the *Natural History*'s representation of the colonialist as one "whom the unavoidable accidents of life, or frowns of fortune, have . . . induced to seek an asylum in distant countries" (366).

17 James Clifford, "Traveling Cultures" in *Cultural Studies* ed. with intro. Lawrence Greenberg, Cary Nelson, Paula Treichler (New York and London: Routledge, 1992), 97.

18 E. P. Thompson, 'Patrician Society, Plebian Culture," *Journal of Social History* 7 (1974), 403.

19 Anon., *The Female American; or, The Adventures of Unca Eliza Winkfield. Compiled by Herself* (1767) (New York and London: Garland Publishing, 1974), 1.2–3.

20 Sarah Osborn, *Political and Social Letters of a Lady of the Eighteenth Century. 1721–1771* ed. Emily F. D. Osborn (New York: Dodd Mead, 1891), 155, 157.

21 Annette Kolodny, *The Lay of the Land: Metaphor as Experience and History in American Life and Letters* (Chapel Hill: University of North Carolina Press 1975), 4.

PART III

INTRODUCTION

1 For historical precedents, see Kate Lilley, "Blazing Worlds: Seventeenth-Century Women's Utopian Writing" in *Women, Texts and Histories 1575–1760* ed. Clare Brant and Diane Purkiss (London and New York: Routledge, 1992), 102–33.

2 William Dodd, *An Account of the Rise, Progress and Present State of the Magdalen Hospital, For the Reception of Penitent Prostitutes. Together with Dr. Dodd's Sermons. To which are added, The Advice to the Magdalens; with the Psalms, Hymns, Prayers, Rules and Lists of Subscribers* 5th edn. (London: 1776), 15.

7 VERSIONS OF COMMUNITY: WILLIAM DODD, SARAH SCOTT, CLARA REEVE

1 For an account of the gendering of eighteenth-century philanthropic discourse and of Scott's alternative de-emphasizing of female sexuality in *Millenium Hall*, see Dorice Williams Elliott, "Sarah Scott's *Millenium Hall* and Female Philanthropy" in *Studies in English Literature* 35 (1995), 535–53. Both George Haggerty and Susan Sniader Lanser have argued that *Millenium Hall* reveals a lesbian sexuality. Lanser contrastively pairs *Millenium Hall* which she reads as an Enlightenment utopia with Mary Wollstonecraft's revolutionary dystopia, *The Wrongs of Woman; or, Maria.* The narrative compromises that make up *Millenium Hall* – the story is told by a "conventional Christian gentleman," but he relies on Mrs. Maynard for the individual histories of the inhabitants – create tensions that are underpinned by what Lanser sees as a sexual contest between indirect "signs of lesbian eroticism" and a "voyeuristic structure by which men 'penetrate' women's secrets." See Susan Sniader Lanser, *Fictions of Authority: Women Writers and Narrative Voice* (Ithaca and London: Cornell University Press, 1992), 230. For a full account of Astell's *Serious Proposal*, see Ruth Perry, *The Celebrated Mary Astell: An Early English Feminist* (Chicago and London: University of Chicago Press 1986), particularly chapter four, "England's First Feminist: *A Serious Proposal to the Ladies.*"

2 Betty Rizzo has recently argued that eighteenth-century charitable societies, in providing women with a "challenging as well as acceptable use for their talents," also testify to the greater likelihood of their meeting on social grounds rather than on aggressive (as in regiments) or judicial or governmental ones, as was characteristic of men. Betty Rizzo, *Companions Without Vows: Relationships Among Eighteenth-Century British Women* (Athens and London: University of Georgia Press 1994), 23. But as Dorice Williams Elliott contends, such philanthropic ventures as the "houses of charity" were usually "organized, supervised and managed by men ... Excluded from the leadership of these new charitable projects, women faced the potential loss of the opportunity that philanthropy had offered them – opportunity not only for useful public activity, but also for an alternative vocation to marriage." Sarah Scott's *Millenium Hall* is seen in this context as a novel which is able to construct a feminized version of male-dominated philanthropy by renouncing the sexuality of the community's inhabitants. Elliott, "Sarah Scott's *Millenium Hall* and Female Philanthropy," 536–7. For accounts of the Magdalen Hospital and of William Dodd, see Stanley Nash, "Prostitution and Charity: the Magdalen Hospital, a Case Study," *Journal of Social History* 17 (1984), 617–28; Vern L. Bullough, "Prostitution and Reform

in Eighteenth-Century England," *Eighteenth-Century Life. Special Issue. Unauthorized Sexual Behaviour during the Enlightenment* 9 (1985), 61–74; and Sarah Lloyd, "'Pleasure's Golden Bait': Prostitution, Poverty and the Magdalen Hospital in Eighteenth-Century London," *History Workshop Journal* 41 (1996), 50–70. Ann Jessie Van Sant's analysis of Magdalen House and the Philanthropic Society focuses on the rhetorical and scientific strategies that underpin the construction of philanthropic institutions in the period. Ann Jessie Van Sant, *Eighteenth-Century Sensibility and the Novel: The Senses in Social Context* (Cambridge University Press, 1993), 16–44.

3 A late eighteenth-century edition of Dodd's 1754 novel, *The Sisters*, appends an account that charts Dodd's life in terms of alternating periods of extravagance and retrenchment, taking the early 1770s as epochal: "At this period, Dr. Dodd appears to have been in the zenith of his popularity and reputation. Beloved and respected by all orders of people, he would have reached, in all probability, the situation which was the object of his wishes, had he possessed patience enough to have waited for it, and prudence sufficient to keep himself out of difficulties which might prove fatal to his integrity. But the habits of dissipation and expence had acquired too much influence over him." William Dodd, *The Sisters; Or, The History of Lucy and Caroline Sanson, Entrusted to a False Friend* (London: Cooke's Edition, 1798), v. He sent an anonymous letter to Lady Apsley, offering 3,000 pounds for the living of St. George's, Hanover Square, an act which resulted in his name being struck from the order of chaplains: "The press teemed with satire and invective; he was abused and ridiculed in the papers of the day; and, to crown the whole, the transaction became a subject of entertainment in one of Mr. Foot's pieces at the Hay-market." Dodd subsequently forged a bond for 4,200 pounds for which he was committed to prison, tried in February 1777, and executed in June of that year, after the failure of appeals for clemency by, among others, Samuel Johnson.

4 Dodd, *Magdalen Hospital*, 52–3, 86–7, 218–19.

5 *The Sisters* represents these habits of industry as both a preventive and (if necessary) a corrective to false dreams of female independence and financial success. The novel charts the disastrous consequences of paternal aspiration in relation to two daughters who are encouraged to believe that their fortunes can be easily made in London. Mr. Sanson's "one great foible ... was family pride ... he could not bear the reflection of placing a son to a mechanic trade, or giving a daughter any notions of those branches of business, by which an industrious young woman may support herself with credit." His failure to school his daughters in acceptance of their lot is compounded by the effects of reading – "the young girls grew vain, foolish, and affected; Cassandra, Cleopatra, Heywood's novels, and above all, the works of the inimitable Fielding, with a thousand more romantic books of the same kind (wherewith the present age so happily abounds) were the constant employment of their days." Their London encounters lead the one to prostitution and disease, the other to an unhappy penitence. Dodd, *The*

Sisters, 7–8.

6 For a discussion of the ideological implications of conduct-book literature with reference specifically to John Fordyce and Hannah More, see Kathryn Kirkpatrick, "Sermons and Strictures: Conduct-Book Propriety and Property Relations in Late Eighteenth-Century England" in *History, Gender and Eighteenth-Century Literature* ed. Beth Fowkes Tobin (Athens and London: University of Georgia Press 1994), 198–226. For a more generalized discussion of propriety, see Mary Poovey, *The Proper Lady and the Woman Writer: Ideology as Style in the Works of Mary Wollstonecraft, Mary Shelley, and Jane Austen* (Chicago and London: University of Chicago Press 1984). In *A Vindication of the Rights of Woman*, Mary Wollstonecraft attacks Magdalen Houses as a symptom of (rather than solution to) patriarchal corruption. The "state of idleness in which women are educated, who are always taught to look up to man for a maintenance, and to consider their persons as the proper return for his exertions to support them," she writes, combined with the absence of "other means of support" than prostitution for women when once "fallen," are the evils that need attention. "Asylums and Magdalens are not the proper remedies for these abuses. It is justice, not charity, that is wanting in the world!" Mary Wollstonecraft, *Political Writings* ed. Janet Todd (Oxford: World's Classics, 1994), 143.

7 Sarah Scott, *Journey Through Every Stage of Life, Described in a Variety of Interesting Scenes, Drawn from Real Characters. By a Person of Quality* (London: 1754), 1.4.

8 The recognition that romantic love often serves as a mask for the presumptive exercise of power in marriage becomes central to the debunking of sensibility in conservative novels of the 1790s. Richard Dudley thus warns his credulous daughter in Jane West's *A Gossip's Story*: "'Have you observed so little of real life as not to perceive, that the kind of [romantick] address you talk of, is chiefly practised by the designing part of mankind, upon the woman whose person or fortune is the object of their desire? You must know that marriage divests you of all this assumed consequence. Law and custom leave the husband master of his own actions, and in a certain degree arbiter of his wife's. Whether your lover was a sentimental sniveller, or an artful designer, the mock majesty with which you were invested, could not continue in the married state'." *A Gossip's Story, and a Legendary Tale* (New York: Garland Publishing, 1974), 1.95–6. In the same vein, Hannah More urges that men avoid choosing a wife from assemblies and ballrooms since such a wife will continue to desire display "just as if she were not become private property, and had never been definitively disposed of." Hannah More, *Strictures on the Modern System of Female Education* (1799) (New York: Garland Publishing, 1974), 11.163.

9 Ruth Perry, "Bluestockings in Utopia" in *History, Gender and Eighteenth-Century Literature* ed. Beth Fowkes Tobin (Athens and London: University of Georgia Press 1994), 167.

10 Both George Cumberland's *The Captive of the Castle of Sennaar. Part II. The Reformed* and Mary Wollstonecraft's *Mary, A Fiction* offer late eighteenth-

century versions of the idea of community explored in *Millenium Hall*, the former, utopian, the latter, sentimental. Like Sir George Ellison in the pendant volume to *Millenium Hall*, *The History of Sir George Ellison*, Cumberland's narrator, Memmo, realizes the principles of the alternative society he encounters in Africa by establishing on the estate he builds in Italy factories, schools, and libraries. See George Cumberland, *The Captive of the Castle of Sennaar* ed. G. E. Bentley Jr. (Montreal and Kingston: McGill–Queen's University Press, 1991), 275–96. In Wollstonecraft's novel, the long-suffering heroine's activities contrast with the restrictive emotional life she endures as a consequence of her unhappy marriage. At novel's end, she "visited the continent, and sought health in different climates; but her nerves were not to be restored to their former state. She then retired to her house in the country, established maunfactories, threw the estate into small farms; and continually employed herself this way to dissipate care, and banish unavailing regret." See Mary Wollstonecraft, *"Mary" and "The Wrongs of Woman"* ed. Gary Kelly (Oxford University Press, 1980), 67.

11 For a wide-ranging discussion of the colonial motif in women's writing, see Moira Ferguson, *Subject to Others:. British Women Writers and Colonial Slavery, 1670–1834* (New York and London: Routledge, 1992).

12 Sarah Scott, *A Description of Millenium Hall* ed. Gary Kelly (Peterborough, Ont.: Broadview Press, 1995), 53. While Lamont is named in *Millenium Hall*, the identity of the narrator, Sir George Ellison, is revealed only in the sequel, *The History of Sir George Ellison*.

13 While, as Ruth Perry notes, the title of the novel "convey[s] in [its] very name the feudal manorial ideal" on which the novel is based, it is significant that this name is provided by the male narrator and through his generic reading of the estate linked to a pastoral order that is imagined as existing apart from history. As with other women-authored utopias, Perry notes, *Millenium Hall* defends "women's capacity for art and learning and for the production of culture," activities, as we saw in *Clarissa*, generically allied with georgic. ("Bluestockings in Utopia," 159, 161.)

14 As Mrs. Morgan comments, "The care of our virtue we owe to ourselves, the preservation of our characters is due to the world, and both are required by Him, who commands us to preserve ourselves pure and unpolluted, and to contribute as far as we are able to the well-being of all his creatures. Example is the means given universally to all whereby to benefit society" (125).

15 James Cruise, "A House Divided: Sarah Scott's *Millenium Hall*," *Studies in English Literature* 35 (1995), 556. Cruise goes on to detail the connections between the women's utopian order and the four-fold stadial model of civil progress endorsed by Scottish Enlightenment thinkers. For discussion of the imperial theme in the novel, see chapter six, "Feminotopias: the Seraglio, the Homoerotic, and the Pleasures of 'Deformity'," of Felicity Nussbaum's *Torrid Zones: Maternity, Sexuality, and Empire in Eighteenth-Century English Narratives* (Baltimore and London: Johns Hopkins University Press,

1995), 135–62.

16 Mrs. Morgan provides the men with an object lesson in the distinction between the apparent and the real when she stops the tour "in one spot, saying, "from hence, as Lady Mary observed, you may behold our riches, that building, (pointing to what we thought a pretty temple) which perhaps you imagine designed only for ornament or pleasure, is a very large pidgeon house, that affords a sufficient supply to our family, and many of our neighbours. That hill on your right-hand is a warren, prodigiously stocked with rabbits; this canal, and these other pieces of water, as well as the river you saw this morning, furnish our table with a great profusion of fish. You will easily believe from the great number of deer you see around us, that we have as much venison as we can use, either in presents to our friends, or our own family. Hares, and all sorts of game likewise abound here; so that with the help of a good dairy, no situation ever more amply afforded all the necessaries of life. These are, indeed, our riches; here we have almost everything we can want, for a very small proportion of that expense which others are at to procure them'" (110). The attention to the aesthetic dimension of georgic is evident here, as throughout the novel, in the women's equal commitment to beauty and utility.

17 For an analysis of this process of negation in eighteenth-century painting, see John Barrell, *The Dark Side of the Landscape: The Rural Poor in English Painting 1730–1840* (Cambridge University Press, 1980) and Ann Bermingham, *Landscape and Ideology: The English Rustic Tradition, 1740–1860* (Los Angeles: University of California Press 1986).

18 For a reading of *Millenium Hall* as the most fully realized representation of the eighteenth-century "ideal of a feminized and intimate conversational community" (88), see "Authorizing the Marginalized Circle in Sarah Scott's *Millenium Hall*," chapter six of Betty A. Schellenberg, *The Conversational Circle: Re-Reading the English Novel, 1740–1775* (Lexington: University Press of Kentucky, 1996), 88–101. Leland E. Warren has a number of interesting discussions of conversation within the period including, "The Conscious Speakers: Sensibility and the Art of Conversation Considered" in *Sensibility in Transformation: Creative Resistance to Sentiment from the Augustans to the Romantics* ed. Syndy M. Conger (Rutherford, N.J.: Farleigh Dickinson University Press, 1990), 25–42, and "'Turning Reality Round Together': Guides to Conversation in Eighteenth-Century England," *Eighteenth-Century Life* 8 (1983), 65–85.

19 In Scott's pendant piece to *Millenium Hall, The History of Sir George Ellison* (1766), this vision of separate spheres is subjected to the scrutiny of two different but finally complementary male perspectives: Lamont's overtly misogynistic and Ellison's paternalistic, which together are dedicated to undercutting the notion of women's authority. They suggest that within a propertied economy, women's capacity for self-making is necessarily restricted, an insight that Clara Reeve's *The School for Widows* (1791) will indirectly confirm in her novel's association of women's independence with

"*bourgeois* habits." The degree of attention Scott dedicates to specifying Lamont and Ellison's arguments, however, testifies to her sense of their authoritative status. A brief rehearsal of these arguments will help to position both Clara Reeve's countervailing "bourgeois" stance and the one defined by notions of confederacy which will be considered in chapter 8.

In *The History of Sir George Ellison*, Lamont overcomes the mortification provoked by the encounter with the women of Millenium Hall by arguing that their accomplishments are not appropriate for a man, "who, formed with more extensive capacity, deeper penetration, and more exalted courage, was designed to govern the world, to regulate the affairs of kingdoms, and penetrate into the most mysterious arts of human policy." (Sarah Scott, *The History of Sir George Ellison* ed. Betty Rizzo [Lexington: University Press of Kentucky, 1996], 40–1.) The greater power of men, as the imperfectly veiled sexual allusions confirm, derives from their "deeper penetration," a capacity linked to the sustained exercise of political authority. George Ellison's response to this special pleading neatly sidesteps the issue of different capacities by focusing instead on the deflation of Lamont's vision of male potential. In order to do so, he counters his friend's gendered analysis with one that purports to be historically authentic, invoking the terms of political economy to argue that the emergence of "political institutions" hampered the free development and articulation of individual capacity: "'When in regard to property,' (said he) 'all men were in a state of equality, a superiority of parts and courage were sufficient to raise a man to power and command; but since nature's Agrarian law has been abolished by political institutions, few men have a chance of filling those important offices you seem to think the property of all. Poverty is an impenetrable cloud, which will conceal the greatest merit from the rest of mankind; rank and fortune are such steps to honour, that it is difficult for a man to climb to any height who is not possessed of them: Some degree of one, or both, is absolutely necessary to bring the highest talents into such a light as can render them conspicuous...'" (41). Central to the logic of this position is a metaphorical and literal reading of property relations which will ultimately be used to redefine social responsibilities. When there was no private property, Ellison suggests in an echo of Adam Ferguson, those inner properties (superiority of parts and courage) unique to each individual determined his access to authority. Now private property intercedes between desire and completion, functioning as a barrier to those who possess only intrinsic merit. The novel's ending implicitly advocates that this rift between virtue and authority be addressed by a reversion to an older, almost feudal, sense of community. Sir George acts on his belief in "marriage as a state commanded by God, and very useful to the community; he respected it therefore both on religious and political motives" (202). In the patriarchal order he and his wife establish on their estate, their regulatory control is secured through a division of duties: Sir George attends to the economic life of the community, Lady Ellison to its standards of dress and behavior.

20 For a detailed account of the middle-class idiom in the 1790s, see Dror Wahrman, *Imagining the Middle Class: The Political Representation of Class in Britain, c.1780–1840* (Cambridge University Press, 1995).

21 Clara Reeve, *The School for Widows* (Dublin: 1791), I.38.

22 This pattern of male oppression as a spur to female friendship had long served as a premise for novelistic plots. See for example, Eliza Haywood's *The British Recluse* (1722) where two women meet accidentally, discover they've been seduced by the same man and resolve to retire and live together in peace, and Charlotte Smith's *Emmeline* (1788), in which Lady Adeline and Mrs. Stafford are united by their victimization and consequent nurturing of each other.

23 In its focus on the origins of a community which will make the domestic and economic reciprocal, *The School for Widows* complicates Nancy Armstrong's supposition that eighteenth-century conduct books and educational treat- ises for women "portrayed aristocratic women along with those who har- bored aristocratic pretensions as the very embodiments of corrupted desire, namely, desire that sought its gratification in economic and political terms. The books all took care to explain how this form of desire destroyed the very virtues essential to a wife and mother... [They] severed the language of kinship from that of political relations, producing a culture divided into the respective domains of domestic woman and economic man." See *Desire and Domestic Fiction*, 60.

24 For an account of the taint attaching to epistolary narrative in the 1790s, see Nicola J. Watson, *Revolution and the Form of the British Novel, 1790–1825: Intercepted Letters, Interrupted Seductions* (Oxford: Clarendon Press 1994).

8 CONFEDERACIES OF WOMEN: PHEBE GIBBES AND JOHN TRUSLER

1 Clara Reeve, *Plans of Education; with Remarks on the Systems of Other Writers In a Series of Letters Between Mrs. Darnford and Her Friends* (London: 1792), 19, 2.

2 Phebe Gibbes, *The Life and Adventures of Mr. Francis Clive* (1764) (New York: Garland Publishing, 1974), I.111.

3 Janet Todd discusses the ways in which female gesture operates in the contemporary novel as a "potent fantasy" of the authority exerted by "displays of femininity"; Mrs. Smith is clearly attuned to the convention and able to manipulate it for her own material ends. See *The Sign of Angellica*, 185.

4 This concluding emphasis on the child serves to displace attention from the woman as agent of the narrative's resolution. Charlotte Lennox's *Euphemia* (1790) will offer a similar implicit defense of what the novel wants finally to represent as untoward female activity by casting it as maternal in origin. On occasion, as in Charlotte Palmer's *It Is and It Is Not a Novel* (1792), the trope is applied to authorship: "my ultimate wish will be fulfilled, if those who have the honour to support the maternal character, with exemplary prudence and virtue, should permit it [the novel] to be placed in the hands of their daughters" (I.ix). For a more sinister version of the mother's plot, see Mary

Hays's *The Victim of Prejudice* (1799).

5 The intriguing parallel between the female picaro and authorship can also be seen in Charlotte Charke's *A Narrative of the Life of Mrs. Charlotte Charke (Youngest Daughter of COLLEY CIBBER, Esq;) Written by HERSELF* London: 1755. Charke's summary of her life before she commences author involves forays "into men's cloaths": "being Gentleman to a certain Peer; after my Dismission, becoming *only an Occasional Player*, while I was playing at *Bo-peep with the World*. My turning Pork-Merchant; broke, through the inhuman Appetite of a hungry Dog. Went a Strolling... My Return, and setting up an Eating-House in *Drury-Lane*; undone again, by pilfering Lodgers. Turning Drawer, at St. *Mary-la-Bonne*... Going a Strolling a second Time, and staying near nine Years... Hired myself to a Printer at *Bristol*, to write and correct the Press. Made a short Stay there. Vagabondized again, and last *Christmas* returned to *London*, where I hope to remain as long as I live" (273–74). Quoted in Turner, *Living by the Pen*, 81.

6 For analyses of cross-dressing in eighteenth-century literature, see Diane Dugaw, *Warrior Women and Popular Balladry, 1650–1850* (Cambridge University Press, 1989) and Madeline Kahn, *Narrative Transvestitism: Rhetoric and Gender in the Eighteenth-Century English Novel* (Ithaca and London: Cornell University Press, 1991). Cross-dressing as an admissible release from conventional female behavior (especially tolerated when temporary and followed by martyrdom) is also found in S. J. Pratt's *Emma Corbett; or, The Miseries of Civil War. Founded on Some Recent Circumstances Which Happened in America* (London: 1780). The eponymous heroine pleads without success that she be allowed to marry her lover despite the opposition between his politics and those of her father. The constancy of female tenderness, she asserts, transcends political division. When her father disdains her sensibility as "romance," she decamps to America dressed as a boy and there effects a further transformation by staining her face with berries in order to search Indian territory for her beloved Henry Hammond. He is discovered pierced with an arrow which she "extracted... and sucked the wound... applied to it her lovely lips without hesitation" (257–8). They are married only to discover six months later that the arrow was poisoned. Henry dies of grief and Emma survives only long enough to bear their child and return to England. "I am childless" her father declares over her corpse: "Behold what CIVIL WAR has done for me" (298).

7 Blake to George Cumberland (August 26, 1799) in *The Letters of William Blake. With Related Documents* ed. Geoffrey Keynes 3rd edn. (Oxford: Clarendon Press 1980), 10–11. See also Ruthven Todd, "The Rev. Dr. John Trusler," *Blake Newsletter* 23 (1972–3), 71.

8 John Trusler, *Life; or, The Adventures of William Ramble, Esq.* (London: 1793), 1.3–4.

9 [John Trusler] *Modern Times, Or, The Adventures of Gabriel Outcast. Supposed to be Written By Himself in Imitation of Gil Blas* 3rd edn. (London: 1786), 1.2.

10 Paulson, *Breaking and Remaking*, 251.

11 John Trusler, *Life; or The Adventures of William Ramble, Esq.* 1.61–2.
12 For an account of the complicated, and shifting, meanings attaching to
   "middle-class consciousness" in the 1790s (interpreted as an outgrowth of
   the nation's changing political responses to the French Revolution) see Dror
   Wahrman's *Imagining the Middle Class.*
13 Despite their significant differences, conservatives such as Robert Bisset and
   Elizabeth Hamilton consistently revert to this critique of radicalism: like
   Trusler, they maintain that republicans don't want a better system; they
   want a system in which their narrow understanding of personal betterment
   will prevail over the good of the state as a whole (a good the conservatives
   insist can only be achieved through the rule of the privileged).
14 The contradictory statements which are produced by this stance are much
   in evidence in Trusler's earlier *The Way to be Rich and Respectable* (1775). After
   decrying the advance of luxury and the "effeminacy" it produces, Trusler
   details the means by which a family can "make an appearance equal to
   1,000l. a year, for half the money..." John Trusler, *The Way to Be Rich and
   Respectable, Addressed to Men of Small Fortune* (London: no date) [1775], 14.
15 Edmund Burke, *Reflections on the Revolution in France* ed. Conor Cruise
   O'Brien (Harmondsworth: Penguin, 1969), 171.

PART IV
INTRODUCTION

1 Robert Bisset, *Sketch of Democracy* (London: 1796), 349.
2 Robert Bisset, *Douglas: or, The Highlander* (London: 1800), III.34.
3 Anon. *Dorothea: Or A Ray of the New Light* (London: 1801), I.1.

9 THE DISCOURSE OF MANLINESS: SAMUEL JACKSON PRATT AND
ROBERT BAGE

1 [Samuel Jackson Pratt], *Shenstone-Green; or, The New Paradise Lost. Being a
   History of Human Nature. In Three Volumes. Written by the Proprietor of the Green. The
   Editor Courtney Melmoth* (London: 1779), I.3. For an account of sentimental
   reading and its implications for historiography, see Mark Salber Phillips,
   "'If Mrs. Mure Be Not Sorry for Poor King Charles': History, the Novel,
   and the Sentimental Reader," *History Workshop Journal* 43 (1977), 111–31.
2 Ruth Perry, "Bluestockings in Utopia" in *History, Gender and Eighteenth-
   Century Literature*, 166.
3 [Samuel Jackson Pratt], *Liberal Opinions upon Animals, Man, and Providence*
   (London: 1775–6), II.64.
4 For an account of the effect of the economic downturn on the book trade,
   see Raven, *Judging New Wealth*, especially pp. 19–41, "Publishing Profiles."
5 Robert Bage, *Man As He Is* (1792) (New York and London: Garland Publishing, 1979), 1.30.
6 Kramnick's *Republicanism and Bourgeois Radicalism* and Raven's *Judging New
   Wealth* dispute the claims of Thompson, Perkins, Neale, and Clark that

there was no distinctive bourgeois culture in eighteenth-century Britain.

7 Anna Laetitia Barbauld, *The Works of Anna Laetitia Barbauld* (London: 1825), "An Address to the Opposers of the Repeal of the Corporation and Test Acts" (1790), II.369.

8 Helen Maria Williams, *Julia, A Novel; Interspersed with some Poetical Pieces* (1790) (New York: Garland Publishing, 1974), I.172. The seemingly obligatory reference to middle-class virtue was often complicated by casting its representatives as highly born. Lady Mary Walker's *Letters from the Duchess of Crui* (London: 1776) thus argues (in an interesting amendment of Shaftesburian civic humanism) that "the *flippante* of both sexes may think otherwise; but, in my opinion, real worth and companionable qualities are most generally found in middle life, where people are less actuated by ambition or necessity, or influenced by dissipation or oeconomical attention to the minutiae of their little concerns, which souring the temper, render people selfish and unsociable" (IV.138). But the ostentatious parade of titles in the novel when combined with this paean to middle-classness suggest the degree of Walker's responsiveness to her readers' desire for vicarious experience of high rank and validation of their actual status.

9 The distinction follows Gary Kelly's location of Bage's satire within the late eighteenth-century tradition of Cowper and Goldsmith whose work lacks the "animus" that typifies Augustan or French Enlightenment writers. For an account of Bage's background and his satiric methods, see Gary Kelly, *The English Jacobin Novel 1780–1805* (Oxford: Clarendon Press 1976), 20–3, 26.

10 Robert Bage, *Mount Henneth* (1782) (New York and London: Garland Publishing, 1979), I.67–8. While acknowledging Steeves's dating of the novel to 1782 (*Notes and Queries* [ccx, Jan. 1965]), Kelly suggests a date of 1781 in *English Jacobin Novel*, 25.

11 Kelly suggests that in the absence of a class vocabulary Bage "phrases his argument in familiar eighteenth-century moral–philosophical terms rather than social or economic ones." *English Jacobin Novel*, 35.

12 In *Barham Downs* (1784) (London and New York: Garland Publishing, 1979) Bage's "boldness" is repeated. The Kitty Ross sub-plot gains additional interest from its multiple contraventions of novelistic protocols: the plebeian Kitty Ross, seduced and abandoned by the Hon. Mr. Corrane, becomes the virtuous, wealthy wife of an honest lawyer; the novel's Quaker is neither sly nor lascivious, but rather persistently loyal to his ideals; the seducer ultimately confesses the error of his ways and makes what restitution he can.

13 In "Bluestockings in Utopia," Ruth Perry couples *Millenium Hall* with Lady Mary Hamilton's *Munster Village*, and *Shenstone-Green* with *Mount Henneth* to argue for the differences between male- and female-authored utopias. While representations of class and colonial power form part of the matrix that substantiate these differences, attitudes to gender, she argues, are key to "determining how radical the utopian vision actually is" (176).

14 Robert Bage, *Man As He Is* (1792) 1.30,29. *The Monthly Review* draws on the

same vocabulary for its praise of *Mount Henneth*: "Its sentiments are liberal and manly, the tendency of it is perfectly moral; for its whole design is to infuse into the heart, by the most engaging examples, the principles of honour and truth, social love, and general benevolence." 1st series (Feb. 1782), 130.

15 Robert Bage, *Hermsprong, or, Man As He Is Not* (1796) (New York and London: Garland Publishing, 1979), 1.3.

16 *Oxford English Dictionary*. And according to Johnson's *Dictionary*: "A restitution of one that hath two titles to lands or tenements, and is seized of them by his latter title, under the title that is more ancient, in case where the latter is defective."

17 Thomas Holcroft, *Anna St. Ives* ed. with intro. Peter Faulkner (London: Oxford University Press, 1970), 172.

18 See H. T. Dickinson, *Liberty and Property: Political Ideology in Eighteenth-Century Britain* (London: Methuen, 1977), 232–69. Richard Polewhele, *The Unsex'd Females; A Poem, addressed to the author of The Pursuits of Literature* (London: 1800), 7.

19 Gary Kelly suggests that in *Anna St. Ives* Holcroft in fact "anticipated all the major precepts which Godwin was to teach in his philosophical *Enquiry Concerning Political Justice,* published exactly a year and a week later." *English Jacobin Novel,* 117.

20 Spacks has written eloquently in *Desire and Truth* of the principle of "energy of mind" which seems to her to displace the emphasis on power that shaped plot before the 1790s. While Jacobin novels do "imply a new view of gender relations" (184), their inability to shake free of the constraints of the narrow view of female agency imposed by the associations of women with property (despite their avowed hostility to conventional property relations) is what particularly interests me here.

10 THE GENDERING OF RADICAL REPRESENTATIOON

1 *Monthly Review* 2nd series x (March 1793), 297.

2 [Thomas Holcroft], review of *The Castle of St. Vallery* in *Monthly Review* 2nd series ix (November 1792), 337.

3 Chris Jones's *Radical Sensibility: Literature and Ideas in the 1790s* (London and New York: Routledge, 1993) argues that the common focus for radical and conservative novelists of the 1790s was the contest over the meaning and implications of sensibility.

4 William Hazlitt, *Memoirs of the late Thomas Holcroft,* iii. 133.

5 The passage could also be read as a vindication of the novel, whose efficacy as an agent of opinion is in part a function of its freedom from the strictures of inherited genres. As Godwin suggests in *Political Justice,* a "revolution of opinions is the only means of attaining to [the] inestimable benefit" of "equality of conditions"; the novel was particularly well placed to effect such a revolution. See William Godwin, *Enquiry Concerning Political Justice and its Influence on Modern Morals and Happiness* ed. Isaac Kramnick (Harmonds-

worth: Pelican Books, 1976), 716.

6 Mary Wollstonecraft, *Vindication of the Rights of Woman* in *Political Writings*, 84.

7 Burke, *Reflections*, 125.

8 Luce Irigaray, "Women on the Market" in *This Sex Which Is Not One* trans. Catherine Porter with Carolyn Burke (Ithaca: Cornell University Press, 1985), 171.

9 Hazlitt, *Memoirs*, III.129.

10 The ambivalence of "want" in this context – it could refer equally to desire or its lack – emphasizes Anna's exclusion from the full range of meanings that will be developed in the exchange between Coke and Frank that follows her comment.

11 As works such as Mary Hays's *Victim of Prejudice* confirm, the unacknowledged constraints that novelistic conventions (especially sentimental ones) impose on fictional representations of the radical programme also shape the writing of avowedly feminist authors.

12 Kelly, *English Jacobin Novel*, 145. See also Marilyn Butler's comments on *Hugh Trevor*'s indebtedness to the picaresque tradition, especially the version developed by Smollett, in *Jane Austen and the War of Ideas* (Oxford: Clarendon Press 1975, rpt. 1987), 46–9.

13 Thomas Holcroft, *The Adventures of Hugh Trevor* ed. Seamus Deans (Oxford University Press, 1978), 127.

14 [William Enfield] *Monthly Review* 2nd series 23 (1797), 281–2.

11 HISTORY, ROMANCE, AND THE ANTI-JACOBINS' "COMMON SENSE"

1 George Walker, *The Vagabond* (London: 1799), I.vi–vii.

2 Linda Colley, citing Mark Harrison, argues for the consideration of loyalist as well as dissident popular demonstrations as evidence of the "dramatic rise in the number of Britons and also the kinds of Britons who were getting involved in public politics." See *Britons: Forging the Nation, 1707–1837* (New Haven and London: Yale University Press, 1992), 228.

3 Thomas Paine, *Rights of Man* ed. with intro. Henry Collins (Harmondsworth: Pelican Books, 1979), 181.

4 Godwin, *Enquiry Concerning Political Justice*, 148–9.

5 Godwin's previously unpublished essay, "Of History and Romance" appears as Appendix IV in William Godwin, *Things As They Are, or, The Adventures of Caleb Williams* ed. Maurice Hindle (London: Penguin, 1988), 359–73.

6 Thomas Mathias, *Pursuits of Literature. A Satirical Poem, In Four Dialogues with notes* (London: 1800), 16. The quote is from Dialogue One, published in 1794. David Bindman notes that before 1794 the radical London Corresponding Society and the Society for Constitutional Information relied on verbal rather than visual means of persuasion, feeling perhaps that "caricature would have harmed their image of seriousness and respectability." After the Treason Trials of 1794, this changes and there emerges "a

distinctive and more obviously popular iconography, deriving from the language used by such pamphleteers as Daniel Eaton and Thomas Spence." See "Introduction" to *The Shadow of the Guillotine: Britain and the French Revolution* (London: British Museum Publications, 1989), 54, 56. The conservatives, in contrast, made full use of visual satire from the beginning of the revolutionary period.

7 Quoted in Emily Lorraine de Montluzin, *The Anti-Jacobins 1798–1800: The Early Contributors to the "Anti-Jacobin Review"* (London: Macmillan Press 1988), 2. Thomas Mathias elaborates on the figure in his *Pursuits of Literature*: "We must indeed be sensible, that it is *now* no longer a mere sport of the pen, a light skirmish, or a random shaft, the Apollineae *bellum puerile* pharetrae, which is *alone* demanded; but our weapons must be instruments of war, able to break down the strongholds of anarchy, impiety and rebellion, and mighty to vindicate the powers of legitimate authority. In every region of Europe there should have been a common cause. But in no kingdom, except Great Britain, has that cause been maintained in *full integrity*. While I am writing, we are convulsed to our centre; and yet in the midst of fear, we are impudently and wickedly told, there is no cause of alarm . . .

We may (for we can) all of us contribute to the assistance, and the comfort, and the good of others and to the stability of social happiness. The sword, the voice and the pen must be resolutely and decisively called into action, for defence, for counsel, for admonition, and for censure" (42–3).

8 [William Beckford], *Azemia, A Novel: Containing Imitations of the Manner, Both in Prose and Verse, of Many of the Authors of the Present Day; With Political Strictures. By J. A. M. Jenks. In Two Volumes. The Second Edition* (London: 1798, 2nd edn.), I.90–1.

9 David C. Streatfield, *Art and Nature in the English Landscape Garden: Design Theory and Practice, 1700–1818* in *Landscape in the Gardens and Literature of Eighteenth-Century England* (Los Angeles: William Andrews Clark Memorial Library, 1981), 67. See also chapter 5, "Sense and Sensibility in the Landscape Designs of Humphry Repton" in John Dixon Hunt, *Gardens and the Picturesque: Studies in the History of Landscape Architecture* (Cambridge, Mass. and London: MIT Press 1992), 139–68. Repton continues to figure satirically in nineteenth-century fiction, appearing as Marmaduke Milestone in Peacock's *Headlong Hall*.

10 Robert Bisset, *Douglas; Or, The Highlander* (London: 1800), III.33.

11 See Gerald Newman, *The Rise of English Nationalism: A Cultural History, 1740–1830* (New York: St. Martin's Press, 1987) and Linda Colley, *Britons*, for the contributions of the unifying terms of nationalism and patriotism to the definition of a coherent public sphere. Wildcodger, of course, illustrates their thesis with his declaration that the "great and patriotic sentiment of rejoicing in the prosperity of their country" will encourage the poor not to repine at their own privations. For the contemporary response to the increase in taxation, see Dror Wahrman, *Imagining the Middle Class*.

12 Dickinson, *Liberty and Property*, 292.

13 Quoted in Dickinson, *Liberty and Property*, 306.
14 David Bindman, "Introduction" to *The Shadow of the Guillotine*, 27. See also Marcus Wood, *Radical Satire and Print Culture, 1790–1822* (Oxford: Clarendon Press 1994) and Jeffrey Cox, "Ideology and Genre in the British Anti-revolutionary Drama of the 1790s," *ELH* 58 (1991), 579–610.
15 Robert Bisset, *Douglas; Or, The Highlander*, III.35; Elizabeth Hamilton, *Memoirs of Modern Philosophers*, III.164; George Walker, *The Vagabond*, I.x.
16 Paine, *Rights of Man*, 207.
17 Quoted in Dickinson, *Liberty and Property*, 201. Although the supposed time scheme of *The Vagabond* – references to the Gordon Riots and the ending of hostilities with America suggest the early 1780s – complicates the identification of Alogos with Priestley, Alogos' house, like Priestley's, is burned by a mob "amidst shouts of liberty and equality" (II.100), after which he emigrates to Philadelphia.
18 Godwin, *Enquiry*, 89.
19 For an analysis of those who regarded the French Revolution not as unprecedented, but as part of a distinctive "typology of revolution" (9), see Marilyn Butler, "Revolving in Deep Time: the French Revolution as Narrative" in *Revolution and English Romanticism: Politics and Rhetoric* ed. Keith Hanley and Raman Selden (Hassocks: Harvester Wheatsheaf; New York: St. Martin's Press 1990), 1–22.
20 Cox, "Ideology and Genre," 584.
21 The cluster of ideas invoked by Walker recur in Anna Seward's letter to Samuel Johnson on the subject of Knight's poem *The Landscape*: "Knight's system appears to me the Jacobinism of taste ... Mr. Knight would have nature as well as man indulged in that uncurbed and wild luxuriance, which must soon render our landscape-island rank, weedy, damp, and unwholesome as the incultivate savannas of America ... save me, good Heaven, from living in tangled forests and amongst men who are unchecked by those guardian laws, which bind the various orders of society in one common interest. May the lawns I tread be smoothed by healthful industry, and the glades opened by the hands of picturesque taste, to admit the pure and salutary breath of heaven! – and may the people, amongst whom I live, be withheld by stronger repellants than their own virtue, from invading my property and shedding my blood!! – and so much for politics and pleasure grounds." Quoted in Tom Williamson and Liz Bellamy, *Property and Landscape: A Social History of Land Ownership and the English Countryside* (London: George Philip, 1987), 154.
22 *Oxford English Dictionary*.
23 The anonymous *Berkeley Hall: Or, The Pupil of Experience* (1796) makes similar comic capital out of George Berkeley's immaterialist philosophy.
24 One of the ironies that attaches to this change in the representation of Laura (from verbal to visual, from moral center to marginal wife) involves the parallel between it and the ending of Thomas Holcroft's *Anna St. Ives*. In both the radical and the conservative fiction, the final emphasis is on the

achievement of a masculine identity through conversion and through sub-ordination of female integrity.

25 *Monthly Review* 2nd series 34 (1801), 413.

1 2 JANE WEST AND THE POLITICS OF READING

1 Jane West, *A Tale of the Times* (1799) (New York and London: Garland Publishing, 1974), III.388.

2 For those unfamiliar with West's novels of the 1790s, brief plot summaries may be helpful. In *Advantages of Education*, the recently widowed and impecunious Amelia Williams settles with her daughter Maria in the neighborhood of the latter's wealthy and indulged friend, Charlotte Raby. Maria, pursued by the libertine Sir Henry Neville, recognizes, with the gentle guidance of her mother, his many faults and rejects him in favor of the worthy Edmund Herbert. Charlotte Raby, in contrast, is allowed to act on her passion for Major Pierpoint and makes a disastrous marriage. In *A Gossip's Story*, Louisa, raised by her father, Richard Dudley, possesses the solid virtues which her more flighty sister Marianne lacks as a result of sustained indulgence by her grandmother. Marianne rejects as dull the eminently virtuous Pelham in favor of the more "romantic" Lord Clermont, only to discover that sentimental excess cannot be sustained in marriage. After the death of her father, Louisa's quiet steadiness is rewarded with marriage to Pelham. In *A Tale of the Times*, the ubiquitous paired heroines are Geraldine Powerscourt, who marries the unworthy Earl of Monteith, is seduced by the Jacobin villain Fitzosborne, and dies, and Lucy Evans, whose successful marriage to Henry Powerscourt is founded on mutual esteem and abilities.

3 Jane West, *A Gossip's Story, and a Legendary Tale* (1796) (New York: Garland Publishing, 1974), I.13, 2.

4 Adam Smith, *The Theory of Moral Sentiments* ed. D. D. Raphael and A. L. Macfie (Oxford: Clarendon Press 1976), 247.

5 Jane West, *The Advantages of Education: or, The History of Maria Williams* (1793) (New York: Garland Publishing, 1974), I.3–4.

6 Todd, *Sign of Angellica*, 233. Claudia L. Johnson also locates West "among conservative novelists of Austen's generation." While she characterizes her as "the most distinguished to dramatize Burkean fictions," her emphasis is on West's "idealiz[ation of] authority per se," rather than on the ironic qualifications for which I argue. See *Jane Austen: Women Politics and the Novel* (Chicago and London: University of Chicago Press 1988), 6, 8.

7 In Virginia Blain, Isobel Grundy, Patricia Clements, (*The Feminist Companion to Literature in English: Women Writers from the Middle Ages to the Present* [New Haven and London: Yale University Press, 1990], 1151), Grundy suggests that West took the name from Charlotte McCarthy's *Letter* to the Bishop of London (?1767); Homespun is also the patronymic of the gentry exemplar in Mackenzie's *Lounger* essays.

8 [Samuel Jackson Pratt], *The Pupil of Pleasure; or, The New System Illustrated*

(London: 1776), 1.30, 1.32, 1.26.

9 The vilification of "fashion" as destructive of social distinction is consistent with reaction against the growing commercialization of English society as documented by Neil McKendrick, John Brewer, and J. H. Plumb, *The Birth of a Consumer Society: The Commercialization of Eighteenth-Century England* (Bloomington: Indiana University Press, 1982). See also Colin Campbell, *The Romantic Ethic and the Spirit of Modern Consumerism* (Oxford: Basil Blackwell, 1977) and Raven, *Judging New Wealth*.

10 See for instance, the narrator's definition of a "generous spirit," which, in the manner of Fielding's *Covent-Garden Journal* entries, is glossed as "a man, who squanders, with indiscriminating prodigality, the superflux of wealth, which he knows not properly how to bestow." Such an epithet, Prudentia adds with typical acerbity, is contingent on the person in question possessing "rank and birth" (*Advantages* II.4–5).

11 In Mary Robinson's *The Widow, or A Picture of Modern Times. A Novel in a Series of Letters* (London: 1794) Lord Woodly, a banal Lovelace, is similarly identified as pernicious through his associations with pastoral and contempt for the poor: "It is no very difficult undertaking to break the fetters of a *romantic* passion, which is only inspired by the pure air of the mountains! Cherished by the odours of enamelled meadows! and sanctioned by the pastoral simplicity of the children of *nature*! Unhappy beings! how I pity them! they are the very cart horses of creation; formed to labour for *our* use; to drag their heavy souls through a life of toil, and, when worn out in our service, to sink unnoticed to their native clod! While *we*, of higher blood, race full speed over the course of delight; the wonder of the multitude, the pride of pedigree, and the ornaments of the pleasurable scene!" (II.89–90). Again, as in West's novels, his aristocratic contempt for the poor complements his overt misogyny: "since I cannot tyrannize over my vassals, I will over the *women*; they shall at least, feel my dominion, and be subservient to my pleasures" (II.91).

12 See "Socializing Desire and Radiating the Exemplary in Samuel Richardson's *Sir Charles Grandison*" in Schellenberg, *Conversational Circle*, 51–68.

13 Patricia Meyer Spacks, *Gossip* (Chicago and London: University of Chicago Press 1986), 46.

14 Thomas MacDonald, *Thoughts on the Public Duties of Private Life with Reference to Present Circumstances and Opinions* (London: 1795), 1–2.

15 Edmund Burke, *Second Letter on a Regicide Peace* vol. IX. ed. R. B. McDowell of *The Writings and Speeches of Edmund Burke* ed. Paul Langford (Oxford: Clarendon Press 1991), 291.

16 Marilyn Butler's reading of this passage suggests that West's allusions to "domestic confidence" and "private worth" are accidental rather than integral to her meaning: ". . . her reference to the successful 'arms of France' has given the larger part of her case away. The immediate events which provoked the reaction headed in 1798 by the *Anti-Jacobin* were surely political and military rather than private or theoretical." See *Jane Austen,*

105. I argue that West's narratorial stance formally replicates and so confirms the connection of private and political, theoretical and actual. For an analysis of the Scottish moralists' engagement with the notion that private life "was the proper school of virtue" (100), see John Dwyer, *Virtuous Discourse: Sensibility and Community in Late Eighteenth-Century Scotland* (Edinburgh: John Donald, 1987).

17 J. G. A. Pocock, "The political economy of Burke's analysis of the French Revolution" in *Virtue, Commerce, and History*, 194, 209.

18 Jane West, *An Elegy on the Death of the Right Honourable Edmund Burke* (London: 1797), 15.

19 [William Beckford], *Azemia, A Novel: Containing Imitations of the Manner, Both in Prose and Verse, of Many of the Authors of the Present Day; With Political Strictures. By J. A. M. Jenks.* 2nd edn. (London: 1798), 1.64–5.

20 This division of labor according to class reveals an entirely characteristic distinction between West's adaptation of georgic and those of earlier eighteenth-century novelists. Arthur Young's *The Adventures of Emmera, Or, The Fair American* (London: 1767), for instance, typically represents the possibility of social regeneration through the active farming of both husband and wife.

21 For analysis of the paired sisters motif, see Patricia Meyer Spacks, "Sisters" in *Fetter'd or Free?: British Women Novelists, 1670–1815*, 136–151, and Eleanor Ty, "Jane West's Feminine Ideal of the 1790s" in *1650–1850: Ideas, Aesthetics, and Inquiries in the Early Modern Era* 1 (1994), 1–19.

22 This argument has a long-standing place in conservative novels, as evidenced by Fielding's comment in *Joseph Andrews* on Lady Booby's arrival in the country; she was greeted by the "Acclamations of the Poor, who were rejoiced to see their Patroness returned after so long an Absence, during which time all her Rents had been drafted to *London*, without a Shilling being spent among them, which tended not a little to their utter impoverishing." Henry Fielding, *Joseph Andrews* ed. Martin C. Battestin (Middletown, Conn.: Wesleyan University Press, 1967), 277. Prudentia aligns her writing with the "simple elegance and rational amusement" of "Addison, Goldsmith, and Fielding," which she distinguishes from the "high-sounding phrases and inconceivable wonders, signifying nothing" (*Tale* 1.164) of contemporary novelists. In her treatment of the issue of residence, however, she attends explicitly to the potential threat of the poor in ways that distinguish her from those she claims as models.

EPILOGUE

1 See Mark Salber Phillips's forthcoming *Society and Sentiment: Genres of Historical Writing in Britain, 1740–1820* for an analysis of historiography's intersections with such associated genres as biography, literary history, and memoirs.

2 For a representative discussion of issues relating to sensibility and sociability across a range of genres see John Dwyer and Richard B. Scher (eds.),

Sociability and Society in Eighteenth-Century Scotland (Edinburgh: Mercat Press, 1993).

3 An intriguing perspective on this process is afforded by a key marginal genre, conduct literature. In a representative text, the anonymous *The Polite Lady. Or, A Course of Female Education* (1760), Portia writes to her daughter Sophia that when she was young she was told by her parents "that truth was the only thing I was to expect in history, and that pleasure, delight, and entertainment, were only to be found in plays, novels, and romances." Smollett's *History of England*, however, has disproven this, "for in the perusal of his book, I received all the knowledge, information, and instruction, that could be derived from the most accurate history; and all the pleasure, delight, and entertainment, that could be expected from the most ingenious romance" (138). She later commends William Robertson's *History of Scotland* for its "taste, genius, and judgment" (142).

4 The most striking instances of this phenomenon, discussed above, are George Walker's *Vagabond* and William Godwin's essay on "History and Romance."

5 Leonore Davidoff and Catherine Hall, *Family Fortunes: Men and Women of the English Middle Class 1780–1850* (London and Chicago: University of Chicago Press 1987).

6 Walter Scott, *Waverley; Or, 'Tis Sixty Years Since* ed. Claire Lamont (Oxford University Press, 1986), 283.

7 For a discussion of Scott's adaptation of "manliness" to the legitimation of the novel, see Ina Ferris, *The Achievement of Literary Authority: Gender, History and the Waverley Novels* (Ithaca and London: Cornell University Press, 1991).

Bibliography

Anon. *Berkeley Hall: or, The Pupil of Experience* London: 1796.

Anon. *Critical Remarks on "Sir Charles Grandison," "Clarissa," and "Pamela"* (1754), Augustan Reprint Society, no. 21. Los Angeles: William Andrews Clark Memorial Library, University of California, 1950.

Anon. *Dorothea; Or, A Ray of the New Light* London: 1801.

Anon. *The Female American; or The Adventures of Unca Eliza Winkfield. Compiled by herself* (1767) New York and London: Garland Publishing, 1974.

Anon. *Fordyce Delineated. A Satire* London: 1767.

Anon. *Henry Willoughby. A Novel* London: 1798.

Anon. *The Polite Lady. Or, A Course of Female Education* London: 1760.

Alexander, William. *The History of Women, From the Earliest Antiquity, to the Present Time; Giving Some Account of almost every interesting Particular concerning the Sex, among all Nations, ancient and modern* London: 1779.

Amory, Thomas. *The Life of John Buncle, Esq; Containing Various Observations and Reflections, Made in several Parts of the World, and Many Extraordinary Relations* London: 1766.

Anderson, Patricia. *The Printed Image and the Transformation of Popular Culture, 1790–1860* Oxford: Clarendon Press, 1991.

Appleby, Joyce Oldham. *Economic Thought and Ideology in Seventeenth-Century England* Princeton University Press, 1978.

Liberalism and Republicanism in the Historical Imagination Cambridge, Mass.: Harvard University Press, 1992.

Armstrong, Nancy. *Desire and Domestic Fiction: A Political History of the Novel* Oxford University Press, 1987.

Bacon, Francis. *The Advancement of Learning and New Atalantis* intro. Thomas Case. London: Oxford University Press, 1957, rpt. 1974.

Philosophical Works of Francis Bacon, ... Methodiz'd, and made English, from the Originals with Occasional Notes, to explain what is obscure. In Three Volumes ed. Peter Shaw. London: 1733.

Bage, Robert. *Barham Downs* (1784) New York and London: Garland Publishing, 1979.

The Fair Syrian (1787) New York and London: Garland Publishing, 1979.

Hermsprong or, Man As He Is Not (1796) New York and London: Garland Publishing, 1979.

James Wallace (1788) New York and London: Garland Publishing, 1979.

Man As He Is (1792) New York and London: Garland Publishing, 1979.

Mount Henneth (1782) New York and London: Garland Publishing, 1979.

Ballaster, Ros. *Seductive Forms: Women's Amatory Fiction from 1684 to 1740* Oxford: Clarendon Press, 1992.

Bancroft, Edward. *An Essay on the Natural History of Guiana, in South America* London: 1769.

Experimental Researches concerning the Philosophy of Permanent Colours and the Best Means of Producing Them (1794) London: 1813.

Facts and Observations, briefly stated, in Support of an Intended Application to Parliament London: 1798.

The History of Charles Wentworth (1770) New York and London: Garland Publishing, 1975.

Remarks on the Review of the Controversy Between Great Britain and her Colonies London: 1769.

Barbauld, Anna Laetitia. *The Works of Anna Laetitia Barbauld* London: 1825.

Barker-Benfield, G. J. *The Culture of Sensibility: Sex and Society in Eighteenth-Century Britain* Chicago and London: University of Chicago Press, 1992.

Barrell, John. "'The Dangerous Goddess': Masculinity, Prestige, and the Aesthetic in Early Eighteenth-Century Britain," *Cultural Critique* 12 (1989), 101–31.

The Dark Side of the Landscape. The Rural Poor in English Painting 1730–1840 Cambridge University Press, 1980.

English Literature in History, 1730–80: An Equal, Wide Survey London: Hutchinson, 1983.

The Political Theory of Painting from Reynolds to Hazlitt. "The Body of the Public" New Haven and London: Yale University Press, 1986.

[Beckford, William], *Azemia, A Novel: Containing Imitations of the Manner, Both in Prose and Verse, of Many of the Authors of the Present Day; With Political Strictures. By J. A. M. Jenks. In Two Volumes. The Second Edition* London: 1798.

Modern Novel Writing, or The Elegant Enthusiast; and Interesting Emotions of Arabella Bloomville. A Rhapsodical Romance; Interspersed with Poetry. In Two Volumes. By the Rt. Hon. Lady Harriet Marlow London: 1796.

Beebee, Thomas O. *"Clarissa" on the Continent: Translation and Seduction* University Park and London: Pennsylvania University Press, 1990.

Belanger, Terry. "Publishers and Writers in Eighteenth-Century England" in *Books and their Readers in Eighteenth-Century England* ed. Isobel Rivers. New York and London: St. Martin's Press; Leicester University Press, 1982, 5–15.

Bellamy, Liz and Tom Williamson. *Property and Landscape: A Social History of Land Ownership and the English Countryside* London: George Philip, 1987.

Bemis, Samuel Flagg. "British Secret Service and the French–American Alliance," *American Historical Review* 29 (1924), 474–95.

Benedict, Barbara. *Framing Feeling: Sentiment and Style in English Prose Fiction 1745–1800* New York: AMS Press, 1994.

Benger, Elizabeth. *Memoirs of the Late Mrs. Elizabeth Hamilton. With a Selection from her Correspondence, and other Unpublished Writings* London: 1818.

Bermingham, Ann. *Landscape and Ideology: The English Rustic Tradition, 1740–1860* Los Angeles: University of California Press, 1986.

Bindman, David. "Introduction" to *The Shadow of the Guillotine: Britain and the French Revolution* London: British Museum Publications, 1989, 26–78.

Bisset, Robert. *Douglas; Or, The Highlander* London: 1800.

    Sketch of Democracy London: 1796.

    The Life of Edmund Burke. Comprehending an Impartial Account of his Literary and Political Efforts, and a Sketch of the Conduct and Character of his most eminent Associates, Coadjutors, and Opponents (2nd edn.) London: 1800.

Blackstone, William. *Commentaries on the Laws of England* New York and London: Oceana Press, 1966.

Blake, William. *The Letters of William Blake. With Related Documents* ed. Geoffrey Keynes, 3rd edn. Oxford: Clarendon Press, 1980.

Blain, Virginia, Grundy, Isobel, Clements, Patricia. *The Feminist Companion to Literature in English. Women Writers from the Middle Ages to the Present* New Haven and London: Yale University Press, 1990.

Blair, Hugh. *Lectures on Rhetoric and Belles Lettres* (1783) ed. Harold F. Harding. Carbondale and Edwardsville: Southern Illinois University Press, 1965.

Bohls, Elizabeth. *Women Travel Writers and the Language of Aesthetics, 1716–1818* Cambridge University Press, 1995.

Braudy, Leo. "The Form of the Sentimental Novel," *Novel* 7 (1973), 5–13.

    "Penetration and Impenetrability in *Clarissa*" in *Modern Essays on Eighteenth-Century Literature* ed. Leopold Damrosch, Jr. New York and Oxford: Oxford University Press, 1988.

Brewer, John. "'This Monstrous Tragi-comic Scene': British Reactions to the French Revolution" in *The Shadow of the Guillotine: Britain and the French Revolution* ed. David Bindman. London: British Museum Publications, 1989, 11–25.

Briscoe, Sophia. *Miss Melmoth; Or, The New Clarissa* London: 1771.

Brophy, Elizabeth Bergen. *Women's Lives and the Eighteenth-Century English Novel* Tampa: University of South Florida Press, 1991.

Brown, John. *An Estimate of the Manners and Principles of the Times* London: 1757.

    An Estimate of the Manners and Principles of the Times, Volume II London: 1758

    An Explanatory Defence of the Estimate of the Manners and Principles of the Times. Being an Appendix to that Work, occasioned by the Clamours lately raised against it among certain Ranks of Men. Written by the Author of the Estimate, In a Series of Letters to a Noble Friend London: 1758.

Brown, Laura. *Ends of Empire: Women and Ideology in Early Eighteenth-Century English Literature* Ithaca and London: Cornell University Press, 1993.

Bullough, Vern L. "Prostitution and Reform in Eighteenth-Century England," *Eighteenth-Century Life. Special Issue. Unauthorized Sexual Behaviour during the Enlightenment* 9 (1985), 61–74.

Burke, Edmund. *An Account of the European Settlements in America. In Six Parts. In*

Two Volumes (1770) New York: Arno Press, 1972.

Reflections on the Revolution in France ed. Conor Cruise O'Brien. Harmondsworth: Penguin, 1969.

Letters on a Regicide Peace vol.IX ed. R. B. McDowell in *The Writings and Speeches of Edmund Burke* ed. Paul Langford. Oxford: Clarendon Press, 1991.

Burney, Frances. *Evelina Or The History of a Young Lady's Entrance into the World* ed. with intro. Edward A. Bloom and Lillian D. Bloom. Oxford University Press, 1968, rpt. 1991.

Butler, Marilyn. *Jane Austen and the War of Ideas* Oxford: Clarendon Press, 1975, rpt. 1987.

"Revolving in Deep Time: the French Revolution as Narrative" in *Revolution and English Romanticism: Politics and Rhetoric* ed. Keith Hanley and Raman Selden. Hassocks: Harvester Wheatsheaf; New York: St. Martin's Press, 1990, 1–22.

Campbell, Colin. *The Romantic Ethic and the Spirit of Modern Consumerism* Oxford: Basil Blackwell, 1977.

Carretta, Vince. "Utopia Limited: Sarah Scott's *Millenium Hall* and *The History of Sir George Ellison*," *The Age of Johnson: A Scholarly Annual* 5 (1992), 303–25.

Castle, Terry. *Clarissa's Ciphers: Meaning and Disruption in Richardson's "Clarissa"* Ithaca and London: Cornell University Press, 1982.

Chalker, John. *The English Georgic: A Study in the Development of a Form* Baltimore: Johns Hopkins University Press, 1969.

Chapone, Hester. *Letters on the Improvement of Mind* (1773) Edinburgh: 1821.

Clark, J. C. D. *English Society, 1688–1832 Ideology, Social Structure and Political Practice during the Ancien Regime* Cambridge University Press, 1985.

Clifford, James. "Traveling Cultures" in *Cultural Studies* ed. with intro. Lawrence Greenberg, Cary Nelson, Paula Treichler. New York and London: Routledge, 1992.

Cogan, Thomas. *John Buncle, Junior, Gentleman* London: 1776–8.

Cohen, Ralph. *Innovation and Variation: Literary Change and Georgic Poetry* in *Literature and History. Papers Read at a Clark Library Seminar. March 3, 1973.* Los Angeles: William Andrews Clark Memorial Library, 1974.

Colley, Linda. *Britons: Forging the Nation, 1707–1837* New Haven and London: Yale University Press, 1992.

Cox, Jeffrey. "Ideology and Genre in the British Antirevolutionary Drama of the 1790s," *ELH* 58 (1991), 579–610.

Crabbe, George. *Tales, 1812 and Other Selected Poems* ed. with intro. Howard Mills. Cambridge University Press, 1967.

Cruise, James. "A House Divided: Sarah Scott's *Millenium Hall*," *Studies in English Literature*," 35 (1995), 555–73.

Cumberland, George. *The Captive of the Castle of Sennaar* ed. G. E. Bentley Jr. Montreal and Kingston: McGill–Queen's University Press, 1991.

Cumberland, Richard. *Arundel* London: 1789.

Dickinson, H. T. *Liberty and Property. Political Ideology in Eighteenth-Century Britain* London: Methuen, 1977.

Dodd, William. *An Account of the Rise, Progress, and Present State of the Magdalen Hospital, For the Reception of Penitent Prostitutes. Together with Dr. Dodd's Sermons. To which are added, The Advice to the Magdalens; with the Psalms, Hymns, Prayers, Rules and Lists of Subscribers* 5th edn. London: 1776.

The Sisters; Or, The History of Lucy and Caroline Sanson, Entrusted to a False Friend London: Cooke's Edition, 1798.

Doederlein, Sue Warrick. "Clarissa in the Hands of the Critics," *Eighteenth-Century Studies* 16 (1983), 401–14.

Doody, Margaret Anne. "The Man-made World of Clarissa Harlowe and Robert Lovelace" in *Samuel Richardson: Passion and Prudence* ed. Valerie Grosvenor Myer. London: Vision P; Totowa, N.J.: Barnes and Noble Books, 1986.

A Natural Passion: A Study of the Novels of Samuel Richardson Oxford: Clarendon Press, 1974.

Dryden, John. *The Works of Virgil: Containing his Pastorals, Georgics and Aeneis. Translated into English Verse* in *The Poems of John Dryden Volume II* ed. James Kinsley. Oxford: Clarendon Press, 1958.

Dugaw, Diane. *Warrior Women and Popular Balladry, 1650–1850* Cambridge University Press, 1989.

Dwyer, John. *Virtuous Discourse: Sensibility and Community in Late Eighteenth-Century Scotland* Edinburgh: John Donald, 1987.

Dwyer, John and Richard B. Scher (eds.). *Sociability and Society in Eighteenth-Century Scotland* Edinburgh: Mercat Press, 1993.

Eagleton, Terry. *The Rape of Clarissa: Writing, Sexuality and Class Struggle in Samuel Richardson* Oxford: Basil Blackwell, 1982.

Eddy, Donald D. *A Bibliography of John Brown* New York: The Bibliographical Society of America, 1971.

Elliott, Dorice Williams. "Sarah Scott's *Millenium Hall* and Female Philanthropy," *Studies in English Literature* 35 (1995), 535–53.

Ettin, Andrew. *Literature and the Pastoral* New Haven and London: Yale University Press, 1984.

Favret, Mary. *Romantic Correspondence: Women, Politics and the Fiction of Letters* Cambridge University Press, 1993.

Feingold, Richard. *Nature and Society: Later Eighteenth-Century Uses of the Pastoral and Georgic* New Brunswick, N.J.: Rutgers University Press, 1978.

Ferguson, Adam. *An Essay on the History of Civil Society* intro. Louis Schneider. New Brunswick, N.J. and London: Transaction Publishers, 1980.

Ferguson, Moira. *Subject to Others: British Women Writers and Colonial Slavery, 1670–1834* New York and London: Routledge, 1992.

Ferris, Ina. *The Achievement of Literary Authority: Gender, History, and the Waverley Novels* Ithaca and London: Cornell University Press, 1991.

Fielding, Henry. *Joseph Andrews* ed. Martin C. Battestin. Middletown, Conn.: Wesleyan University Press, 1967.

"Joseph Andrews" and "Shamela" ed. with intro. Martin Battestin. Boston: Houghton Mifflin, 1961.

Flint, Christopher. "The Anxiety of Affluence: Family and Class (Dis)order in *Pamela: or, Virtue Rewarded*," *Studies in English Literature* 29 (1989), 489–514.

Fordyce, James. *The Character and Conduct of the Female Sex* London: 1776.

Sermons to Young Women, In Two Volumes. The Third Edition, Corrected London: 1766.

Fowler, Alastair. *Kinds of Literature: An Introduction to the Theory of Genres and Modes* Cambridge, Mass.: Harvard University Press, 1982.

Gallagher, Catherine. *Nobody's Story: The Vanishing Acts of Women Writers in the Marketplace, 1670–1820* Berkeley and Los Angeles: University of California Press, 1994.

Gibbes, Phebe. *The Life and Adventures of Mr. Francis Clive* (1764) New York and London: Garland Publishing, 1974.

Girouard, Mark. *Life in the English Country House: A Social and Architectural History* New Haven and London: Yale University Press, 1978.

Gisborne, Thomas. *An Inquiry into the Duties of the Female Sex* London: 1797.

Godwin, William. *Enquiry Concerning Political Justice and its Influence on Modern Morals and Happiness* ed. Isaac Kramnick. Harmondsworth: Pelican Books, 1976.

Things As They Are, or, The Adventures of Caleb Williams ed. Maurice Hindle. London: Penguin, 1988.

Gregory, John. *A Father's Legacy to his Daughters* (1774) Edinburgh: 1821.

Grieder, Josephine. "'Amiable Writer' or 'wretch'? The Elusive Samuel Jackson Pratt," *Bulletin of Research in the Humanities* 81 (1978), 464–84.

Guillén, Claudio. *Literature as System: Essays Toward the Theory of Literary History* Princeton University Press, 1971.

Gunning, Susannah Minifie. *Barford Abbey, A Novel: In a Series of Letters* London: 1768.

Coombe Wood London: 1783.

The Cottage; A Novel: In a Series of Letters London: 1769.

Haggerty, George. "'Romantic Friendship' and Patriarchal Narrative in Sarah Scott's *Millenium Hall*," *Genders* 13 (1992), 108–22.

Hamilton, Elizabeth. *Letters on the Elementary Principles of Education* 2nd London edn. Alexandria: 1803.

Memoirs of Modern Philosophers (1800) New York and London: Garland Publishing, 1974.

Popular Essays, Illustrative of Principles Essentially Connected with the Improvement of the Understanding, the Imagination, and the Heart Edinburgh: 1813.

Hanway, Mary Ann. *Ellinor; Or, The World As It Is* (1798) New York and London: Garland Publishing, 1974.

Hays, Mary. *An Appeal to the Men of Great Britain in Behalf of Women* (1798) New York and London: Garland Publishing, 1974.

Memoirs of Emma Courtney London: 1796.

The Victim of Prejudice ed. Eleanor Ty. Peterborough, Ont.: Broadview Press, 1994.

Haywood, Eliza. *Betsy Thoughtless* London: 1751.

Hazlitt, William. "Memoirs of the late Thomas Holcroft" in *The Complete Works of William Hazlitt* ed. P. P. Howe (after the edition of A. R. Waller and Arnold Glover) London and Toronto: J. M. Dent, 1932.

Hecht, J. Jean. *The Domestic Servant Class in Eighteenth-Century England* London: Routledge and Kegan Paul, 1956.

Hill, Christopher. "Clarissa Harlowe and her Times," *Essays in Criticism* 5 (1955), 315–40.

Hilliard, Raymond F. "*Clarissa* and Ritual Cannibalism," *PMLA* 105 (1990), 1083–97.

Hirschman, Albert O. *The Passions and the Interests: Political Arguments for Capitalism Before its Triumph* Princeton University Press, 1977.

Hirschon, Renée. "Introduction: Property, Power and Gender Relations" in *Women and Property: Women as Property* ed. Renée Hirschon. New York: St. Martin's Press; London, Canberra: Croom Helm, 1984.

Holcroft, Thomas. *Anna St. Ives* ed. with intro. Peter Faulkner. Oxford University Press, 1970.

The Adventures of Hugh Trevor ed. Seamus Deans. Oxford University Press, 1978.

Homes, Henry, Lord Kames. *Sketches of the History of Man. A Second Edition* (1778 edn.) Hildesheim: Georg Olms Verlagsbuchhandlung, 1968.

Horne, Thomas A. *Property Rights and Poverty: Political Argument in Britain, 1605–1834* Chapel Hill and London: The University of North Carolina Press, 1990.

Hulme, Peter. *Colonial Encounters: Europe and the Native Caribbean, 1492–1797* London and New York: Methuen, 1986.

Hulme, Peter and Whitehead, Neil L. (eds.). *Wild Majesty. Encounters with Caribs from Columbus to the Present Day. An Anthology* Oxford: Clarendon Press, 1992.

Hunt, John Dixon. *Gardens and the Picturesque: Studies in the History of Landscape Architecture* Cambridge, Mass. and London: MIT Press, 1992.

Hunter, J. Paul. "Clocks, Calendars, and Names: the Troubles of Tristram and the Aesthetics of Uncertainty" in *Rhetorics of Order / Ordering Rhetorics in English Neoclassical Literature* ed. J. Douglas Canfield and J. Paul Hunter. Newark: University of Delaware Press; London and Toronto: Associated University Presses, 1989, 173–98.

"'The Young, the Ignorant, and the Idle': Some Notes on Readers and the Beginnings of the English Novel" in *Anticipations of the Enlightenment in England, France, and Germany* ed. A. C. Kors and P. J. Korshin. Philadelphia: University of Pennsylvania Press, 1987, 259–82.

Irigaray, Luce. "Women on the Market" in *This Sex Which is Not One* trans. Catherine Porter with Carolyn Burke. Ithaca: Cornell University Press, 1985.

Jacob, Margaret C. "Scientific Culture in the Early English Enlightenment: Mechanisms, Industry, and Gentlemanly Facts" in *Anticipations of the Enlightenment in England, France, and Germany* ed. A. C. Kors and P. J. Korshin. Philadelphia: University of Pennsylvania Press, 1987.

Johnson, Claudia L. *Jane Austen: Women Politics and the Novel* Chicago and London: University of Chicago Press, 1988.

Jones, Chris. *Radical Sensibility: Literature and Ideas in the 1790s* London and New York: Routledge, 1993.

Kahn, Madeline. *Narrative Transvestitism: Rhetoric and Gender in the Eighteenth-Century English Novel* Ithaca and London: Cornell University Press, 1991.

Kaufman, Paul. *Borrowing from the Bristol Library, 1773–1784: A Unique Record of Reading Vogues* Charlottesville: Bibliographical Society of the University of Virginia, 1960.

"In Defence of Fair Readers" in *Libraries and their Users: Collected Papers in Library History* London: The Library Association, 1969, 223–8.

Kelly, Gary. *The English Jacobin Novel 1780–1805* Oxford: Clarendon Press, 1976.

Women, Writing, and Revolution 1790–1827 Oxford: Clarendon Press, 1993.

Kernan, Alvin. *Printing Technology, Letters, and Samuel Johnson* Princeton University Press, 1987.

Kibbie, Anne Louise. "Sentimental Properties: *Pamela* and *Memoirs of a Woman of Pleasure*," *ELH* 58 (1991), 561–77.

Kirkpatrick, Kathryn. "Sermons and Strictures: Conduct-Book Propriety and Property Relations in Late Eighteenth-Century England" in *History, Gender and Eighteenth-Century Literature* ed. Beth Fowkes Tobin. Athens and London: University of Georgia Press, 1994, 198–226.

Klancher, Jon. *The Making of English Reading Audiences, 1790–1832* Madison: University of Wisconsin Press, 1987.

Kolodny, Annette. *The Lay of the Land: Metaphor as Experience and History in American Life and Letters* Chapel Hill: University of North Carolina Press, 1975.

Kramnick, Isaac. *Republicanism and Bourgeois Radicalism: Political Ideology in Late Eighteenth-Century England and America* Ithaca and London: Cornell University Press, 1990.

Langbauer, Laurie. *Women and Romance: The Consolations of Gender in the English Novel* Ithaca and London: Cornell University Press, 1990.

Langford, Paul. *Public Life and the Propertied Englishman, 1689–1798* Oxford: Clarendon Press, 1991.

Lanser, Susan Sniader. *Fictions of Authority: Women Writers and Narrative Voice* Ithaca and London: Cornell University Press, 1992.

Lennox, Charlotte. *Euphemia* (1790) ed. Mary Anne Schofield. Delmar, N.Y.: Scholars Facsimiles, 1989.

Lilley, Kate. "Blazing Worlds: Seventeenth-Century Women's Utopian Writing" in *Women, Texts and Histories 1575–1760* ed. Clare Brant and Diane Purkiss. London and New York: Routledge, 1992, 102–33.

Linebaugh, Peter. *The London Hanged: Crime and Civil Society in the Eighteenth Century* Cambridge University Press, 1992.

Lloyd, Sarah. "'Pleasure's Golden Bait': Prostitution, Poverty and the Magdalen Hospital in Eighteenth-Century London," *History Workshop Journal* 41 (1996), 50–70.

Locke, John. *Two Treatises of Government* ed. with intro. and notes Peter Laslett. Cambridge University Press, 1988.

London, April. "Historiography, Pastoral, Novel: Genre in *The Man of Feeling*," *Eighteenth-Century Fiction* 10 (1997), 43–62.

Lonsdale, Roger (ed.). *The Poems of Thomas Gray, William Collins, and Oliver Goldsmith* London: Longmans, Green, 1969.

Low, Anthony. *The Georgic Revolution* Princeton University Press, 1985.

MacDonald, Thomas. *Thoughts on the Public Duties of Private Life with Reference to Present Circumstances and Opinions* London:1795.

McKendrick, Neil, Brewer, John and Plumb, J. H. *The Birth of a Consumer Society: The Commercialization of Eighteenth-Century England* Bloomington: Indiana University Press, 1982.

Mackenzie, Henry. *Julia de Roubigné. A Tale. In a Series of Letters. Published by the Author of The Man of Feeling, and The Man of the World. In Two Volumes* (1777) New York and London: Garland Publishing, 1979.

Literature and Literati: The Literary Correspondence and Notebooks of Henry Mackenzie. Volume I. Letters, 1766–1827 ed. Horst W. Drescher. Frankfurt am Main: Verlag Peter Lang, 1989.

The Man of Feeling ed. Brian Vickers. London: Oxford University Press, 1967.

The Man of the World. In Two Parts. The Second Edition Corrected London: 1773.

McKeon, Michael. "Historicizing Patriarchy: the Emergence of Gender Difference in England, 1660–1760," *Eighteenth-Century Studies* 28 (1995), 295–322.

The Origins of the English Novel, 1600–1740 Baltimore and London: Johns Hopkins University Press, 1987.

McLaughlin, Thomas. "Figurative Language" in *Critical Terms for Literary Study* ed. Frank Lentricchia and Thomas McLaughlin. Chicago and London: University of Chicago Press, 1990, 80–90.

Macpherson, C. B. *Political Theory of Possessive Individualism* Oxford: Clarendon Press, 1962.

Markley, Robert. "Sentimentality as Peformance: Shaftesbury, Sterne and the Theatrics of Virtue" in *The New Eighteenth Century: Theory, Politics, English Literature* ed. Felicity Nussbaum and Laura Brown. New York and London: Methuen, 1987, 210–30.

Mathias, Thomas. *Pursuits of Literature. A Satirical Poem, In Four Dialogues with notes* London: 1800.

Meek, Ronald L. *Social Science and the Ignoble Savage* Cambridge University Press, 1976.

Millar, John. *The Origin of the Distinction of Ranks* (1806 edn.) intro. John Valdimir Price. Bristol: Thoemmes Antiquarian Books, 1990.

Miller, Nancy K. *The Heroine's Text: Readings in the French and English Novel, 1722–1782* New York: Columbia University Press, 1980.

Montluzin, Emily Lorraine de. *The Anti-Jacobins 1798–1800: The Early Contributors to the "Anti-Jacobin Review"* London: Macmillan Press, 1988.

More, Hannah. *Strictures on the Modern System of Female Education* (1799) New York and London: Garland Publishing, 1974.

Murdoch, John. "The Landscape of Labor: Transformations of the Georgic" in *Romantic Revolutions: Criticism and Theory* ed. Kenneth R. Johnston, Gilbert Chaitin, Karen Hanson, and Herbert Marks. Bloomington and Indianapolis: Indiana University Press, 1990, 176–93.

Nash, Stanley. "Prostitution and Charity: the Magdalen Hospital, a Case Study," *Journal of Social History* 17 (1984), 617–28.

Newbery, John. *The Art of Poetry on a New Plan* (1762) New York and London: Garland Publishing, 1970.

Newman, Gerald. *The Rise of English Nationalism: A Cultural History, 1740–1830* New York: St. Martin's Press, 1987.

Newman, Peter. *British Guiana. Problems of Cohesion in an Immigrant Community* London and New York: Oxford University Press, 1964.

Nussbaum, Felicity. *Torrid Zones. Maternity, Sexuality, and Empire in Eighteenth-Century English Narratives* Baltimore and London: Johns Hopkins University Press, 1995.

Okin, Susan Moller. "Patriarchy and Married Women's Property in England: Questions on Some Current Views," *Eighteenth-Century Studies* 17 (1983–4), 121–38.

Osborn, Sarah. *Political and Social Letters of a Lady of the Eighteenth Century. 1721–1771* ed. Emily F. D. Osborn. New York: Dodd Mead, 1891.

Paine, Thomas. *Rights of Man* ed. with intro. Henry Collins. Harmondsworth: Pelican Books, 1979.

Palmer, Charlotte. *It Is and It Is Not a Novel* London: 1792.

Pateman, Carol. *The Sexual Contract* Stanford University Press, 1988.

Paulson, Ronald. *Breaking and Remaking: Aesthetic Practice in England, 1700–1820* New Brunswick and London: Rutgers University Press, 1989.

Pennington, Lady. *A Mother's Advice to her Absent Children* (1761) Edinburgh: 1821.

Perry, Ruth. "Bluestockings in Utopia" in *History, Gender and Eighteenth-Century Literature* ed. Beth Fowkes Tobin. Athens and London: University of Georgia Press, 1994.

The Celebrated Mary Astell: An Early English Feminist Chicago and London: University of Chicago Press, 1986.

"Mary Astell and the Feminist Critique of Possessive Individualism," *Eighteenth-Century Studies* 23 (1990), 444–57.

Phillips, Mark Salber. "Macaulay, Scott, and the Literary Challenge to Historiography," *Journal of the History of Ideas* 50 (1989), 117–33.

"'If Mrs. Mure Be Not Sorry for Poor King Charles'; History, the Novel, and the Sentimental Reader," *History Workshop Journal* 43 (1997), 111–31.

Phillipson, Nicholas. "The Scottish Enlightenment" in *The Enlightenment in National Context* ed. Roy Porter and Mikulas Teich. Cambridge University Press, 1981, 19–40.

Playfair, William. *The History of Jacobinism, Its Crimes, Cruelties and Perfidies* Philadelphia: 1796.

Pocock, J. G. A. *The Ancient Constitution and the Feudal Law: A Study of English*

Historical Thought in the Seventeenth Century Cambridge University Press, 1957.

The Machiavellian Moment: Florentine Political Thought and the Atlantic Republican Tradition Princeton University Press, 1975.

Virtue, Commerce, and History: Essays on Political Thought and History, Chiefly in the Eighteenth Century Cambridge University Press, 1985.

Polewhele, Richard. *The Unsex'd Females; A Poem, addressed to the author of The Pursuits of Literature* London: 1800.

Poovey, Mary. *The Proper Lady and the Woman Writer: Ideology as Style in the Works of Mary Wollstonecraft, Mary Shelley, and Jane Austen* Chicago and London: University of Chicago Press, 1984.

Pope, Alexander. *Imitations of Horace* vol. IV ed. John Butt. *Twickenham Edition of The Poems of Alexander Pope* London: Methuen, New Haven: Yale University Press, 2nd edn. rpt. 1961.

Pratt, Mary Louise. *Imperial Eyes: Travel Writing and Transculturation* London and New York: Routledge, 1992.

[Pratt, Samuel Jackson]. *Emma Corbett; or, The Miseries of Civil War. Founded on Some Recent Circumstances Which Happened in America* London: 1780.

Liberal Opinions upon Animals, Man, and Providence London: 1775–6.

The Pupil of Pleasure; or, The New System Illustrated London: 1776.

Shenstone-Green; or, The New Paradise Lost. Being a History of Human Nature. In Three Volumes. Written by the Proprietor of the Green. The Editor Courtney Melmoth London: 1779.

Raven, James. *Judging New Wealth: Popular Publishing and Responses to Commerce in England, 1750–1800* New York: Oxford University Press, 1992.

Ray, William. *Story and History. Narrative Authority and Social Identity in the Eighteenth-Century French and English Novel* Oxford: Basil Blackwell, 1990.

Reeve, Clara. *Destination. Or, Memoirs of a Private Family* Dublin: 1799.

The Exiles; Or, Memoirs of the Count Cronstadt London: 1788.

Memoirs of Sir Roger de Clarendon, The Natural Son of Edward Prince of Wales, Commonly Called the Black Prince; with Anecdotes of Many Other Eminent Persons of the Fourteenth Century London: 1793.

Plans of Education; with Remarks on the Systems of Other Writers In a Series of Letters Between Mrs. Darnford and Her Friends London: 1792.

The Progress of Romance Through Times, Countries, and Manners (1785) New York and London: Garland Publishing, 1970.

The School for Widows Dublin: 1791.

The Two Mentors. A Modern Story. The Second Edition London: 1783.

Reeve, Andrew. *Property* London: Macmillan Press, 1986.

Richards, Thomas. *The Imperial Archive: Knowledge and the Fantasy of Empire* London and New York: Verso, 1993.

Richardson, Alan. *Literature, Education, and Romanticism: Reading as Social Practice, 1780–1832* Cambridge University Press, 1994.

Richardson, Alan and Sonia Hofkosh (eds.). *Romanticism, Race, and Imperial Culture, 1780–1834* Bloomington and Indianapolis: Indiana University Press, 1996.

Richardson, Samuel. *Clarissa, or, The History of a Young Lady* ed. Angus Ross. Harmondsworth: Penguin Books, 1985.

The History of Sir Charles Grandison ed. with intro. Jocelyn Harris. Oxford University Press, 1972.

Pamela; Or, Virtue Rewarded London and Melbourne: Dent, 1914, rpt. 1983.

Pamela. Volume II intro. Mark Kinkead-Weekes. London: Dent, New York: Dutton, rpt. 1976.

Selected Letters of Samuel Richardson ed. John Carroll. Oxford: Clarendon Press, 1964.

Richetti, John. "The Public Sphere and the Eighteenth-Century Novel: Social Criticism and Narrative Enactment," *Eighteenth-Century Life* 16 (1992), 114–29.

Rizzo, Betty. *Companions Without Vows: Relationships Among Eighteenth-Century British Women* Athens and London: University of Georgia Press, 1994.

Robbins, Bruce. *The Servant's Hand: English Fiction from Below* New York: Columbia University Press, 1986.

Robinson, Mary. *The Widow, or A Picture of Modern Times. A Novel in a Series of Letters* London: 1794.

Rose, Mark. *Authors and Owners: The Invention of Copyright.* Cambridge, Mass.: Harvard University Press, 1993.

Ross, Trevor. "Copyright and the Invention of Tradition," *Eighteenth-Century Studies* 26 (1992), 1–27.

Sack, James J. *From Jacobite to Conservative: Reaction and Orthodoxy in Britain, c. 1760–1832* Cambridge University Press, 1993.

Said, Edward. *Culture and Imperialism* New York: Alfred A. Knopf, 1993.

Salvaggio, Ruth. *Enlightened Absence: Neoclassical Configurations of the Feminine* Urbana and Chicago: University of Illinois Press, 1988.

Schellenberg, Betty A. *The Conversational Circle: Re-Reading the English Novel, 1740–1775* Lexington: University Press, of Kentucky, 1996.

Scheuermann, Mona. *Her Bread to Earn: Women, Money, and Society from Defoe to Austen* Lexington: University Press, of Kentucky, 1993.

Schnorrenberg, Barbara Brandon. "A Paradise Like Eve's: Three Eighteenth-Century English Female Utopias," *Women's Studies* 9 (1982), 263–73.

Schofield, Mary Anne and Macheski, Cecilia (eds.). *Fetter'd or Free: British Women Novelists, 1670–1815* Athens, Ohio and London: Ohio University Press, 1986.

Schomburgk, Robert H. *A Description of British Guiana, Geographical and Statistical: Exhibiting its Resources and Capabilities, together with the present and future condition and prospects of the colony* (1840) London: Frank Cass, 1970.

Schott, Robin May. "The Gender of Enlightenment" in *What is Enlightenment? Eighteenth-Century Answers and Twentieth-Century Questions* ed. James Schmidt. Berkeley: University of California Press, 1996, 471–87.

Scott, Sarah. *Agreeable Ugliness: Or, The Triumph of the Graces. Exemplified in the Real Life and Fortunes of a young Lady of some Distinction* London: 1754.

A Description of Millenium Hall ed. Gary Kelly. Peterborough, Ont.: Broadview

Press, 1995.

The History of Cornelia Dublin: 1750.

The History of Sir George Ellison ed. Betty Rizzo. Lexington: University Press, of Kentucky, 1996.

Journey Through Every Stage of Life, Described in a Variety of Interesting Scenes, Drawn from Real Characters. By a Person of Quality London: 1754.

A Test of Filial Duty London: 1772.

Scott, Walter. *Waverley; Or, 'Tis Sixty Years Since* ed. Claire Lamont. Oxford University Press, 1986.

Sheriff, John. *The Good-Natured Man: The Evolution of a Moral Ideal, 1660–1800* University: University of Alabama Press, 1982.

Sitter, John. *Literary Loneliness in Mid-Eighteenth-Century England* Ithaca and London: Cornell University Press, 1982.

Skinner, Quentin. *The Foundations of Modern Political Thought* Cambridge University Press, 1978.

Smith, Adam. *The Theory of Moral Sentiments* ed. D. D. Raphael and A. L. Macfie. Oxford: Clarendon Press, 1976.

Smith, Raymond T. *British Guiana* London and New York: Oxford University Press, 1962.

Spacks, Patricia Meyer. *Desire and Truth. Functions of Plot in Eighteenth-Century English Novels* Chicago and London: University of Chicago Press, 1990.

Gossip Chicago and London: University of Chicago Press, 1986.

"Sisters" in *Fetter'd or Free?: British Women Novelists, 1670–1815* ed. Mary Anne Schofield and Cecilia Macheski. Athens, Ohio and London: Ohio University Press, 1986, 136–51.

Spadafora, David. *The Idea of Progress in Eighteenth-Century Britain* New Haven and London: Yale University Press, 1990.

Spencer, Jane. *The Rise of the Woman Novelist From Aphra Behn to Jane Austen* Oxford: Basil Blackwell, 1986.

Spurr, David. *The Rhetoric of Empire. Colonial Discourse in Journalism, Travel Writing, and Imperial Administration* Durham, N.C. and London: Duke University Press, 1993.

Stafford, William. "Narratives of Women: English Feminists of the 1790s," *History* 82 (1997), 24–42.

Stanton, Judith Phillips. "Statistical Profile of Women Writing in English from 1660 to 1800" in *Eighteenth-Century Women and the Arts* ed. Frederick M. Keener and Susan E. Lorsch. New York: Greenwood Press, 1988, 247–54.

Starr, G. A. "'Only a Boy': Notes on Sentimental Novels," *Genre* 10 (1977), 501–27.

"Sentimental De-education," in *Augustan Studies: Essays in Honour of Irvin Ehrenpreis* ed. Douglas Lane Patey and Timothy Keegan. Newark: University of Delaware Press; London and Toronto: Associated University Presses, 1985, 253–62.

Staves, Susan. "British Seduced Maidens," *Eighteenth-Century Studies* 14 (1980), 109–34.

Married Women's Separate Property in England, 1660–1833 Cambridge, Mass.: Harvard University Press, 1990.

Sterne, Laurence. *The Life and Opinions of Tristram Shandy* ed. Ian Campbell Ross. Oxford University Press, 1983.

Stevenson, John Allen. "The Courtship of the Family: Clarissa and the Family Once More," *ELH* 48 (1981), 757–77.

"'A Geometry of his Own': Richardson and the Marriage Ending," *Studies in English Literature* 26 (1986), 469–83.

Streatfield, David C. *Art and Nature in the English Landscape Garden: Design Theory and Practice, 1700–1818* in *Landscape in the Gardens and Literature of Eighteenth-Century England* Los Angeles: William Andrews Clark Memorial Library, 1981.

Taylor, Charles. *The Sources of the Self: The Making of the Modern Identity* Cambridge, Mass.: Harvard University Press, 1989.

Tenger, Zeynep and Paul Trolander. "The Politics of Literary Production: the Reaction to the French Revolution and the Transformation of the English Literary Periodical," *Studies in Eighteenth-Century Culture* 24 (1995), 279–95.

Thaddeus, Janis Farrar. "Elizabeth Hamilton's Domestic Politics," *Eighteenth-Century Culture* 23 (1994), 265–84.

Thomas, Nicholas. *Colonialism's Culture: Anthropology, Travel and Government* Princeton University Press, 1994.

Thompson, E. P. "Patrician Society, Plebian Culture," *Journal of Social History* 7 (1974), 382–405.

Thomson, James. *Poetical Works* ed. J. Logie Robertson. London: Oxford University Press, rpt. 1971.

Tobin, Beth Fowkes. "Arthur Young, Agriculture, and the Construction of the New Economic Man" in *History, Gender and Eighteenth-Century Literature* ed. Beth Fowkes Tobin. Athens and London: University of Georgia Press, 1994, 179–97.

Superintending the Poor: Charitable Ladies and Paternal Landlords in British Fiction, 1770–1860 New Haven and London: Yale University Press, 1993.

Todd, Janet. *Sensibility. An Introduction* London and New York: Methuen, 1986.

The Sign Of Angellica: Women, Writing and Fiction, 1660–1800 New York: Columbia University Press, 1989.

Todd, Ruthven. "The Rev. Dr. John Trusler," *Blake Newsletter* 23 (1972–3), 71.

Tomaselli, Sylvana. "The Enlightenment Debate on Women," *History Workshop Journal* 20 (1985), 101–24.

Trapp, Joseph. *Lectures on Poetry, Read in the Schools of Natural Philosophy at Oxford* (1742) New York and London: Garland Publishing, 1970.

Trusler, John. *The Complete Works of William Hogarth, in a Series of One Hundred and Fifty-Seven Engravings, From the Original Pictures, Including Many of the Author's Minor Pieces, Not in Any Other Edition, With Descriptions and Comments on their Moral Tendency. By the Rev. John Trusler.* London: H. Fowkes, [1860].

Elements of Modern Gardening: Or, The Art of Laying out of Pleasure Grounds, Ornamenting Farms, and Embellishing the Views About our Houses (1784) London and New York: Garland Publishing, 1982.

Life; or The Adventures of William Ramble, Esq. London: 1793.

Modern Times, Or, The Adventures of Gabriel Outcast. Supposed to be Written By Himself in Imitation of Gil Blas 3rd edn. London: 1786.

Principles of Politeness, and Of Knowing the World. By the late Lord Chesterfield. Methodised and digested under distinct Heads, with Additions, by the Rev. Dr. John Trusler … To Which is Now First Annexed. A Father's Legacy to his Daughters: By the late Dr. Gregory of Edinburgh. The whole admirably calculated for the IMPROVEMENT OF YOUTH, yet not beneath the attention of any Portsmouth, New Hampshire, 1786.

The Progress of Man and Society. Illustrated by upwards of One Hundred and Twenty Cuts. Opening the Eyes, and Unfolding the Mind of Youth Gradually London: 1791.

Proverbs Exemplified, and Illustrated By Pictures from Real Life (1790) East Ardley, Yorkshire and New York: S. R. Publishers and Johnson Reprint Corp., 1970.

The Way to Be Rich and Respectable, Addressed to Men of Small Fortune London: no date [1775].

Tucker, Irene. "Writing Home: *Evelina*, the Epistolary Novel, and the Paradox of Property," *ELH* 60 (1993), 419–39.

Turner, Cheryl. *Living by the Pen: Women Writers in the Eighteenth Century* London and New York: Routledge, 1992.

Ty, Eleanor. "Female Philosophy Refunctioned: Elizabeth Hamilton's Parodic Novel," *Ariel* 22 (1991), 111–29.

"Jane West's Feminine Ideal of the 1790s," *1650–1850: Ideas, Aesthetics, and Inquiries in the Early Modern Era* 1 (1994), 1–19.

Van Sant, Ann Jessie. *Eighteenth-Century Sensibility and the Novel: The Senses in Social Context* Cambridge University Press, 1993.

Vincent, David. *Literacy and Popular Culture: England 1750–1914* Cambridge University Press, 1989.

Waddell, D. A. G. *The West Indies and the Guianas* Englewood Cliffs, N.J.: Prentice-Hall, 1967.

Wahrman, Dror. *Imagining the Middle Class: The Political Representation of Class in Britain, c.1780–1840* Cambridge University Press, 1995.

Walker, George. *The Surprising travels and adventures of Sylvester Tramper through the interior of South Africa* London: 1816.

Theodore Cyphon; Or The Benevolent Jew: A Novel London: 1796.

The Three Spaniards, A Romance London: 1800.

The Vagabond London: 1799.

Walker, Lady Mary. *Letters from the Duchess of Crui* London: 1776.

Wall, Cynthia. "Gendering Rooms: Domestic Architecture and Literary Acts," *Eighteenth-Century Fiction* 5 (1993), 349–72.

Warner, William. *Reading "Clarissa": The Struggles of Interpretation* New Haven and London: Yale University Press, 1979.

Warren, Leland E. "The Conscious Speakers: Sensibility and the Art of Conversation Considered" in *Sensibility in Transformation: Creative Resistance to Sentiment from the Augustans to the Romantics* ed. Syndy M. Conger. Rutherford, N.J.: Farleigh Dickinson University Press, 1990, 25–42.

"'Turning Reality Round Together': Guides to Conversation in Eighteenth-Century England," *Eighteenth-Century Life* 8 (1983), 65–85.

Watson, Nicola J. *Revolution and the Form of the British Novel, 1790–1825: Intercepted Letters, Interrupted Seductions* Oxford: Clarendon Press, 1994.

Watt, Ian. *The Rise of the Novel: Studies in Defoe, Richardson, and Fielding* Berkeley and Los Angeles: University of California Press, 1957.

West, Jane. *The Advantages of Education: or, The History of Maria Williams* (1793) New York and London: Garland Publishing, 1974.

An Elegy on the Death of the Right Honourable Edmund Burke. London: 1797.

A Gossip's Story, and a Legendary Tale (1796) New York and London: Garland Publishing, 1974.

A Tale of the Times New York and London: Garland Publishing, 1974.

Williams, Helen Maria. *Edwin and Eltruda* London: 1782.

Julia, A Novel; Interspersed with some Poetical Pieces (1790) intro. Gina Luria. New York: Garland Publishing, 1974.

Letters Written in France, in the Summer 1790, To a Friend in England (1790) Oxford: Woodstock Books, 1989.

Williams, Ioan (ed.). *Novel and Romance 1700–1800. A Documentary Record* London: Routledge & Kegan Paul, 1970.

Williams, Raymond. *The Country and the City* New York: Oxford University Press, 1973.

Williamson, Tom and Bellamy, Liz. *Property and Landscape: A Social History of Land Ownership and the English Countryside* London: George Philip, 1987.

Wilt, Judith. "He Could Go No Farther: A Modest Proposal about Lovelace and Clarissa," *PMLA* 92 (1977), 19–32.

Wollstonecraft, Mary. *Political Writings* ed. Janet Todd. Oxford: World's Classics, 1994.

"Mary" and "The Wrongs of Woman" ed. Gary Kelly. Oxford University Press, 1980.

Wood, Marcus. *Radical Satire and Print Culture, 1790–1822* Oxford: Clarendon Press, 1994.

Young, Arthur. *The Adventures of Emnera, Or, The Fair American* London: 1767.

Young, Robert C. *Colonial Desire. Hybridity in Theory, Culture and Race* London and New York: Routledge, 1995.

Zimmerman, Everett. *The Boundaries of Fiction. History and the Eighteenth-Century British Novel* Ithaca and London: Cornell University Press, 1996.

Zomchick, John. *Family and the Law in Eighteenth-Century Fiction. The Public Conscience in the Private Sphere* Cambridge University Press, 1993.

Index

258